WEST METRO BIKE ROUTES

See inside back cover for EAST METRO BIKE ROUTES

RIDES
1-20 BIKE TOURS
See pages 26 to 63

RIDES

A-G MOUNTAIN BIKE RIDES
See pages 104 to 111

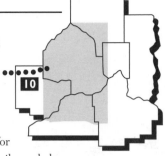

RATINGS FOR BIKE TOURS

🌊 **Easier** – Mostly paved, off-road trails

〽 **Moderate** – Mostly on bike-friendly streets

💠 **Experienced** – On roads, longer, less protected

LENGTH

Mileage listed below is for a full tour, loop, or distinct area. OW (one way) and RT (round trip) mileage is given for linear trails. Note: Longer rides are easily made by connecting two or more routes.

Sample Description (tour user guide pages 26 & 27)

O BIKE TOUR with RATING and LENGTH
   Oa. Regional Park/Trail or shorter loop described and mapped within tour.

---

1 COON RAPIDS RIDER — 〽 20.5 MILES
- 🌊 1a. Coon Rapids Dam Regional Park — 3.3 miles
- 🌊 1b. Bunker Hills Regional Park — 5.7 miles

2 NORTH HENNEPIN REGIONAL TRAIL 🌊 14.0 MILES RT
- 🌊 2a. Elm Creek Park Reserve — 9.0 miles
- 🌊 2b. N. Henn. Trail plus adjacent parks — 27.0 miles

3 FRIDLEY FLYER — 〽 17.7 MILES
- 🌊 3a. Long Lake Regional Park — 5.0 miles
- 🌊 3b. Rice Creek West Regional Trail — 5.5 miles RT

4 MINNEAPOLIS GRAND ROUNDS — 〽 32.7 MILES
- 🌊 4a. Minnehaha Parkway — 9.8 miles RT
- 🌊 4b. West River Parkway — 9.2 miles RT
- 🌊 4c. Wirth and Memorial Parkways — 12.7 miles RT

5 ST. ANTHONY FALLS SPECTACULAR 🌊 3.8 MILES

6 MINNEAPOLIS LAKE DISTRICT 🌊 15.8 MILES
- 🌊 6a. Cedar Lake Trail — 7.0 miles RT
- 🌊 6b. Lake of the Isles — 2.9 miles
- 🌊 6c. Lake Calhoun — 3.1 miles
- 🌊 6d. Lake Harriet — 2.8 miles

7 HENNEPIN EXPLORER — 💠 39.6 MILES
- 🌊 7a. Palmer Lake Loop — 2.7 miles
- 🌊 7b. Shingle Creek Path — 7.0 miles RT
- 🌊 7c. Elm Creek Park Reserve — 9.0 miles

8 EVERY WHICH WAY TO THE LUCE — 〽 31.2 MILES
- 🌊 8a. Medicine Lake Loop — 8.1 miles
- 〽 8b. Big Loop without Medicine Lake — 24.4 miles

9 ON THE ROAD TO FREEDOM — 💠 31.9 MILES
- 🌊 9a. Baker Park Reserve — 6.0 miles
- 〽 9b. Road Route without Baker Park — 23.8 miles
- 🌊 9c. Lake Rebecca Park Reserve — 6.1 miles

10 LUCE LINE STATE TRAIL — 〽 69.8 MILES OW
- 🌊 10a. Medicine Lake Road to Winsted — 31.8 miles
- 〽 10b. Winsted to Thompson Lake (Cosmos) — 38.0 miles

11 BLOOMINGTON OR BUST — 〽 19.2 MILES
- 🌊 11a. Hyland Lake Park Reserve — 5.0 miles
- 〽 11b. All mapped routes to Hyland Park — 31.1 miles OW

12 SWIM ROUND LAKE MINNETONKA 💠 29.2 MILES

13 LRT NORTH TRAIL — 🌊 18.0 MILES OW
- 💠 13a. LRT North and LRT South Loop — 41.4 miles
- 🌊 13b. Carver Park Reserve — 8.2 miles

14 LRT SOUTH TRAIL — 🌊 14.2 MILES OW
- 〽 14a. LRT South to MN Valley Trail — 17.2 miles OW

15 CHASKA CHASER — 🌊 13.2 MILES
- 🌊 15a. Total miles of paved path — 23.0 miles

16 MINNESOTA VALLEY STATE TRAIL 💠 44.0 MILES RT
- 🌊 16a. Chaska to Shakopee — 8.0 miles RT

17 EDEN PRAIRIE – BIKES & BOMBERS 〽 20.8 MILES
- 🌊 17b. Short Loop — 11.1 miles

18 BURNSVILLE BIKE BYWAYS — 〽 18.4 MILES

19 BIKING FOR THE BIRDS — 〽 29.5 MILES
- 🌊 19a. Short Loop — 10.0 miles

20 PLANES, TRAINS & AUTOMOBILES 〽 17.0 MILES

MOUNTAIN BIKE RIDES Rating for terrain/distance

16 MINNESOTA VALLEY STATE TRAIL — 💠 44.0 MILES RT

19 BIKING FOR THE BIRDS — 〽 29.5 MILES
   19a. Short Loop — 10.0 miles

A ELM CREEK PARK RESERVE — 🌊 5.0 MILES

B HYLAND HILLS SKI AREA — 💠 2.0 MILES

C BLOOMINGTON BLUFF TRAIL — 〽-💠 20 MILES RT

D TERRACE OAKS PARK — 〽-💠 3.4 MILES

E BUCK HILL SKI AREA — 〽-💠 3.0 MILES

F MURPHY HANREHAN REGIONAL PARK — 💠 6.0 MILES

G LOUISVILLE SWAMP — 🌊 11.5 MILES

When I see an adult on a bicycle, I do not despair for the future of the human race.

H.G. Wells

Fred's Best Guide to

TWIN CITIES BICYCLING

By
Richard 'Fred' Arey

MINNESOTA

OUTDOORS
PRESS

Fred's Best Guide to
TWIN CITIES BICYCLING

Minnesota Outdoors Press
Richard Fred Arey • 534 Laurel Avenue #6

612-290-0309
Saint Paul, Minnesota 55102

Additional copies of this book may be obtained by sending $18.50 per copy – or two copies for just $32! – (price includes tax, shipping and handling) to the publisher at the above address. Make checks payable to Minnesota Outdoors Press. Allow up to four weeks for delivery.

I GET BY WITH A LITTLE HELP FROM MY FRIENDS.
Cover art and design – David Mataya
Production and design – Rob Schanilec – my main man
Word processing – Rob Schanilec and Lisa Beller
Text, maps and some illustrations – Fred
Editing – Paula Schanilec, Julie Lund and Patricia Frazier
Photos – Credits adjacent to each photograph

First printing, 1995
10   9   8   7   6   5   4   3   2   1

Library of Congress Cataloging-in-Publication Data

Arey, Richard
    Twin Cities Bicycling
    Fred's Best Guide to Twin Cities Bicycling
    Richard Arey
    p.   cm.
ISBN 0-9620918 - 1 - 2 $14.50

1. Bicycle touring – Twin Cities Metropolitan Area – Guide books
2. Minnesota – Twin Cities – Bicycling Guide
3. History – Bicycling – Minnesota

Watch for these upcoming Minnesota Outdoors Press books.
1. A Pictorial History of Twin Cities Parks and Recreation
2. Twin Cities Winter Outside Recreation
3. Twin Cities Summer Outside Recreation

Dakota and Ojibway place names are from Paul Durand's excellent book, *Where the Waters Gather and the Rivers Meet*. Send $17.00 to Paul at 15341 Red Oaks Road SE, Prior Lake, MN 55372, to obtain your copy. Many of the geographical place name histories are from Warren Upham's landmark book, *Minnesota Geographic Names*, available from the Minnesota Historical Society. The Thomas McGrath poem (How could I have come so far?…) is from *Selected Poems: 1938-1988* © 1988 by Thomas McGrath. Reprinted by permission of Copper Canyon Press. PO Box 271, Port Townsend, WA 98368. I would also like to thank everyone that reviewed and commented on my text and maps.

LIABILITY DISCLAIMER

Routes described and mapped in this book were compiled from a variety of sources. Minnesota Outdoors Press and Richard Arey assume no liability for bicyclists travelling on these routes. The maps and descriptions are intended to aid in the selection of routes, but do not guarantee safety while riding these routes.

HAVE FUN, WEAR A HELMET, RIDE AT YOUR OWN RISK

DEDICATIONS

To Mom and Dad — who have always kept the faith
and been there when I needed them. This is for you,
finally.

> *How could I have come so far?*
> *(And always on such dark trails!)*
> *I must have travelled by the light*
> *Shining from the faces of all those I have loved.*
>
> Thomas McGrath

And for everyone else who has heard me talk about a
Twin Cities Parks and Recreation book for the last
decade or so — Voila! This doesn't seem that tough
does it? One down, three to go.

This is for those who were there at the beginning —
Jerry Hass, Roxanne Hart and Marty Bucher.

And for all those who have biked, skied, paddled,
walked and sailed along with me through the years.

Hey, Ho. Let's Go!

Do you remember your first bike?

PICTORIAL HISTORY OF BICYCLING

B icycling, until lately, has been looked upon by many as a sport for the youth, or as a "craze," soon to pass out of fashion. But slowly and surely it has been dawning upon the public mind that this great invention is really a vehicle that is destined to supplant, in many instances, the horse and buggy — is doing so and pointing to greater possibilities.

MINNESOTA WHEELMAN, September, 1885

Do you remember your first bicycle?

The history of bicycling goes back some 500 years, but for me, nothing is more memorable than the first view of my bright red Schwinn under the Christmas tree. Except, perhaps, the first ride on my second bike, when I became so enamored with how the gears were shifting that I rode smack into a parked car.

The bicycle, the most efficient form of transportation ever devised, has a long and colorful history. In the 1890s, cyclists led the national "Good Roads" movement. Summit Avenue became the first paved street in St. Paul at the urging of local bike racers.

The first road maps were developed by bicyclists looking for the best roads out of town. The bicycle also helped energize the movement for women's emancipation. In 1896, Susan B. Anthony declared, "I stand and rejoice every time I see a woman ride by on a wheel."

Technical innovations were legion and included the development of gears, cyclometers, sprockets and pneumatic tires. Cecil Behringer, a Minnesotan and former bicycle racer, patented a titanium treatment process he used in building an ultralight racing bike.

What goes around comes around. Separated bike paths seemed like a good innovation in the 1970s — about 80 years after the first ones were built on Como Avenue and around Lake Harriet. Bicycle cops, bike couriers, mandatory bike registration, and bike tours that span the globe have all made the news over the last few years. They also made the news a century ago.

And what about those nutty winter bicyclists who seem to have popped up out of every other snowdrift? If they're really serious they'll revive another old Twin Cities tradition. At the stroke of midnight each New Year's Eve, cyclists from Minneapolis and St. Paul would race over the High Bridge, to Northfield and back, to see who would complete the year's first century ride.

Will history repeat itself yet again?

1493	Leonardo da Vinci produces a rough sketch of a bicycle. It has two spoked wheels, pedals, cranks, sprocket and a chain. The sketch is lost to history (only recently was it rediscovered) and the world must wait 400 years to realize its successor.
1817	German inventor Karl von Drais patents the two-wheel hobbyhorse with a pivoting front wheel for steering. It is propelled by the feet while straddling the vehicle — like a 19th century Fred Flintstone.
1843	Kirkpatrick Macmillan, a Scottish blacksmith, adds pedals attached to connecting rods and crank arms on the rear wheel hub. He takes this bicycle on a 140-mile, round-trip test ride from his home in Dumfries to Glasgow. Crowds gather on his return and in the confusion he knocks over a child and is fined five schillings, the bicycle's first moving violation. Historians still have not decided if this is a true story or simply a good story.
March 1861	Controversy surrounds Pierre Michaux' claims for creating the first "practical bicycle." He is, however, the first known manufacturer (starting in 1867) of two-wheeled velocipedes that are driven by cranks and pedals attached to the front wheel.

Pierre Lallement on his 1866 velocipede — arguably the world's first true bicycle.

Smithsonian Institute.

Nov. 20 1866	Pierre Lallement, a New Haven, Connecticut resident and recent U.S. immigrant from France, takes out the first patent anywhere for a rotary-action, crank-driven velocipede. The bicycle has arrived in America.

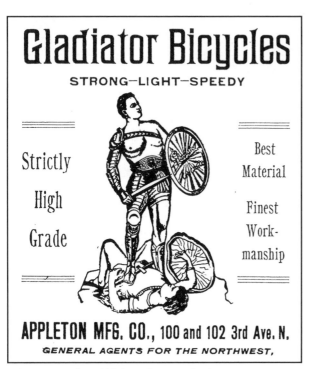

Advertisement from 1896 Northwest Cycle Show program.

One of the famous Bell Brothers bicyclists, c. 1885.

1869
The first bicycle craze hits the wilds of Minnesota, a mere decade after statehood's arrival on May 11, 1858. Velocipedes, also known as boneshakers, are reported to have raced in St. Paul at Armory Hall.

Aug. 11 1870
James Starley patents the "Ariel," an all metal, mass produced high-wheeler from England, considered by some historians to be the first real bicycle. The high-wheeler, also known as an "ordinary," is similar to a velocipede but employs a far larger front wheel for greater speed.

1877-1878
The first known "safety" bike (high-wheelers being notoriously difficult to ride and subject to "headers" that catapulted the bicyclist headfirst into the ground) was built by H. Bate of England. Both wheels are the same size, there is a center saddle, and pedals drive the rear wheel like today's bikes. Four centuries after da Vinci, the bike is back on track.

May 1881
The Minneapolis Cycling Club organizes with 12 members. It claims affiliation with the League of American Wheelmen (LAW) that began in Boston the previous year.

Sept. 24 1884
The second annual meet of the Minnesota Wheelmen includes a one mile — bicycle against roller skate race — with cup to winner. Any doubt about who won?

1885
James Starley returns with a refined version of the safety bike using a diamond frame, direct steering and a brake. Of even greater importance, frame modifications now allow women to be bicyclists.

Sept. 22 1885
The third annual meeting of the Minnesota division of the LAW is marked by the publication of volume one of the *Minnesota Wheelman*. The 16-page pamphlet notes that there are 408 bicycles in the state including "about 150 in Minneapolis." And a section on the Rights of Wheelmen points out that "bicycles and tricycles are carriages subject to the same rules and regulations and enjoying the same rights and privileges in the public highways as those drawn by horses."

The pamphlet also mentions that the Minneapolis Parks Commission has passed a law prohibiting bicyclists. But they note that "Minneapolis wheelmen are serene as yet, for the parks are good places to keep out of with a bicycle. About the time they are ripe for the wheelmen, the wheelmen will enjoy them. Mark the prediction."

1886 High-wheeler catalog has chapter on "Learning to Fall." Mark Twain says, "Get a bicycle. You will not regret it, if you live."

1888 John Dunlop takes a piece of rubber tubing, like a garden hose, joins the ends together and glues it onto the rim of his son's bike. He attaches a baby's milk bottle tube as a valve and the pneumatic tire is born. On June 18, 1891, Edouard Michelin goes the next step and produces a removable tire that is attachable without glue. Today's bike is now complete.

1890 By the early 1890s, safety bicycles become common, and prices fall (high wheelers could be as expensive as a house!) to the point where the middle class can enjoy them. Bicycle clubs like Flour City Cyclists sprout up around the Twin Cities. Bicycle theft becomes a matter of no small concern and one thief who claimed he was, "just giving it a try," is sent to the workhouse at Como Park for three months.

1892 *The Bicycle: Its Selection, Riding and Care* is issued by F.L. Korns and dedicated "to the Ladies Cycling League, Minneapolis, Minnesota."

Jan. 24 1894 Farmers and bicyclists join together at the first Minnesota Good Roads Convention held in St. Paul. Professor Pendergast addresses the congress saying, "Wheelmen are no longer confined to the cities. Bicycles, now within the reach of all, are no strangers among farmers. The golden days of which the poets have sung are upon us."

1895 The Minneapolis YWCA sponsors an all-women bicycle club with 60 members.

April 2 1896 Henry Ford takes his first handmade "car" out for a spin in Detroit. The gasoline "quadricycle" consists of a buggy frame mounted on four bicycle wheels and powered with a two-cylinder engine.

1890 Flour City Cyclists Clubhouse at 1611 Park Avenue, Minneapolis

Three women bicyclists and friend on 1896 bicycle path around Lake Harriet.

Dottie Farnsworth

1896 The first bicycle path is installed around Lake Harriet by the Minneapolis Park Board. Not to be outdone, the St. Paul Park Board installs seven-foot-wide bike paths on both sides of Como Avenue Parkway and installs racks for 1,500 bicycles at Como Park. Local bicycle clubs get excited about these prospects and propose a bikeway linking Minneapolis and St. Paul funded by user fees from the estimated 25,000 local cyclists.

1896 Deere and Webber Co. is just one of the many local bike manufacturers that pop up during this first heyday of bicycling.

1896 Bicycle speed records are being set constantly and Minneapolis racer Dottie Farnsworth edges out Mate Christopher, "breaking the world record all to pieces by making 21 miles and seven laps" in an hour. The understated report continues by exclaiming, "a gait of 21 miles an hour is an encroachment on an express train that would excite enthusiasm anywhere."

1896 Longtime Lyndale Avenue South resident, John S. Johnson, is one of Minnesota's all-time great bicycle racers. He is said to be the first person in the world to ride one mile in under two minutes. In England, in 1896, he breaks the European record for the paced, flying start mile with a time of 1:44. Minnesota nice is no advantage overseas, however. Johnson loses a one-on-one race in front of 15,000 spectators when he stops to allow his adversary to change a punctured tire.

JOHN S. JOHNSON
THE
FLOUR CITY FAVORITE.

John S. Johnson, "The White Flyer"

*Mrs. Archie Matheis, winner of the Minnesota
"Special Meritorious Medal" 1897 competition.*

Advertisement from 1896 magazine. Deere and Webber later became the John Deere Co.

1896   Susan B. Anthony proclaims, "the wheel has done more to emancipate women than anything else in the world. I stand and rejoice every time I see a woman ride by on a wheel. It gives a woman a feeling of freedom and self-reliance."

April 1897   The Minneapolis Park Board decides to equip two of its officers with bicycles for the Lake Harriet–Minnehaha Boulevard beat. Reports say, "there is a lively scramble among the officers to see who will do the Board's riding this season."

Aug. 8 1897   Mrs. Archie Matheis becomes the first woman in Minnesota to ride a double century — 200 miles! — in a single day.

Aug. 3 1899   At 2:54 a.m., Gus "Rainmaker" Hansen sets the American record for 1,000 miles on a bicycle with a time of 92 hours and 36 minutes. Known for his knack of bringing rain at the start of a long ride, Gus is also remarkable for eating rhubarb pie as part of his training regiment. He sets the 1,000 mile record riding loops on the cycle path network connecting Fort Snelling with Chowan's Corners near Lake Minnetonka.

1896 bicycle path, Minnehaha Parkway

Josephine Parquette and Charles Affleck on a bicycle built for two. St. Paul, 122 W. Congress, 1900. (They married in 1901.)

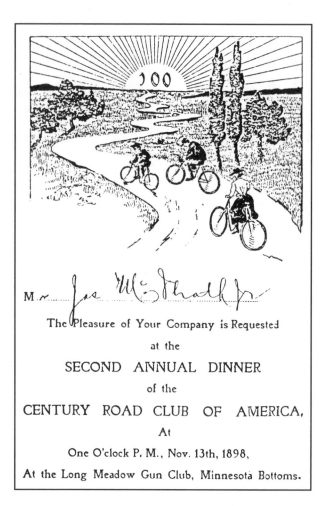

1899-1900   The St. Paul City Council passes a bicycle ordinance requiring a lighted lantern at night while the Minneapolis City Council passes a law requiring bike licenses. Over 33,000 are sold the first year at 50 cents apiece.

Jan. 1 1900   The annual 100-mile, midnight race between Minneapolis and St. Paul riders is hotly contested. This year, the first century of the new century is at stake and St. Paul cyclists Thomas Bird and James McIlrath take the prize.

June 1902   The *Guide to Minneapolis Bicycle Paths* is published by Rev. Isaac Houlgate. The 57 miles of mapped paths mark the zenith of the Minneapolis path system. "Minneapolis is recognized as a wheelman's paradise," says the *Minneapolis Journal*.

M ~ Jas McStrath Jr

The Pleasure of Your Company is Requested

at the

SECOND ANNUAL DINNER

of the

CENTURY ROAD CLUB OF AMERICA,

At

One O'clock P. M., Nov. 13th, 1898,

At the Long Meadow Gun Club, Minnesota Bottoms.

1904   Just two years later, the *Minneapolis Journal* reports the beginning of the end for the first '90s bicycle craze. It reports that "several local paths will be destroyed this summer," and trees planted in their place. Trolleys and the arrival of the automobile mark the transition.

Taylors Falls was a popular destination for Twin Cities cyclists in 1900.

6
Day
Bike
Race

Sixth
International
Race

Feb. 20
thru 26
1 9 3 6

15c

MINNEAPOLIS · AUDITORIUM
SPONSORED BY MINNEAPOLIS MILK FUND

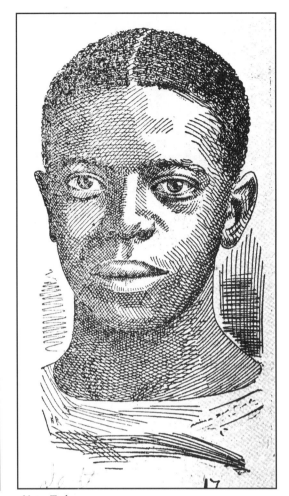

Major Taylor

1905 A *Minneapolis Journal* editorial argues that, "while comparatively few people now go wheeling for pleasure, the bicycle is more than ever the working-man's horse."

1929 The years 1910 to 1930 are the dark ages for bicycling in America. Perhaps the most noteworthy event is the publication of Major Taylor's autobiography, *The Fastest Bicycle Rider in the World: The Story of a Colored Boy's Indomitable Courage and Success Against Great Odds.* Jackie Robinson is generally credited with breaking the color line in professional sports in baseball in 1947, but a half century earlier Major Taylor defied all the odds when he won the world professional sprint championship in 1899 and the U.S. National title in 1900. Taylor first raced in the Midwest.

1931 The Six Day Races begin their run at the Minneapolis Auditorium. Two person teams from throughout Europe and North America compete. The rules provide that one of the racers has to be on the track at all times. The races become extremely popular and in 1936 nearly 40,000 attend the annual event.

1933 Schwinn introduces balloon-tired Excelsior bicycles for kids and helps revive interest in bicycling. With fat tires and ruggedness to spare, Excelsiors reappear in the late 1970s as the first mountain bikes on Mount Tamalpais near San Francisco.

1934 The Gopher Wheelmen bicycle racing club is formed and meets nightly at Lake Calhoun. Today this club is the oldest in Minnesota, and founding member Kenny Woods is still active and bicycling.

1941 With the coming of World War II and fuel rationing, bicycling's fortunes continue to rise. In 1941 a bicycle rental concession is opened near the Lake Harriet Grandstand.

1948 The State of Minnesota produces its first *Bicycle Safety Manual.* There is a section on bike hikes and bike parades. Bicycle accident statistics for 1947 indicate 333 car-bike crashes with eight fatalities (six in the five to fourteen age group). Accidents at intersections account for 69 percent of the total while "disregarding stop signs" and "stunting" are listed among the common causes.

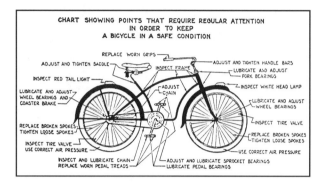

CHART SHOWING POINTS THAT REQUIRE REGULAR ATTENTION IN ORDER TO KEEP A BICYCLE IN A SAFE CONDITION

REPLACE WORN GRIPS
ADJUST AND TIGHTEN SADDLE
INSPECT FRAME
ADJUST AND TIGHTEN HANDLE BARS
INSPECT RED TAIL LIGHT
LUBRICATE AND ADJUST FORK BEARINGS
ADJUST CHAIN
INSPECT WHITE HEAD LAMP
LUBRICATE AND ADJUST WHEEL BEARINGS AND COASTER BRAKE
LUBRICATE AND ADJUST WHEEL BEARINGS
REPLACE BROKEN SPOKES TIGHTEN LOOSE SPOKES
INSPECT TIRE VALVE
INSPECT TIRE VALVE USE CORRECT AIR PRESSURE
REPLACE BROKEN SPOKES TIGHTEN LOOSE SPOKES
USE CORRECT AIR PRESSURE
INSPECT AND LUBRICATE CHAIN REPLACE WORN PEDAL TREADS
ADJUST AND LUBRICATE SPROCKET BEARINGS
LUBRICATE PEDAL BEARINGS

WOODS & LARSON
"Wizards of the Wheel"
FOR
CLUB AND PRIVATE ENTERTAINMENTS
Co. 8547   *Cycliste's Extraordinaire*   Co. 7848

Sept. 25 1955	The Gopher Wheelmen score a major upset by winning the 50-mile Elgin to Chicago Bicycle Race — the oldest in America.
1967	Bicycling's popularity continues to grow for adults as well as for kids. In 1967 the Minneapolis Park Board reopens a bike path around Lake Harriet. The Board also initiates a car-free parkway program on Sundays that is quite popular for the next several years.
Feb. 2 1970	Nearly 800 cyclists complete the First Annual Mid-American Grand Prix Marathon Bicycle Race (otherwise known as the Ground Hog Invitational) around Lake Harriet. Two cyclists decide they have a better route and cut across the lake.
April 18 1972	A bicyclist collides with a pedestrian on a combined bike-walk path around Lake Harriet. The fatal accident spurs the Minneapolis Park Board to separate all walking and biking paths.

Ken Woods, one of the founders of the Gopher Wheelmen, on his "giraffe" unicycle. Ken earned a living from the 1930s into the 1950s bike racing and trick riding around the country.

Oct. 9 1972	The Countryview Bicycle Trail, lauded as Minnesota's first state bike trail, is dedicated. The 22-mile "trail" runs on low traffic roads between Lake Phalen and Stillwater.

MHS Collections - John Runk photographer

Boys bicycling down flooded levee. Stillwater, MN ca. 1945.

© 1972 Star Tribune/Minneapolis – St. Paul, Earl Seubert, photographer

Governor Wendell Anderson, wife Mary and son Brett dedicate the Countryview Bicycle Trail.

1973 The Mideast Oil Embargo hits the United States. Gas lines form, stations are closed on Sundays and Americans first face up to their total dependence on imported oil.

Aug. 22 1973 Carl Ohrn, a transportation planner with Barton-Aschman Associates, presents a proposal for an 1,856-mile bikeway system in the Twin Cities. Stating that the average door-to-door speed for auto trips is only 20 miles per hour, he estimates that 8 percent of the 3 million daily metro area trips would be made by bikes if a good system was built.

Sept. 1974 The Minneapolis Public Works Department installs Minnesota's first dedicated bike lanes along University Avenue and Fourth Street at the University of Minnesota campus.

1976 Packed gravel is laid down on the first 6½ miles of the Luce Line State Trail and this becomes Minnesota's second developed rail-to-trail conversion. (The Douglas Trail near Rochester opened in 1975.) Rail trails have eclipsed state parks in popularity, and to keep up with the demand, there are now over 50 built or planned in Minnesota.

1977 Cecil Behringer builds a 200-meter wood velodrome near Shakopee. A metallurgical engineer with several patents, Behringer got his start as a Western Union bike messenger in 1933 and went on to become the Minnesota bike racing champion in 1936.

1978 Minnesotan Chris Kvale and his brother Kevin bike from California to New York City in a record 14½ days.

Feb. 14 1980 The first annual statewide bicycle conference is held at the ArrowWood Resort in Alexandria. Educating motorists, statewide bicycle licensing, and teens on bike patrols are among the topics discussed.

1982 Designed in America and built in Japan, Specialized comes out with the first production mountain bike — the Stumpjumper. Within two years mountain bikes account for a third of all adult bike sales in the United States.

1984 The Minnesota state legislature gives MN DOT the authority to hire a State Bicycle Coordinator and form the Minnesota State Bicycle Advisory Board. Jim Dustrude bikes to his first day of work on Wednesday, September 5, 1984.

Dipping their front tires into the Pacific Ocean, Dan Buettner and crew conclude their record journey. Along for the ride are, left to right, Dan Buettner, Martin Engel, Ann Knabe and Bret Andersen.

Aug. 8 1986 Roseville resident Dan Buettner leaves Prudhoe Bay, Alaska, on the start of his first continent-spanning excursion. He doesn't stop biking until he reaches Ushuaia, Argentina, on June 14, 1987, where the four-person crew celebrates with a king crab dinner. The 15,536 mile trip establishes the first of his world records.

Summer 1987 Hennepin County opens Minnesota's first pilot mountain bike program at Bryant Lake Park on a 3½ kilometer trail.

Nov. 1 1987 Greg LeMond, the first American to win the Tour de France (1986), purchases his new home in Wayzata. He is still recovering from a hunting accident that nearly kills him and takes up cross-country skiing in the off-season.

May 19 1989 The Hennepin Parks Board continues to lead the way in local parks programming and officially approves the first experimental mountain bike trail season at Murphy Hanrehan Park Reserve.

Courtesy of Flanders Brothers Bikeshop.

A young Greg LeMond leads the pack at the Nature Valley Criterium around Kenwood Park, Minneapolis. August, 1980.

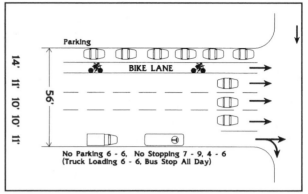

New downtown Minneapolis bike lane diagram.

July 24 1989 Racing from Versailles into Paris in a stunning 26 minutes, 57 seconds, Greg LeMond wins the Tour de France for the second time. In what is one of the most amazing sporting comebacks of all time, LeMond beats out Laurent Fignon of France by eight seconds — the smallest margin of victory ever in the world's greatest bicycle race.

1990 Governor Rudy Perpich puts Minnesota on the world cycling map by building the velodrome at the National Sports Center in Blaine. The facility is hailed as the finest racing track in the country.

1990 Under Minnesota Congressman Martin Sabo's leadership, the 1990 Congress directs the U.S. Department of Transportation to identify the potential of the bike as a mode of transportation. The U.S. DOT releases the multi-volume *National Bicycling and Walking Study* as a result.

Sept. 15 1990 Just weeks after winning his third Tour de France, Greg LeMond enters his first mountain bike race. On "Fire Tower Hill," he pulls away from his competitors and wins the 35-mile Chequamegon Fat Tire Festival.

1991 Looking to expand the alternatives for "Bike to Work Day," Jeff Obst coins the phrase B-BOP (Bike, Bus Or carPool) Day. In direct response to the Gulf War (millions of dollars and lives spent to protect U.S. access to cheap oil and almost nothing spent on methods to limit our addiction), RFA launches the first employer-based B-BOP Challenge where participants pledge to B-BOP twice a month, once a week, or more for a four-month period. Since 1991, B-BOP programs have sprung up around the U.S.

1991 Minnesota Congressman James Oberstar is instrumental in passage of the Intermodal Surface Transportation Efficiency Act (ISTEA or "ice tea") — the most profound national support of bicycling since the Good Roads Movement of a century ago.

Feb. 1992 *PLAN B*, the nation's first Comprehensive State Bicycle Plan, is produced in Minnesota.

Aug. 1992 Bike lanes are striped on Summit Avenue in St. Paul from Lexington Avenue west to the Mississippi River. This is the first Minnesota application of sophisticated "straight-through" bicycle striping that is common in many European cities.

Aug. 17 1993 Fifteen countries, 272 days, 11,877 miles and 4.7 million pedal turns later, Africa Trek, led by Dan Buettner, pulls up to the southern tip of South Africa. Five continents down — two to go.

Sept. 1993 The semi-recumbent, two-wheeled Cheetah smashes the world record for the fastest bicycle when it clocks a speed of 68.73 mph.

July 1994	Tom Becker leads the city of Minneapolis into the 21st century with an unprecedented system of downtown bicycle lanes. Check out Hennepin Avenue, where two-way bicycle lanes share traffic with over 20,000 other vehicles every day.
Feb. 17 1995	A groundbreaking ceremony inaugurates the Cedar Lake Trail. America's first bicycle freeway sports divided, nonstop, one-way lanes heading into and out of downtown Minneapolis. The Cedar Lake Trail (see RIDE 6) connects the city's most popular recreational bike trails with the most concentrated employment node in the state. This is BIG! And once again it shows how history has a way of repeating itself. In 1896 — almost one hundred years earlier — one-way, separated cycle paths first connected downtown St. Paul with Como Park.

Take the B-BOP Challenge! Phone 349-RIDE now.

Jerry Hass, 1995

America's "first bicycle freeway" — the Cedar Lake Trail — offers nonstop service into downtown Minneapolis. See RIDE 6.

Jerry Hass, 1995

BIKE SAFETY – POP QUIZ

Test your knowledge of bicycle safety. The following questions were developed with the help of the **Minnesota Community Bicycle Safety Project** (625-9719) and Cynthia McArthur. Answers below.

1. Bicycles are legal vehicles subject to the same traffic laws as cars.

   True   False

2. What percent of bicycle crashes involve collisions with motor vehicles?

   a. 10%   b. 40%   c. 70%   d. 90%

3. Almost half of the children under age nine killed on bicycles die when they bike out of a driveway without looking or yielding.

   True   False

4. Riding on off-road paths is safer than riding on the street.

   True   False

5. Bicycle registration is required by law in the following cities:

   a. Bloomington   b. Minneapolis   c. St. Paul

6. About three percent of all bicycle riding is at night. What percent of fatalities occur at night?

   a. 4%   b. 25%   c. 60%   d. 75%

7. A white light (visible from 500') and a red reflector (visible to 600') are required by Minnesota law. Why are flashing rear lights so popular?

   a. They meet state law.

   b. They are highly visible.

   c. They last "forever" on one battery.

Match the percent of car-bike collisions that occur in each of the following situations:

8. _____ Cyclists fail to yield (pulling out of driveway, at controlled intersection, etc.).

9. _____ Motorists fail to yield (either at a stop sign or when turning left).

10. _____ Being hit from behind.

11. _____ Riding the wrong way against traffic.

12. _____ No lights on bike at night.

13. _____ Opening car doors.

   a. 5%
   b. 7%
   c. 10%
   d. 18%
   e. 30%
   f. 60%

14. What is wrong with this picture?

15. Could you replace your bike for $10.00?

   Yes   No

QUIZ ANSWERS

1. True
2. a. 10%
3. True
4. Statistics vary, but experts generally agree that bike path collisions are more frequent, whereas on-street accidents result in more injuries.
5. b. Minneapolis
6. c. 60%
7. All of the above
8. e. 30%
9. e. 30%
10. b. 7% Rear-ending often occurs at night. Experienced riders will use a mirror which is also good on country roads where there is no shoulder.
11. c. 10% It is against the law to ride against traffic and motorists will not expect you.
12. d. 18%
13. a. 5%
14. The bicyclist is riding the wrong way, not wearing a helmet, listening to Barry Manilow and singing, "look Ma, no hands."
15. Probably not but registering your bike will significantly increase the chances of recovering your bicycle. It costs a mere $10.00 and can help to quickly identify injured bicyclists, especially kids. Phone 625-9719 or stop by a Motor Vehicle Deputy Registrar, local police department or bike shop to register your bike.

BIKING SAFELY

Minnesota SAFE KIDS in St. Paul (291-9150) has helmets for children and adults for under $20.

If experience is the best teacher then I should be an expert on bike safety. I have been hit by a car at an intersection, run into an opening car door while biking along a line of parked cars, and done a complete flip over the handlebars of a mountain bike after hitting a large rock hidden in some tall grass. Most of my bike accidents happened many years ago, and for the most part, they were my fault. **Truth is, poor cycling skills — not cars — are to blame for most injuries to bicyclists.** In fact, 90 percent of all bike crashes do not involve a motor vehicle.

Bicycling is a fun, life-long activity. Most accidents are easily avoided by following some simple rules. You must be predictable, be seen, and anticipate the worst. However, as Elvis Costello once sang, "accidents will happen," and that is perhaps the best reason to wear a helmet.

BE PREDICTABLE

Obey traffic signs and signals.
Nothing makes motorists more angry than bicyclists blowing past them at a red light. You will run into these same folks later at public bike facility meetings.

Ride on the right with traffic.
Ride in a straight line.

Choose the best way to turn left.
Most experienced cyclists prefer to do it like a car. LOOK, signal, move into the left lane and turn left. At busy, multiple lane intersections you may opt for using cross-walks like a pedestrian.

BE SEEN

Use headlights, taillights, reflectors and reflective vests at night.
Bright neon colors and whites help day or night.

Use hand signals.
Right turns can be signalled in one of two ways. Hold left arm up and bent 90° at elbow or extend right arm straight out. Keep one hand on handlebar.

Go slowly on walks and paths.
Pedestrians have the right of way. Yell, "On your left," when passing.

ANTICIPATE THE WORST

Make eye contact.
Believe that motorists do not see you. Never assume that motorists will:
- Stop at red lights.
- Go straight (even if they have not signaled a turn).
- Look when backing out of a driveway.
- Stay in their lane.

Avoid road hazards.
Slow down. Cross railroad tracks at right angles.

Wear a helmet.

Intersections are dangerous.
Watch for left-turning vehicles and driveway pull-outs.

BICYCLE COMMUTING

Small steps can make a big difference. By using just one less gallon of gas each week you will eliminate over 1,000 pounds of pollution each year.

MN Department of Transportation

I rather enjoy it!

Former Mayor Don Fraser on why he would bike to work occasionally

As many as 2,000 bicyclists now commute into downtown Minneapolis. Bicycling provides no-wait, no-transfer, door-to-door service — just like a car — and this is just one of its attractions.

Most trips (over 75 percent) in the Twin Cities are not work-related. Travelling by bicycle has the same benefits whether you are commuting to the bank, the store or your buddy's place.

It's cheap.

This partly explains the influx into downtown Minneapolis. Some people simply cannot afford to own, operate and park a car downtown.

It's fun.

I would bet this is the number one reason people commute by bike — whether it is to work, the store or a friend's house. As the Cedar Lake Parkway and River Road routes are completed, expect the number of Minneapolis commuters to rise dramatically.

It's good exercise.

You don't have to worry about squeezing in time for the club. And the scenery is a lot better.

CHOOSING A ROUTE

Use the maps on the following pages and any additional street maps (see sidebar on MAP SOURCES page 22) to help choose a good route. Once you have determined a good route, practice it once on a weekend. Consider the following:

- Length (2 to 8 miles is typical)
- Your comfort level in traffic
- Personal safety in unfamiliar neighborhoods
- Scenery (try a prettier route on your way home)
- Combining trips on the way home to include shopping, socializing, etc.

DRESS FOR SUCCESS

Dress for the weather and dress comfortably. Take your time. Europeans wear the most stylish clothes while bicycling and never seem to work up a sweat. Some thoughts:
- Pick a "casual day" as your bike day
- Keep an extra set of clothes/shoes at work
- Wear a bright colored shell or reflective vest at twilight
- Bring a polypropylene head band and gloves
- Wear a helmet

BIKE NECESSITIES
- Bright, white clothing
- Helmet that fits
- U-lock
- Fenders
- Reflectors and lights
- Rear rack, saddlebags
- Bell or horn
- Mirror
- Bike registration tag

The well-dressed, fully-equipped bicycle commuter in action.

SAINT PAUL BIKE COMMUTER ROUTES

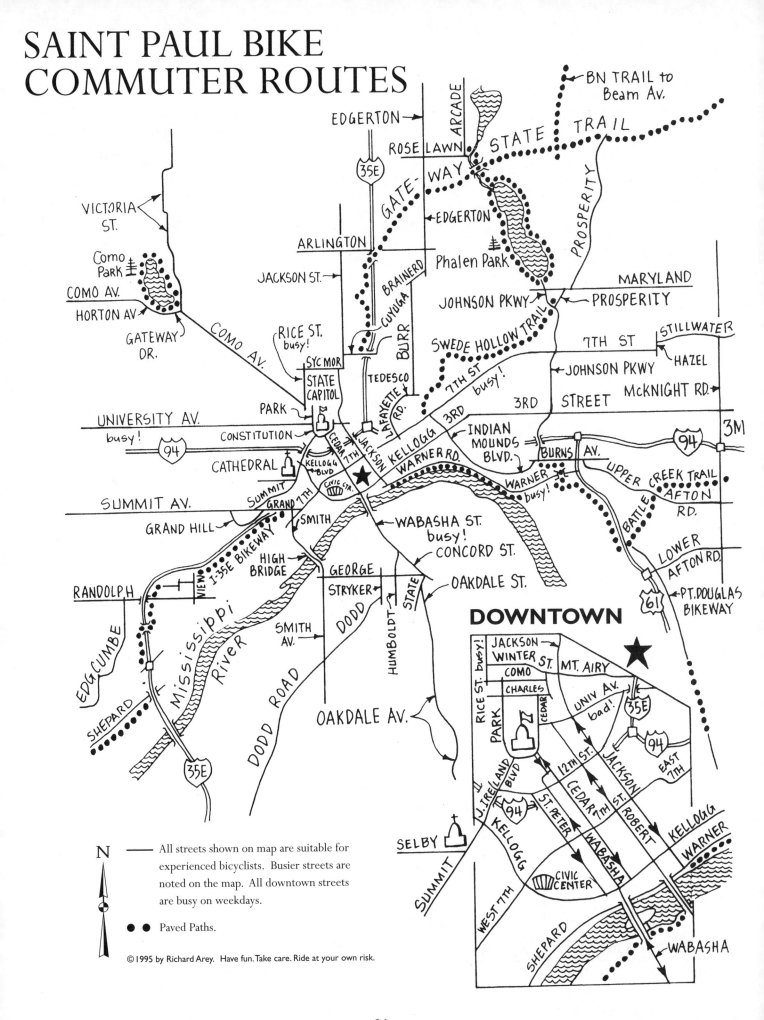

BN TRAIL to Beam Av.

STATE TRAIL

GATE-WAY

ARCADE

EDGERTON →

ROSE LAWN

35E

PROSPERITY

ARLINGTON

← EDGERTON

JACKSON ST.

Phalen Park

BRAINERD

CUYUGA

BURR

MARYLAND

JOHNSON PKWY

← PROSPERITY

VICTORIA ST.

Como Park

Como Av.

HORTON AV.

GATEWAY DR.

COMO AV.

RICE ST. busy!

SWEDE HOLLOW TRAIL

7TH ST

7TH ST

STILLWATER

HAZEL

SYC MOR

STATE CAPITOL

TEDESCO

LAFAYETTE RD.

3RD ST busy!

JOHNSON PKWY

McKNIGHT RD.

PARK

3RD

3RD   STREET

UNIVERSITY AV. busy!

94

CONSTITUTION

CEDAR

7TH

JACKSON

KELLOGG

WARNER RD.

INDIAN MOUNDS BLVD.

BURNS AV.

94   3M

CATHEDRAL

KELLOGG BLVD

★

CIVIC CTR.

WARNER busy!

UPPER CREEK TRAIL

AFTON RD.

SUMMIT AV.

SUMMIT

GRAND   7TH

SMITH

WABASHA ST. busy!

CONCORD ST.

BATTLE

LOWER AFTON RD.

GRAND HILL →

I-35E BIKEWAY

HIGH BRIDGE

GEORGE

OAKDALE ST.

61

PT. DOUGLAS BIKEWAY

RANDOLPH

VIEW

STRYKER

DODD

HUMBOLDT

STATE

DOWNTOWN

EDGCUMBE

Mississippi River

SMITH AV.

DODD ROAD

OAKDALE AV.

JACKSON →

WINTER ST.

COMO

MT. AIRY

★

SHEPARD

35E

RICE ST. busy!

PARK

CHARLES

CEDAR

UNIV AV. bad!

35E

94

J. IRELAND BLVD

94

12TH ST.

ST. PETER

CEDAR

7TH

JACKSON ST.

ROBERT

EAST 7TH

SELBY

SUMMIT

WEST 7TH

KELLOGG

ST. PETER

WABASHA

CIVIC CENTER

KELLOGG

WARNER

SHEPARD

WABASHA

N

── All streets shown on map are suitable for experienced bicyclists. Busier streets are noted on the map. All downtown streets are busy on weekdays.

●●● Paved Paths.

© 1995 by Richard Arey. Have fun. Take care. Ride at your own risk.

MAP SOURCES

Good street maps are often essential companions for bicycle riding and route finding. Check with your local municipality and county for both regular street maps and specific bicycle route maps. Many of the following maps are available at local bike shops, travel and map stores.

Metropolitan Maps

University of Minnesota
Bicycle Guide and Commuter Map
This map shows all streets and color codes good, fair and poor routes within about 8 miles of campus. Very readable and complete. Phone 625-9719.

Metropolitan Council
Regional Parks Map
Phone 296-5029
My favorite seven county car map.

MN DOT

Metro East and Metro West Bikeways
Phone 296-2216
These 1989 maps cover all city streets in a very large area (including Ramsey County, most of Hennepin County, and portions of the other five metro counties.) Map is starting to get dated and scale is quite small, but still a very good back-up map to bring on new rides.

Southeast Bikeways
This 1990 map covers the southeast quadrant of the state and includes detailed maps of Stillwater, Hastings, Red Wing, etc.

Little Transport Maps

Twin Cities' Bike Map
This 1994 map highlights the better bike routes throughout the metro area. It also shows most of the regional parks and many of the mountain bike areas.

Minnesota Bike Atlas

Twin Cities Bike Club (924-2443)
The fourth edition, published in 1995, is especially good for road rides over 40 miles in length.

County Maps

Dakota County (891-7030)
Washington County (439-6058)
Washington County is great for bicycling with miles of broad-shouldered country roads. Northern Dakota County has an expanding network of off-road bikeways. Both maps are regularly updated.

City Maps

Cities that have bikeway maps include Brooklyn Center (569-3400), Brooklyn Park (493-8335), Burnsville (895-4500), Eagan (681-4660), Eden Prairie (949-8300), Lakeville (985-4600) and Roseville (628-0088).

DO PARK

BIKE RACKS

SIGN POSTS

BIKE LOCKERS

DON'T PARK ⊗

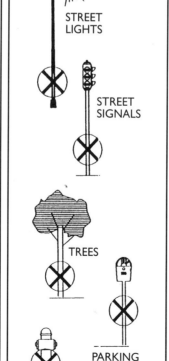

STREET LIGHTS

STREET SIGNALS

TREES

PARKING METERS

FIRE HYDRANTS

BICYCLE PARKING

If you have a four or five hundred dollar (or more!) bicycle, your biggest concern is not how you get to work but whether your bike will be there to get you home. Here are your options.

- Bicycle Registration — This is your best chance to recover a stolen bike should all else fail (625-9719).

- Inside Storage — Some companies allow employees to bring their bicycles into the office. Check with building management as well.

- Bicycle Lockers — Over 200 lockers are now available in downtown Minneapolis. Contact Municipal Parking at 339-2560. Hennepin County (348-2852), various MTC Park-and-Ride lots (349-RIDE), the University of Minnesota (625-9000) and downtown St. Paul (266-6579) all have, or will soon have, bike lockers to rent.

- U-Locks — Case hardened steel and anti-theft designs make these the best. Lock to approved stationary objects.

- Old Bikes — Using a "winter beater" bicycle can save the worry of losing an expensive bike.

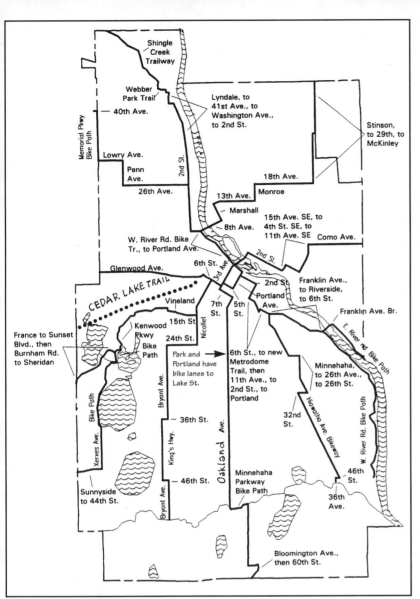

MINNEAPOLIS BIKE COMMUTER ROUTES

The routes shown at left are suggestions only and individual streets vary considerably in their ability to accommodate bicyclists. Use this map in combination with a more detailed street map to plan your commute.

BICYCLE REGISTRATION

Bike registration is mandatory in Minneapolis and your bicycle *may be impounded* if you fail to do so. The $10 fee helps pay for facility improvements. Register your bike at one of these locations or call 625-9719.

- Any motor vehicle licensing office
- Hennepin County Government Center
- Minneapolis Parks office at 3800 Bryant Avenue S.

MINNEAPOLIS BICYCLE ADVISORY BOARD

This bike advocacy group consists largely of city staff and has been very successful. Phone 673-2411 for details. See BICYCLE ORGANIZATIONS chapter for bike advocacy groups in St. Paul, Hennepin County and elsewhere.

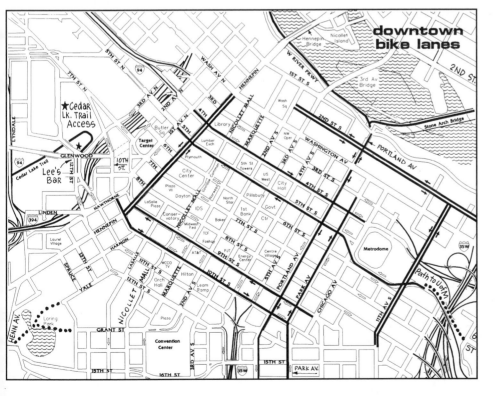

DOWNTOWN BIKE LANES

The striped bike lanes in downtown Minneapolis are almost without precedent for a major American city. They are primarily located on the <u>left</u> side of one-way streets. This feels a little awkward at first but was intentionally designed to avoid conflicts with buses, truck deliveries and opening car doors. The two-way bike lanes amidst Hennepin Avenue may be unique on the planet are definitely worth a try.

NICOLLET MALL

This unique roadway has special rules for safety.

- 10 MPH speed limit for all vehicles including bikes
- No biking on the sidewalk and no passing on the street

Paul Stafford, Minnesota Office of Tourism

There are hundreds of miles of paved off-road trails in the seven county metro area. Most of them are along lakes, parkways, and rivers like the Cannon Valley Trail shown here. See RIDE 38.

RECREATIONAL BIKE TOURS

The Twin Cities are blessed with as great a network of on-road and off-road routes as any metropolitan area in the country. Bicycle riding is a joy. Pick a route you've never done and follow mom's advice.

These routes have been designed to capture the scenic, historic and cultural highlights of each locale while providing a safe biking experience. Since most cycling accidents are the result of poor biking skills, and only 10 percent involve an automobile, you may want to quickly review the chapters on BIKING SAFELY and BIKE COMMUTING.

Use the WEST METRO BIKE ROUTES map (inside front cover) and EAST METRO BIKE ROUTES map (inside back cover) to locate the following rides.

Many regional parks have their own short off-road path systems for families with very young children. Hennepin Parks (559–9000) rents bikes at a number of parks. If you are looking for a longer ride, it is easy to combine two or more routes for as long an excursion as you desire.

The Twin Cities has a number of excellent bicycle shops that can help you select the proper bicycle and help maintain it. Don't get hung up on having the priciest gear or the most stylish clothing — get something that fits and is comfortable. Then get on with it.

If you would like some company on these tours, hook up with one of the local bicycle riding clubs. (See BICYCLE ORGANIZATIONS chapter.) Portions of these routes are included on regularly scheduled club rides or as part of a yearly event. (See ANNUAL BIKE EVENTS chapter.)

A well-maintained bike is essential for safe, comfortable bicycling. You will bike with added confidence if you have taken an introductory bike maintenance class (available at many bike shops, the University and community education courses). At a minimum, carry the equipment and know how to fix a flat.

See RIDE 1, pages 26 and 27, for sample user's guide to bike tour maps and descriptions.

EVERY TIME YOU RIDE

- Check tire pressure and inflate properly
- Spin each wheel to be sure it doesn't rub
- Be certain any quick release mechanisms are tight
- Test brakes
- Make sure bicycle lights are working if night riding

DON'T LEAVE HOME WITHOUT

- Helmet and sunglasses
- Water bottle(s) filled!
- Handlebar bag with plastic map holder
- Maps (one of route and one detailed street map)
- U–Lock and key
- Spare quarters, identification
- Snacks and/or cash
- Windbreaker — white, bright or with reflective stripes
- Gloves, hat
- Handkerchief, paper towels
- Suntan lotion and bug spray

Tool Kit and Skills to Use

- Tire pump
- Tire irons
- Spare tube
- Patch kit
- 6" crescent wrench
- Swiss army knife
- Allen keys, spoke wrench
- Chain link remover

Remember — headlights, tail-lights and reflectors are required by law at night.

BIKING FOR COMFORT

1. Ride a bike that has the right size frame and seat height.

2. Stoke up with a good meal that is rich in carbohydrates and low in fat.

3. Stretch before riding, using smooth gentle movements and holding each stretch for 20 or 30 seconds. Repeat at the end of your ride.

4. Pedal easy the first (and last) ten minutes of each ride.

5. Most cyclists pedal far too slowly and in too high a gear. Gear down to make it easier to pedal and get your cadence up to 70 or 80 pedal revolutions per minute.

6. Drink water before you are thirsty and at least one bottle every hour.

7. Shift your hand positions often and/or use padded bars or gloves to keep hands relaxed.

8. Avoid saddle sores by using a gel–filled or sheepskin seat. Position the seat parallel to the ground. Lift your butt off the seat when the ride is bumpy. Buy a good pair of cycling shorts — the sleek fit is for comfort more than looks.

9. Keep feet level on pedals. Avoid pointing toes downward while pedaling.

10. Ride downhill with the wind at your back and a Dairy Queen on the horizon.

RIDE
1

COON RAPIDS RIDER

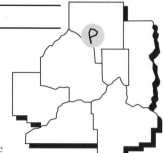

TOUR USER GUIDE

Anoka County. Connects with RIDES 2 and 7.

LENGTH
RATING

- 20.5 mile loop described includes both paved path systems
- 3.3 mile round trip path at Coon Rapids Dam Regional Park
- 5.7 miles of off-road path at Bunker Hills Regional Park
  Dedicated bike space on all roads makes it good for most riders.
  Route is flat with a couple small hills.

CAUTION   Take the sidewalk path on Hanson Boulevard and take care crossing the Highway 10 interchange. Car parking fee at Coon Rapids Dam. Walkway across dam closed through 1997.

An easy route, family approved, that connects the two main recreation destinations in the city. The paved path along the river in Coon Rapids Dam Regional Park is a delight and it is well worth walking your bike across the dam to feel the power of the Mighty Mississippi. And cowa bunga! On the north end of the town the surfs up at the Bunker Hills Wave Pool.

GO!

Start your ride at the **COON RAPIDS DAM REGIONAL PARK** (757-4700). To reach the park take Coon Rapids Boulevard northwest 2 miles from the intersection of Highways 10 and 47. Turn left (south) on Egret Boulevard to park entrance.

NSP donated the dam to Hennepin Parks in 1969 and this continues to be both the park's biggest highlight and a recurring headache. Walkway across dam will be closed for two years and rebuilt starting in 1995. If you happen to have a really long fishing pole in your tool bag, try trolling for carp on the river or stocked trout in **CENAIKO LAKE**.

After a warm-up lap at the Coon Rapids Dam Park head north on Egret Boulevard and left on Robinson Boulevard. Pretty **SUBURBAN** through here.

6.7 mi

Take the bridge over the creek in **LION'S COON CREEK PARK** and turn right onto the paved **SAND CREEK TRAIL**. This path has a wooded intimate feeling that is not necessarily enhanced by the neighborhood kids zipping through here. The path has recently been resurfaced but if you are in a hurry you will save 1.7 miles if you continue up Hanson and take **121st AVENUE** over to Foley.

Mileage given is cumulative and generally to the first bold faced **PLACE** mentioned in text. In this instance the rider will have cycled 3.3 miles in Coon Rapids Dam Regional Park and 3.4 miles further to Lion's Coon Creek Park for a total of 6.7 miles.

11.2 mi   Enter **BUNKER HILLS REGIONAL PARK** (757-3920) and go up the road a couple hundred feet until you see the paved path on the right. In the distance you may hear the soft strains of a Beach Boys medley. Kendall Bunker had a homestead here in the 1850s. Bunker Hills, like much of Anoka County, lies on the low, sandy topography of the Anoka sandplain. The "hills" are actually sand dunes that have been stabilized by planting pine and spruce trees.

For the biggest loop, ride through the park and take County Road 116 over to where the trail starts in the northwest corner. If you time your ride just right, you should be able to **CATCH THE WAVE** on your return.

17.6 mi   The sand, waves and stables may have you itching for a "surf and turf" meal but, hey, this is a **DAIRY QUEEN!** Go for the peanut buster parfait.

19.3 mi   Take note of **ERLANDSON PARK** and call your Coon Rapids council member to speed the completion of the trail that will someday connect Sand Creek with a trail to Coon Rapid Dam Park along Coon Creek.

20.5 mi   **BACK TO GO!** Heck, take another spin along the river.

→ **Total miles bicycled.**

RATINGS FOR RIDES
- Easier – Mostly paved, off-road trails
- Moderate – Mostly on bike-friendly streets
- Experienced – On roads, longer, less protected

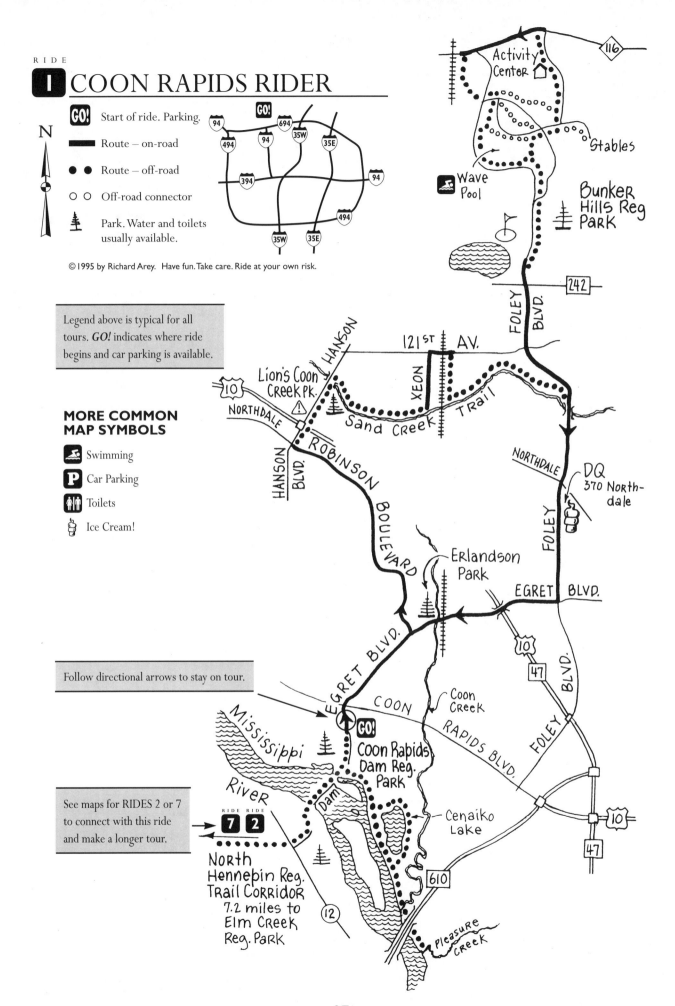

NORTH HENNEPIN REGIONAL TRAIL

Hennepin and Anoka County. Connects with RIDES 1, 7 and A.

**LENGTH
RATING**

14 miles – North Hennepin Trail round trip
9 miles – Elm Creek Park Reserve
27 miles – North Hennepin Trail and both county parks

All three rides are excellent for families.

CAUTION Walkway across dam will be closed for two years and rebuilt starting in 1995. Hennepin Parks annual or daily parking fee required.

The North Hennepin Regional Trail joins Elm Creek Park Reserve and the Coon Rapids Dam Regional Park to provide a seamless recreational experience for all levels of cyclists. Elm Creek won Mpls. St. Paul magazine's 1994 award for Best Suburban Bike Ride. The North Hennepin Trail is one of the area's oldest separated paths. When first proposed in 1972, demographic studies showed it to be an iffy deal at best. Now these types of trails are the hottest thing going.

GO! Start at **COON RAPIDS DAM REGIONAL PARK** (424-8172) on the <u>west</u> side of the river in Brooklyn Park. Take Highway 252 north from I-694 about four miles. Turn left (west) on 93rd Avenue, proceed three blocks and take a right (north) on Russell Av. (County Road 12) to park entrance.

Check out the West Visitor Center that offers a number of programs and displays relating to the natural history of the Mississippi. Live animal displays include bullheads, a fox snake and the "state threatened" Blanding's turtle.

If the walkway is open be sure to check out the Anoka County park facility which includes some great shore fishing and scenic bike paths.

1.5 mi Head west on the **NORTH HENNEPIN TRAIL** (424-5511). You can make a short detour to visit Brooklyn Park's **HISTORICAL FARM**. It is open for tours on summer Sunday afternoons from 1 to 4 p.m. (493-8368).

3 mi **OAK GROVE CITY PARK** has picnic facilities, some nice woods and two ponds.

Large stands of trees break up the flat landscape that was once used for potato farming. The sandy soil is favored by pocket gophers that like to tunnel underneath the path and cause the occasional sag. The suburbs are largely kept at bay until you approach **ZACHARY LANE**.

7 mi Crossing over Zachary Lane you enter **ELM CREEK PARK RESERVE** (424-5511). There are 9 miles of paved trails and a 5-mile mountain bike course that provides an easy introduction to the sport. Wildlife is abundant in Hennepin Parks' largest reserve. Herons, duck, beaver and deer can all be seen from the rolling trail.

The **EASTMAN NATURE CENTER** in the northwest corner of Elm Creek Park offers numerous displays, programs and an observation deck over a large marsh. The center was named for Whitney Eastman, a conservation advocate and charter member of the 600 (bird species sighted) Club in North America. Butterfly tagging is just one of the many programs offered. A monarch butterfly tagged here was later discovered by a researcher in Mexico some 2,000 miles away.

Elm Creek offers many other diversions including a creative play area, swimming, picnicking and bike rentals.

23 mi BACK TO *GO!*

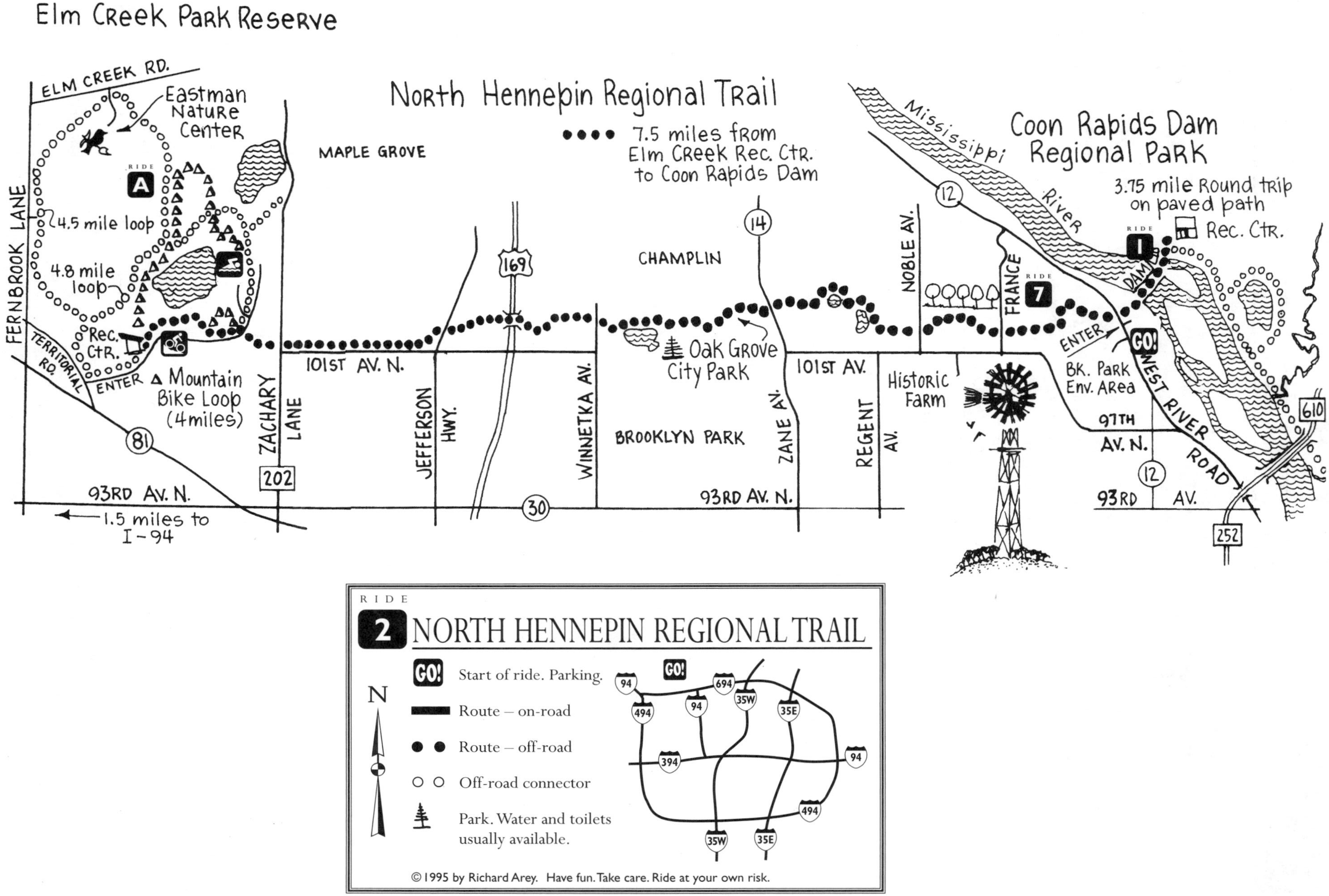

Elm Creek Park Reserve

Coon Rapids Dam
Regional Park

North Hennepin Regional Trail

3.75 mile Round trip on paved path

••• 7.5 miles from Elm Creek Rec. Ctr. to Coon Rapids Dam

Mississippi River

Rec. Ctr.

RIDE 1

ENTER

GO!

WEST RIVER ROAD

Bk. Park Env. Area

97TH AV. N.

93RD AV.

12

252

610

FRANCE

RIDE 7

NOBLE AV.

Historic Farm

REGENT AV.

101ST AV.

ZANE AV. N.

CHAMPLIN

Oak Grove City Park

BROOKLYN PARK

WINNETKA AV.

93RD AV. N.

169

JEFFERSON HWY.

101ST AV. N.

MAPLE GROVE

ZACHARY LANE

202

30

Eastman Nature Center

ELM CREEK RD.

RIDE A

4.5 mile loop

4.8 mile loop

Mountain Bike Loop (4 miles)

Rec. Ctr.

ENTER

TERRITORIAL RD.

FERNBROOK LANE

81

93RD AV. N.

1.5 miles to I-94

RIDE 2 NORTH HENNEPIN REGIONAL TRAIL

GO! Start of ride. Parking.

Route — on-road

••• Route — off-road

OO Off-road connector

Park. Water and toilets usually available.

N

Have fun. Take care. Ride at your own risk.

© 1995 by Richard Arey.

94   35E   494   35E   35W   694   94   35W   GO!   394   494   94

- 29 -

FRIDLEY FLYER

Anoka and Ramsey Counties. Connects with RIDES 4 and 25.

LENGTH
RATING

〰 17.7 miles – Full loop as described

⬤ 5 miles – Paved paths in Long Lake Regional Park

⬤ 5.5 miles – Round trip on Rice Creek Regional Trail from Aldrich Arena to Stinson

Beginners fine on off-road paths, but experience best for full loop.

CAUTION Some gravel paths and short steep pitches along Rice Creek east of Central. Careful crossing Highway 65. East River Road is busy but has a wide bike lane. Use sidewalk for two blocks along Silver Lake Road.

Beautiful stretches of paved paths along Long Lake, Rice Creek and the Mississippi River are now safely linked. Instead of doing a loop you may prefer to retrace your steps upon reaching 42nd Avenue, or continue south along the Mississippi River until you reach St. Anthony Parkway and the Minneapolis Grand Rounds bike loop.

GO! Start at **LONG LAKE REGIONAL PARK** (777-1707). Take I-694 to 35W north to Highway 96. Exit 96 and go west to Old Highway 8. Turn left (south) on 8 and proceed to park entrance on right.

This is a full-service park with plenty to do even if you don't go bicycling. There is a swimming beach with modern bath house, a picnic pavilion, creative play area, and nature trails for hiking. Stop by the old New Brighton train station for a dose of history. Cross the new footbridge over Rice Creek on the north end of the park and follow Mississippi Street a short distance to the path that starts on your right.

1.2 mi Beginning at Long Lake Road the paved path parallels the railroad tracks. Follow this until you reach the intersection of 69th Avenue and Stinson. Head left (south) and you will intersect **RICE CREEK REGIONAL TRAIL**. The first stretch of trail is gravel so you may prefer to take the paved path on 69th Avenue to Central where Rice Creek Trail paving begins.

4.0 mi Bike up out of the ravine and cross Central Avenue at 69th. Rice Creek was named for **HENRY M. RICE**, a United States Senator. Rice was a resident of St. Paul but in 1849 (the same year Minnesota became a territory) he acquired a considerable amount of land and built a country residence near here.

Follow the swiftly flowing stream as it oxbows through the pretty wooded ravine. Canoeing the creek is more difficult than it may appear. I have seen two canoes broken in half on visits here.

5.6 mi **COLUMBIA ARENA** appears as you approach University Avenue. There is public parking here.

6.4 mi You leave Rice Creek as it tumbles over a rocky rapids below a train trestle.

8.5 mi The path ends at Mississippi Street. Bike east over to East River Road and then south past **ISLANDS OF PEACE** county park. (The riverside paths were designed as a retreat for handicapped people and biking is not allowed.) You will pick up a path again just before reaching I-694 and take this under the freeway.

Enjoy the ride along the Mississippi through the **ANOKA COUNTY RIVERFRONT PARK**. Picnic facilities and an exercise course punctuate the otherwise flat and somewhat uninteresting landscape.

Architecture buffs will enjoy peeking in at the **WATER WORKS** buildings located along the path just south of the park. The romantic brick structures look more like chateaus than utility sheds.

10.5 mi The 42nd Avenue bridge takes you up and over the vast railroad yards. Enjoy the view south to the **MINNEAPOLIS SKYLINE**.

13.9 mi Wide paved shoulders make biking a breeze as you head back home. On a hot summer afternoon you might enjoy a dip at the **MOORE LAKE BEACH**.

17.7 mi Caution is advised at Silver Lake Road. Take the sidewalk for two blocks. **BEACH ROAD** takes you back into Long Lake Park. If you look closely you might spot the stone foundation of an 1880s roundhouse on the right side of the path. **BACK TO GO!**

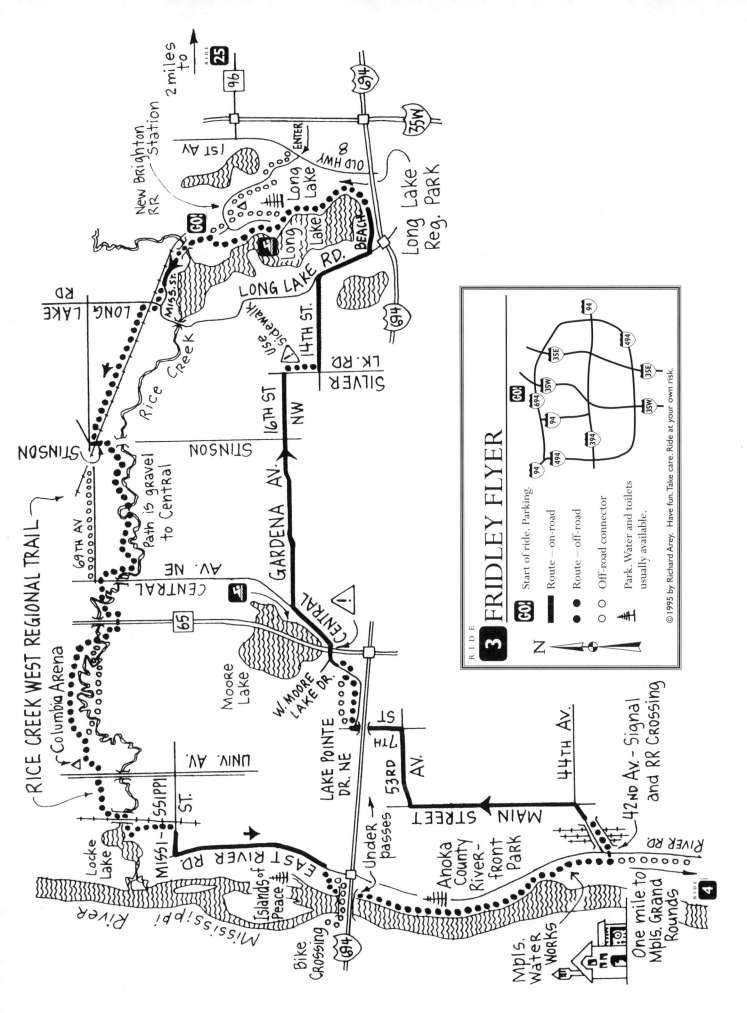

RIDE **3** FRIDLEY FLYER

GO: Start of ride. Parking.

—— Route — on-road

●●● Route — off-road

○○○ Off-road connector

🌲 Park. Water and toilets usually available.

© 1995 by Richard Arey. Have fun. Take care. Ride at your own risk.

RICE CREEK WEST REGIONAL TRAIL

New Brighton RR Station — 2 miles to — RIDE 25 — 96

1ST AV

ENTER — OLD HWY 8

Long Lake

Long Lake

BEACH

Long Lake Reg. Park

LONG LAKE RD.

LONG LAKE RD

Rice Creek

MISS. ST.

Path is gravel to Central

use sidewalk

14TH ST.

SILVER LK. RD.

16TH ST NW

GARDENA AV.

STINSON

STINSON

69TH AV

CENTRAL AV. NE

CENTRAL

65

Columbia Arena

Moore Lake

W. MOORE LAKE DR.

LAKE POINTE DR. NE

UNIV. AV.

MISSI-SSIPPI ST.

Locke Lake

Islands of Peace

EAST RIVER RD.

Mississippi River

Under passes

Bike Crossing

94

Anoka County River-front Park

53RD AV.

7TH ST

MAIN STREET

44TH AV.

42ND AV - Signal and RR Crossing

RIVER RD

Mpls. Water Works

One mile to Mpls. Grand Rounds — RIDE 4

94

35W

94

I94

I94

STINSON

N

© 1995 by Richard Arey.

- 31 -

MINNEAPOLIS GRAND ROUNDS

Hennepin County. Connects with RIDES 3, 6, 7, 8, 11, 19, 20, 27, 30 and 39.

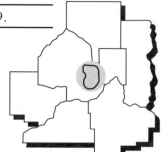

LENGTH
RATING   32.7 miles – Full Grand Rounds as described

9.8 miles – Minnehaha Parkway, round trip

9.2 miles – West River Parkway, round trip

12.7 miles – Wirth and Memorial Parkways, round trip

CAUTION   The 15th Av. SE to Como Av. to Stinson Blvd. section is busy.

> "*I would have the City itself a work of art*"   H.W.S. Cleveland — *Minneapolis, April 20, 1888.*
>
> *And so it is. Here is the bike ride that delivers it all — gleaming lakes, long majestic boulevards, dancing Minnehaha Falls (when running), and the country's third coast — the Mississippi River. On March 14, 1891, a Special Committee of the Minneapolis Parks Commission, under the leadership of Dr. William Watts Folwell, made the first call for enlarging the park system by creating a "Grand Rounds — a main encircling boulevard or parkway, connecting and passing through several of the larger park areas." By 1918, Wirth, Victory Memorial and St. Anthony parkways had all been developed to join The Lakes, Minnehaha Creek and the Mississippi River. This is one of the most impressive systems in the country, and yet, it has never been truly finished. For decades after 1918 there were plans to connect the "Missing Link of the Grand Rounds Parkway System" through the U of M campus. It still hasn't happened. So sing a few stanzas of "Will the Circle be Unbroken" as you wind your way up from the river to Stinson Boulevard.*

GO!   Start your tour at 36th Street and **EAST LAKE CALHOUN PARKWAY.** This is quite near the spiritual, historical and recreational heart of Minneapolis. Within a block or so are the sites of an early Dakota Indian village, the first white residence, and the resting place of H.W.S. Cleveland — the godfather of Minneapolis parks.

1.0 mi   Head south and at the first intersection take William Berry Parkway to **LAKE HARRIET PAVILION.**

2.5 mi   Follow the separated bikeway clockwise around Lake Harriet to **MINNEHAHA PARKWAY.** The bike path along Minnehaha Creek is one of the prettiest in the metro area. A shaded haven in mid-summer, the lively bubbling creek is always a pleasure.

6.1 mi   **LAKE NOKOMIS** is reached. If you missed the **DAIRY QUEEN** on Cedar Avenue you have another **DQ** opportunity shortly. The 2.9 mile bike path around Nokomis is not included in the overall Grand Rounds mileage. Beach is on west shore.

8.2 mi   **MINNEHAHA FALLS** is located about a block south of Godfrey Parkway. The falls were the inspiration for Henry Longfellow's epic poem, *The Song of Hiawatha,* though he never visited here.

8.6 mi   Head up West River Parkway and you will start catching some views of the **MISSISSIPPI RIVER GORGE.** Just north of Franklin Avenue, a long downhill run brings you right next to the river.

13.2 mi   Take **FOURTH STREET** up out of the gorge and across the Washington Avenue bridge. Marvel at

Frank Gehry's stainless steel-clad **WEISMAN ART MUSEUM** gleaming above the Mississippi.

15.5 mi   **STINSON BOULEVARD** is reached after winding through campus. You have just negotiated the "Missing Link of the Grand Rounds."

21.5 mi   St. Anthony Parkway leads to a fine vista at Deming Heights Park. The **CAMDEN BRIDGE** over the Mississippi River allows another distant view of the downtown skyline.

22.4 mi   **VICTORY MEMORIAL PARKWAY** was dedicated on June 11, 1921, in honor of the Hennepin County casualties during World War I.

26.4 mi   Straight and stately Memorial Parkway begins to curve as it approaches Golden Valley Road and the **45th PARALLEL OF LATITUDE.** Locate the marker at the southeast corner of Wirth Parkway and Golden Valley Road. You are now standing halfway between the North Pole and the equator!

28.4 mi   Continue down Wirth Parkway through beautiful **THEODORE WIRTH PARK** — named after the man who took down the "Keep Off the Grass" signs in 1906 and led the Minneapolis park system into the age of recreation. Mileage is to the entrance of **ELOISE BUTLER WILDFLOWER GARDEN.**

29.3 mi   Cross I-394 and in a couple blocks you will cross Cedar Lake Trail and take a left onto the bike path at the head of **CEDAR LAKE.**

32.7 mi   Follow the famous lakes **BACK TO** *GO!*

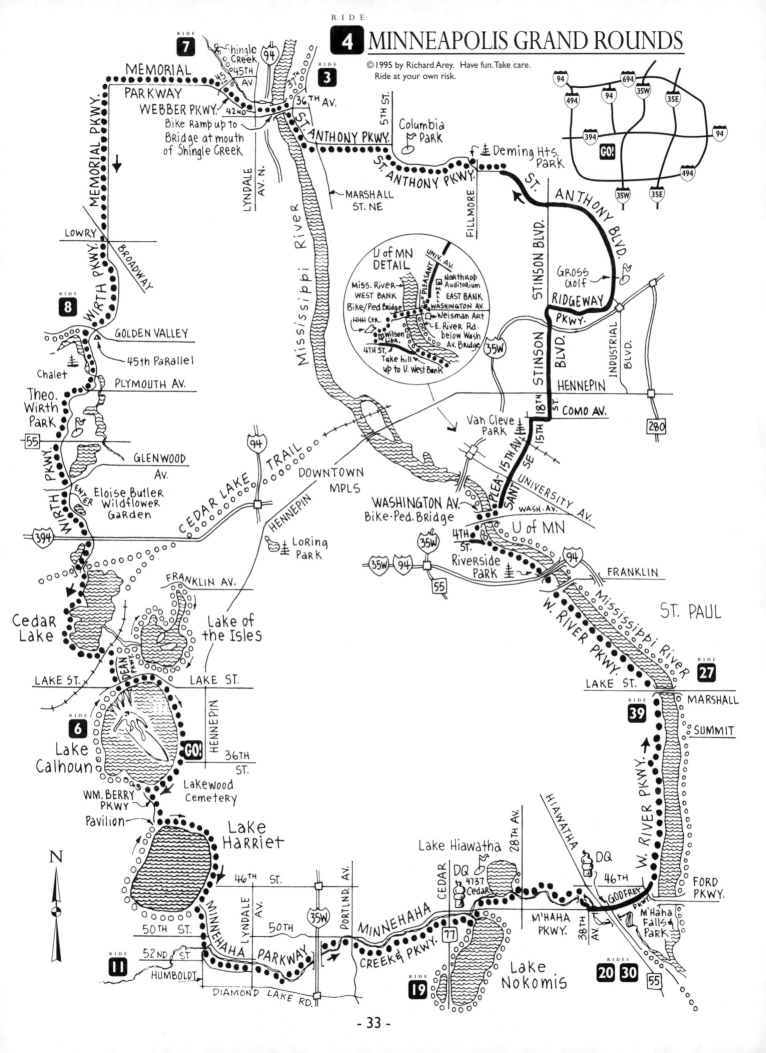

MINNEAPOLIS GRAND ROUNDS

RIDE **4**

© 1995 by Richard Arey. Have fun. Take care.
Ride at your own risk.

ST. ANTHONY FALLS SPECTACULAR

Hennepin County. Connects with RIDES 6 and especially 39.

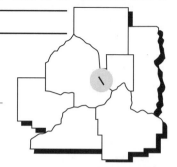

LENGTH A mere 3.8 miles, but take your time to explore

RATING 🌑 Short, flat and easy

CAUTION This is a fairly well used area but bicycling with a friend will ease concerns for personal safety between Hennepin and Plymouth Avenues.

My most memorable image while bicycling in 1994 was gliding across the Stone Arch Bridge on a crisp, blue-sky day — October 31, 1994 — when the historic James J. Hill bridge was reopened and returned to the people. The concrete capped St. Anthony Falls was a revelation, a spectacle. Bold, beautiful and thundering below the sleek Minneapolis skyline. After being hidden from public view for almost a century, the new bikeway and walkway over the bridge have finally unveiled the "waterfall that built a city." For this is no mere tourist attraction. Most historians agree that without these falls Minneapolis would be just another St. Paul suburb today. St. Anthony Falls provided the hydro power that originally drew people to form the small towns of St. Anthony and Minneapolis in the 1850s. The flour mills that sprang up along the river banks can still be seen today. Minneapolis led the world in milling from 1880 to 1930. It is this rich industrial and architectural heritage, combined with the joyful presence of the Mississippi River, that makes this one of the finest, albeit shortest, bike trips in the Upper Midwest.

GO! Start at the **UPPER ST. ANTHONY FALLS LOCK AND DAM** located at the end of Portland Avenue (333-5336). Completed in 1963, this is the uppermost in a series of 29 locks connecting Minneapolis with the Gulf of Mexico. The Visitor Center has a **PANORAMIC VIEW** and interpretive displays.

0.4 mi Head upstream and enjoy the riverside view until you reach the **HENNEPIN AVENUE SUSPENSION BRIDGE.** Completed in 1990, this striking new bridge is historically appropriate (it occupies the site of an 1854-1855 suspension bridge that was the first ever to span the Mississippi), but technically regressive (today's suspension bridges must span at least 1,500 feet to be cost-efficient and this one is just 625 feet across). It does provide a beautiful **GATEWAY** into the city.

1.0 mi Continue northwest along the river and into a more natural setting. A footbridge crosses over **BASSETT CREEK** about 25 yards from the main path. The stone arched outlet can be seen where the creek emerges after travelling 2 miles under the city. (Ask me some day about the time I canoed this stretch.)

1.1 mi A small picnic area is found just before the **PLYMOUTH AVENUE BRIDGE.**

1.6 mi Cross over the bridge and onto **BOOM ISLAND PARK.** This was the site of a log boom in the 1800s and is now enjoyed for its picnic facilities and boardwalk along the river. The **ANSON NORTHRUP EXCURSION BOAT** (227-1100) begins its scenic river tours here.

2.0 mi **NICOLLET ISLAND** is reached via a small footbridge. There are some fine turn-of-the-century homes, the Nicollet Island Inn, and an **OUTDOOR AMPHITHEATER** that hosts the occasional summertime concert.

2.5 mi The fancy ornamental tresses of the 1887 **BROADWAY BRIDGE** (moved here just recently) will take you to the Riverplace and St. Anthony Main complexes. A number of restaurants are located within the sprawling mix of new and historic buildings. Noteworthy buildings include the **LADY OF LOURDES CHURCH** (1857) and **PRACNA ON MAIN** (1890). Stop in at the Minnesota Historical Society's program office at 125 Main Street SE for tour and historic information.

3.0 mi Continue along the path that follows the restored cobblestones of **MAIN STREET.** You will soon reach the **PILLSBURY "A" MILL** (1881). Once the world's largest, it is now the only flour mill still in operation at the falls.

3.2 mi Last stop is **HENNEPIN BLUFFS PARK.** A historical marker commemorates the place where Father Hennepin, the area's first white visitor, first saw the falls in June of 1680. He was led here while a captive of the Dakota Indians, who knew these falls as **O-WA-MNI-YO-MNI.**

3.8 mi The magnificent **GREAT NORTHERN RAILWAY STONE ARCH BRIDGE** (1883) curves gracefully and directly **BACK TO GO!** Enjoy the $2.9 million view along the way.

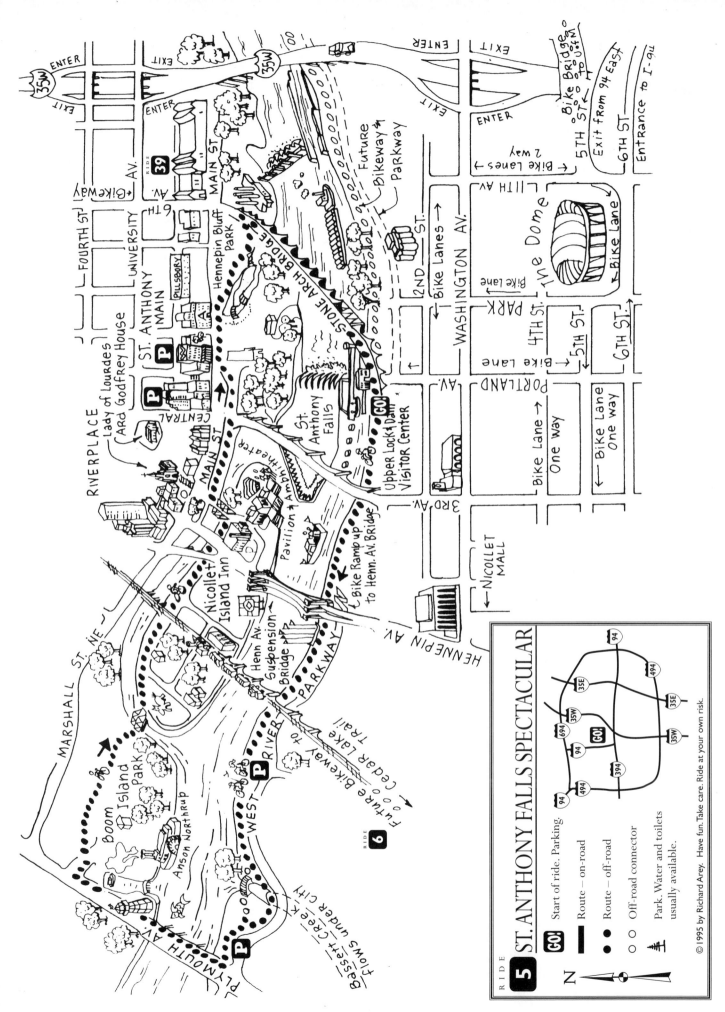

ST. ANTHONY FALLS SPECTACULAR

RIDE 5

N

GO! Start of ride. Parking.

Route — on-road

Route — off-road

o o Off-road connector

Park. Water and toilets usually available.

©1995 by Richard Arey. Have fun. Take care. Ride at your own risk.

MINNEAPOLIS LAKE DISTRICT

Hennepin County. Connects with RIDES 4, 5, 7, 8 and 11.

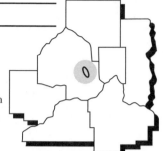

LENGTH   Mileage for each lake given below

RATING   ◗ Everyone loves The Lakes

CAUTION   On nice weekends and weekday afternoons everyone is out here. Watch your speed and yell, "on your left," when passing. New parking fees are easily avoided by bicycling here. (Minneapolis Parks, 661-4800)

The Lakes! We have all been here before. And no wonder. These urban gems are the backyard playground of the Twin Cities. Thanks to the vision of H. W. S. Cleveland, these lakes and surrounding parkways were set aside for public use over a century ago. The unbroken prairie has long since been filled in with large homes, and the lakeside resorts of the 1880s are now the site for swarms of good-looking people circling the shining blue orbs on cycles and skates, strollers and sneakers. Dakota Chief Cloudman established the first village on the southeast shore of Lake Calhoun in 1828. Henry David Thoreau kicked around these same shores in 1861, writer Brenda Ueland grew up here and singer David Pirner wheeled past these lakes before his band Soul Asylum hit it big in the early 1990s.

GO!   Start at the lake of your choice.

1.7 mi one way   **CEDAR LAKE**   Named for the red cedars that once grew alongside the lake and have since been replanted. The **CEDAR LAKE TRAIL** (3.5 miles long) on the north end of the lake provides nonstop service into Minneapolis. This short but spectacular trail has native prairie plantings and an expansive feel with the dramatic Minneapolis skyline looming above. Best access is off of Cedar Lake Road or Kenwood Parkway. See bottom map on page 23 for downtown access point.

2.9 mi loop   **LAKE OF THE ISLES**   Known by the Dakota as **WI-TA TOM NA**, or "Lake of Four Small Islands." Two of the islands were lost when Lake of the Isles was dredged and reshaped prior to 1900. Raspberry Island remains and was the site of a heron rookery until 1992. The curving shoreline and impressive residences make Lake of the Isles the most scenic and stately of the lakes. The nearby **PURCELL HOUSE** is a tour de force prairie-style home, open the second Saturday each month (phone 870-3131 for reservations).

3.1 mi loop   **LAKE CALHOUN**   "Lake of the White Earth," or **MDE MA-KA SKA**, is the name the Dakota used. It was named Lake Calhoun in 1886 after John Caldwell Calhoun, the Secretary of War, who ordered the establishment of Fort Snelling. Gideon and Samuel Pond were missionaries who built a small cabin overlooking the lake (a marker notes the spot on the southeast part of the lake). This was the first white residence in Minneapolis.

Thoreau tromped around here in 1861 and noted the "myriads of mosquitoes and wood ticks," and that the site of Pond's mission was "overgrown with sumac and covered with gopher heaps." The Lake Calhoun Pavilion was built on this spot in 1879, followed by the Lyndale Hotel, a mansion and now the golden dome of St. Mary's Greek Orthodox Church.

Lake Calhoun is the sportiest of the lakes and draws the youngest crowds. There is a refreshment stand on the northeast corner of the lake and some competitive volleyball action takes place in the southwest corner.

2.8 mi loop   **LAKE HARRIET**   Distinguished by the Dakota from Lake Calhoun as **MDE UN-MA** or "The Other Lake." It was later named after Harriet Lovejoy Leavenworth, the wife of Fort Snelling's first Commander. The whimsical **LAKE HARRIET PAVILION** rises from the north end of the lake and concessions can be found here along with a menu of summer concerts. The separated bike and pedestrian paths taken for granted in Minneapolis came as a result of a fatal collision between a bicyclist and a walker on a combined path here in 1972.

There are several other attractions around Lake Harriet including historic **STREET CAR RIDES** (228-0263), the magnificent tile interior of the **LAKEWOOD CEMETERY MEMORIAL CHAPEL**, bird watching at **T.S. ROBERT'S BIRD SANCTUARY,** a stroll through the Lake Harriet **ROCK** or **ROSE GARDENS**, and award-winning ice cream at **SEBASTIAN JOES**. Serious bicyclists, if they venture to The Lakes at all, will simply refill their water bottles at the **SPRING** and move on. See map for specific locations.

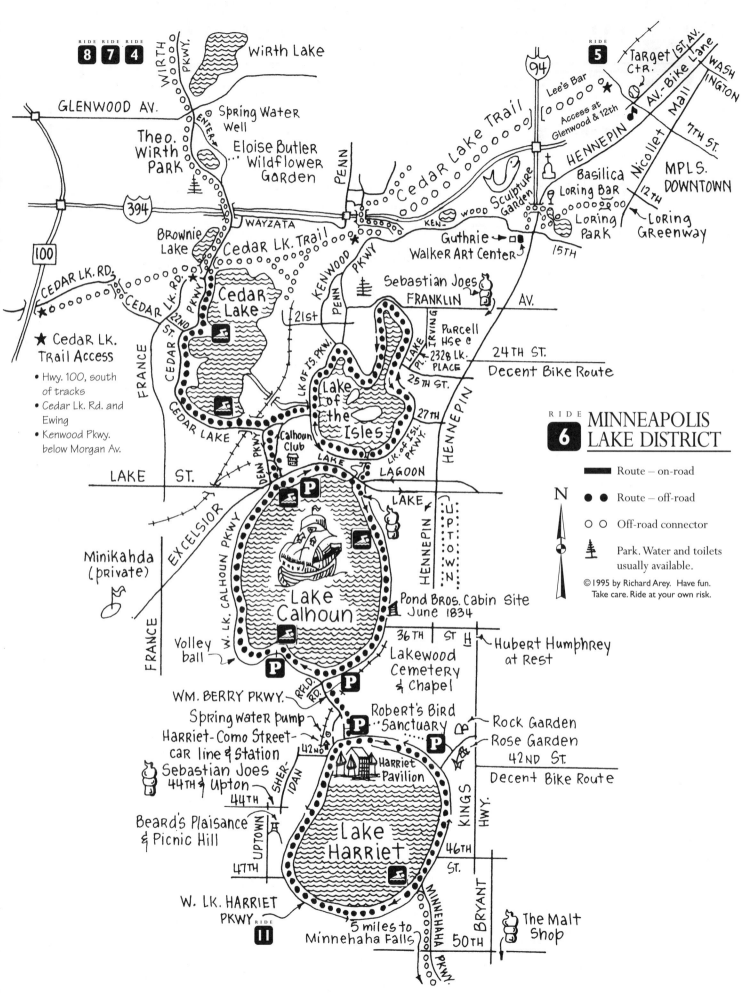

RIDE RIDE RIDE
8 **7** **4**

WIRTH Lake

GLENWOOD AV.

Theo. WiRth Park
Spring Water Well
Eloise Butler Wildflower Garden

WIRTH PKWY.
ENTER

Cedar Lake Trail

Lee's Bar
Access at Glenwood & 12th

94

RIDE
5

Target Ctr.

1ST. AV.
AV.-Bike Lane
WASHINGTON
Mall

HENNEPIN

Nicollet
7TH ST.

MPLS. DOWNTOWN

Basilica
Loring Bar
12TH
Loring Park
15TH
Loring Greenway

Sculpture Garden
KEN-WOOD
394
WAYZATA

100

Brownie Lake
Cedar Lk. Trail

CEDAR LK. RD.

★ Cedar Lk.
Trail Access

• Hwy. 100, south of tracks
• Cedar Lk. Rd. and Ewing
• Kenwood Pkwy. below Morgan Av.

CEDAR LK. RD.
22ND ST.
CEDAR LK. PKWY.
FRANCE

Cedar Lake

21st
PENN
KENWOOD PKWY.

Guthrie
Walker Art Center

Sebastian Joes
FRANKLIN   AV.

Purcell Hse
2328 Lk. PLACE
24TH ST.
Decent Bike Route

IRVING
PT.
LK. OF IS. PKWY.

Lake of the Isles

25TH ST.
27TH
LK. OF ISL. PKWY.

HENNEPIN

CEDAR LAKE
DEAN PKWY.

Calhoun Club

LAKE ST.

LAGOON

LAKE

RIDE
6 MINNEAPOLIS LAKE DISTRICT

———— Route – on-road
•• •• Route – off-road
○ ○ Off-road connector
🌲 Park. Water and toilets usually available.

N

©1995 by Richard Arey. Have fun.
Take care. Ride at your own risk.

Minikahda (private)

EXCELSIOR
FRANCE

W. LK. CALHOUN PKWY.

P
P

Lake Calhoun

Volley ball

P

U P T O W N
HENNEPIN

Pond Bros. Cabin Site
June 1834

36TH   ST. H   Hubert Humphrey at Rest

Lakewood Cemetery & Chapel

WM. BERRY PKWY.
Spring water pump
Harriet-Como Street-car line & Station
Sebastian Joes 44TH & Upton

RFLD. RD.
P

P   Robert's Bird Sanctuary   Rock Garden
Rose Garden
42ND ST.
Decent Bike Route

42ND
SHERIDAN
44TH
UPTOWN
47TH

Beard's Plaisance & Picnic Hill

Harriet Pavilion

Lake Harriet

KINGS HWY.
46TH ST.
BRYANT
50TH

The Malt Shop

W. LK. HARRIET PKWY.
RIDE **II**

5 miles to Minnehaha Falls
MINNEHAHA PKWY.

- 37 -

HENNEPIN EXPLORER

Hennepin County. Connects with RIDES 1, 2, 4, 8 and A.

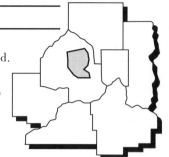

LENGTH Full loop is 39.6 miles. Some traffic and navigational skills required.
RATING Palmer Lake paved path loop (2.7 miles)
            Shingle Creek path from 45th to 63rd avenues (3.5 miles one way)
            Elm Creek Park Reserve paved path (9 miles)

CAUTION Worst stretch is Medicine Lake Road where you may want to use the sidewalk. Fernbrook Lane requires caution as there is new school construction and no shoulder.

A long, scenic tour linking several communities and their best off-road paths. The Shingle Creek and Palmer Lake trails are undiscovered gems. You will be surprised at how rural the North Hennepin Trail is and may want to do an extra loop in Elm Creek Park Reserve. Enjoy the lake vistas as you return through suburban Maple Grove and Plymouth. Hennepin Parks (559-9000) will be improving this route with more off-road trail connections.

GO! Start at the **45TH PARALLEL OF LATITUDE** stone marker on the southeast corner of Golden Valley Road and Wirth Parkway. You are standing exactly halfway between the Equator and the North Pole.

0.9 mi Wirth Parkway becomes **VICTORY MEMORIAL PARKWAY** as you march northward. One elm was planted in honor of each of the 555 (later 568) Hennepin County servicemen who died during World War I. The magnificent living archway of elms has been diminished by disease, at least until the hackberry replacements have time to fill in.

3.8 mi Watch for 45th Avenue on your left. Take this across **SHINGLE CREEK** and immediately turn left onto the paved path next to the creek. (If you like, you can make a detour by continuing <u>east</u> on the paved path to the mouth of Shingle Creek and the Mississippi River. The first shingle mill in the county, built in 1852, was located here.)

Continue north along pretty Shingle Creek and remember that the Dakota knew this as **O-MNI-NA** (a calm place, a shelter), **WA-KAN** (a spirit, sacred), **WA-KPA-DAN** (a small stream).

7.8 mi Just past 69th Avenue you enter the **PALMER LAKE NATURE AREA**. Watch for huge waves of migrating waterfowl should you visit early spring or late fall. The path picks up Shingle Creek again on the north side of the marsh.

10.7 mi At June Avenue you reenter the suburbs.

15.1 mi Brooklyn Park's **HISTORICAL FARM** is a living record of Minnesota farm life from 1890 to 1910. It is open for tours on summer Sunday afternoons from 1 to 4 p.m. Phone 493-8368.

15.4 mi Backtrack to Noble Avenue and connect with the **NORTH HENNEPIN TRAIL**. Strong riders may want to add some more mileage (3.8 miles round trip) by first biking east over to the Coon Rapids Dam and the Mighty Mississippi. Everybody else will head west.

19.8 mi **ELM CREEK PARK RESERVE** is Hennepin Parks' largest preserve with over 5,400 acres. There are 9 miles of paved bike/hike trails and a swimming beach. This ride only crosses a corner of the park.

21.3 mi Exit the park on **TERRITORIAL ROAD** (right) and then head south (left) on Fernbrook. You may want to stop at **CITY HALL** to pick up a map of Maple Grove as the next stretch is a little tricky.

Across the street from City Hall a paved path begins. Follow the route shown. If you get lost you can skip the lakeside trails and take Rice Lake Road and then East Fish Lake Road to Wedgewood. If you don't get lost, take a short detour to **FISH LAKE PARK**. There are picnic facilities overlooking the lake and a short bike trail.

32 mi **CLIFTON FRENCH REGIONAL PARK** is named for Hennepin Parks' first parks superintendent. After stretching out a bit on the creative play area, exit the park and go south on East Medicine Lake Road.

36.2 mi Forget the hassle of Medicine Lake Road with a Brownie Delight at **DAIRY QUEEN**.

39.6 mi After enjoying the occasional skyline views on Sandburg and Golden Valley Roads, its **BACK TO** *GO!*

RIDE

7 HENNEPIN EXPLORER

© 1995 by Richard Arey. Have fun. Take care. Ride at your own risk.

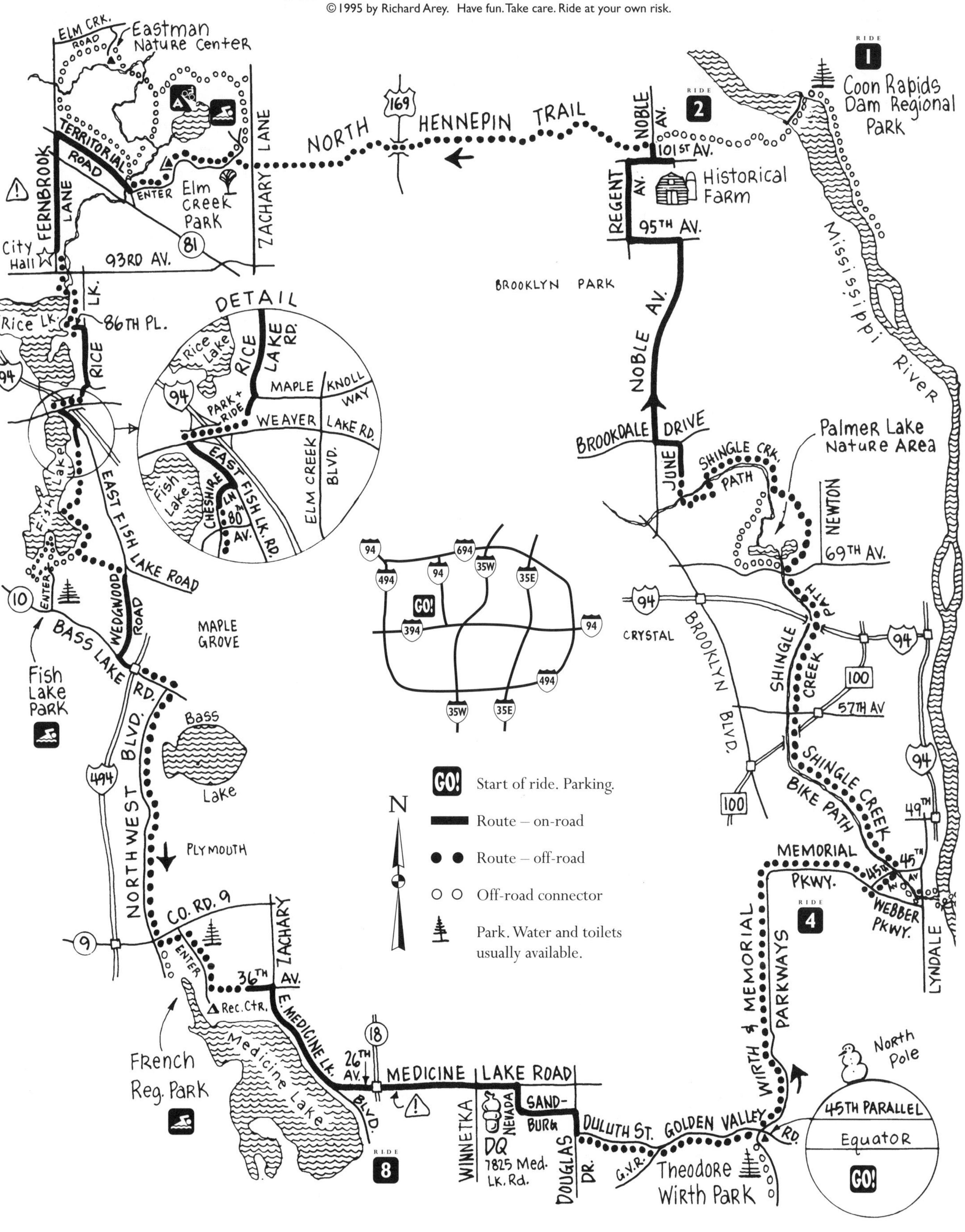

ELM CRK. ROAD

Eastman Nature Center

RIDE 1

Coon Rapids Dam Regional Park

NORTH HENNEPIN TRAIL

169

TERRITORIAL ROAD

FERNBROOK LANE

ZACHARY LANE

ENTER

Elm Creek Park

RIDE 2

NOBLE AV.

101ST AV.

Historical Farm

REGENT AV.

95TH AV.

City Hall

93RD AV.

81

BROOKLYN PARK

Mississippi River

Rice Lk.

86TH PL.

RICE LK.

94

NOBLE AV.

DETAIL

Rice Lake

RICE LAKE RD.

94

PARK + RIDE

MAPLE

KNOLL WAY

WEAVER LAKE RD.

EAST FISH LK. RD.

Fish Lake

CHESHIRE LN.

80TH AV.

ELM CREEK BLVD.

BROOKDALE DRIVE

JUNE

SHINGLE CRK. PATH

Palmer Lake Nature Area

NEWTON

69TH AV.

EAST FISH LAKE ROAD

94

CRYSTAL

BROOKLYN BLVD.

94

100

94

10

ENTER

WEDGWOOD ROAD

MAPLE GROVE

94

494

Fish Lake Park

BASS LAKE RD.

NORTHWEST BLVD.

Bass Lake

SHINGLE CREEK BIKE PATH

57TH AV

100

49TH

494

94

494

94

694

35W

35E

GO!

394

94

45TH

WEBBER PKWY.

LYNDALE

PLYMOUTH

9

CO. RD. 9

ENTER

GO! Start of ride. Parking.

── Route – on-road

●● Route – off-road

○○ Off-road connector

🌲 Park. Water and toilets usually available.

N

35W

35E

MEMORIAL PKWY.

RIDE 4

French Reg. Park

ZACHARY

36TH AV.

Rec. Ctr.

E. MEDICINE LK. BLVD.

18

26TH AV.

Medicine Lake

MEDICINE LAKE ROAD

WINNETKA

NEVADA

DQ 7825 Med. Lk. Rd.

SAND-BURG

DOUGLAS DR.

DULUTH ST.

G.V.R.

GOLDEN VALLEY RD.

Theodore Wirth Park

WIRTH & MEMORIAL PARKWAYS

RIDE 8

North Pole

45TH PARALLEL

Equator

GO!

- 39 -

EVERY WHICH WAY TO THE LUCE

Hennepin County. Connects with RIDES 4, 6, 7, 9 and 10.

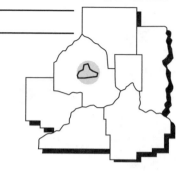

LENGTH
RATING

⚡ 31.2 miles – Big loop plus Medicine Lake as described below

☯ 8.1 mile loop around Medicine Lake

⚡ 24.4 miles – Big loop without Medicine Lake

Intermediate – quite a few hills but no major traffic.

CAUTION Roads have shoulders or low traffic counts. Stone Road to Summer Oaks is tricky to navigate. Sunset Trail has big hills.

This mid-length tour connects the newest rail-to-trail conversion — the Cedar Lake Trail — with the metro area's oldest conversion — the Luce Line State Trail. The route capitalizes on some long stretches of bike-friendly roads for an enjoyable afternoon ride. Highlights include the historic C.H. Burwell House, the Medicine Lake loop and the return ride through Theodore Wirth Park. Nice fall color ride.

GO! The parking lot on the west side of **CEDAR LAKE** is an arbitrary choice and perhaps most people will simply bicycle to the route. See RIDE 6 for detailed map showing location of Cedar Lake.

.8 mi Bike/pedestrian bridge over the Cedar Lake Trail. Nice **SKYLINE VIEW** of downtown Minneapolis.

5.3 mi Penn Cycle Shop is on the corner at Cedar Bend if you need any last minute fine tuning. Down the block is the **CHEEP SKATE ROLLER RINK** for a wheely good time.

7.2 mi The **C.H. BURWELL HOUSE**, built in 1883, is on the National Register of Historic Places. Even better, the grassy slope down to Minnehaha Creek makes for a lovely picnic site. Charles Burwell was manager of the flour and grist mill that was first used for milling lumber in 1852. The lovely East-Lake-style home is open for tours in summer on Thursday and Friday afternoons and the first and third Saturday of the month from noon to 3 p.m.

13.3 mi Follow the winding streets closely and you'll find the trailhead for the **LUCE LINE STATE TRAIL**. Head West young man and don't stop until you have entered the Cosmos. Cosmos, Minnesota, that is. See RIDE 10.

17.7 mi It is another **DQ** moment. Have a Banana Split and think about tackling the Medicine Lake loop.

22.1 mi Stop by the **FRENCH REGIONAL PARK** Visitor Center for more refreshments, take a swim, or goof off a little at the rather amazing creative play area. (My friend thought we were approaching a zoo when she first saw it.) The park is named after Hennepin Parks' first Superintendent, Clifton E. French. Clif guided the acquisition of what has become one of the finest park systems in the country. And he is a great guy to boot.

29.3 mi Enjoy the modern skyline views of Minneapolis — especially nice when reflecting the late afternoon sun — as you cruise down Glenwood Avenue on your way to **THEODORE WIRTH PARK**. Theodore Wirth combined the vision of H.W.S. Cleveland with the park land purchases of Charles Loring to forge the great system of Minneapolis parks and parkways we enjoy today. He came to town in 1906 and ushered in the modern era of recreation. Wirth began by removing the "keep off the grass" signs and ended his career some four decades later with a proposal for a vast metropolitan parks system that is now being realized.

31.2 mi As you bike down the path toward Cedar Lake make one last stop at the small parking lot just north of I-394 (west side of parkway). Across the way is the largest red maple in the city. A short walk behind you is a fascinating tamarack bog. Perhaps another time. **BACK TO** *GO!*

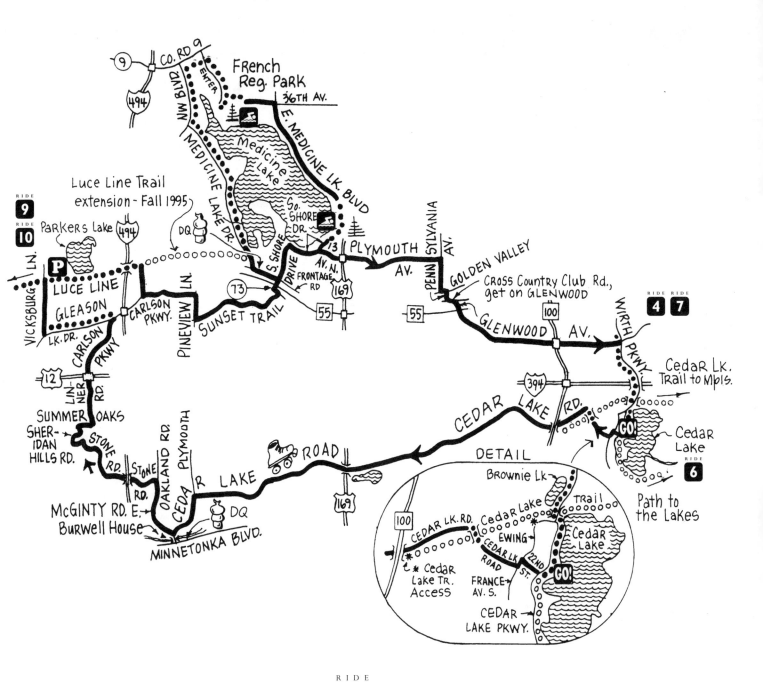

8 EVERY WHICH WAY TO THE LUCE

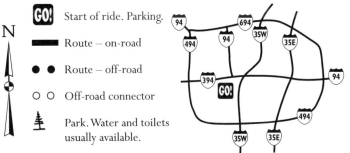

N

GO!   Start of ride. Parking.

─────   Route – on-road

● ●   Route – off-road

○ ○   Off-road connector

🌲   Park. Water and toilets usually available.

RIDE
9
ON THE ROAD TO FREEDOM

Hennepin County. Connects with RIDES 8, 10 and 12.

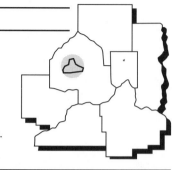

LENGTH
RATING

- 🚴 31.9 miles – Luce Line Trail out plus Baker Park loop
- 🚲 6 mile paved path – Baker Park Reserve
- 🚵 23.8 miles – Road route without Baker Park loop
- 🚲 6.1 miles – Paved path at Lake Rebecca Park Reserve

CAUTION Big hills abound and traffic is moderate but there are good shoulders. County Road 19 has quite a bit of traffic on summer weekends.

A glorious ride when the trees are ablaze. This tour takes you to Lake Independence and stands of mature hardwood are seen on much of the surprisingly rural route. Bicyclists have the option of taking either the Luce Line off-road path or the road out to Baker Park Reserve. Families may just want to do a lap or two at Baker Park Reserve and finish their day with a dipped cone at Dairy Queen or a dip in Lake Independence.

More adventurous bicyclists can go north on County Road 19 and west on County Road 11 to beautiful Lake Rebecca Regional Park. Lake Rebecca sports the finest fall foliage in the Hennepin Parks system.

GO! Start at the **LUCE LINE STATE TRAIL** (832-6170) parking lot on the west side of Vicksburg Lane, south of County Road 6. Take Vicksburg Lane north to County Road 6 and head west. Past Highway 101 the houses are replaced by rolling farms, wetlands and woodlots. NOTE: A second option is to follow the Luce Line out to Budd Street.

5.3 mi First stop is **WOLSFELD WOODS SCIENTIFIC and NATURAL AREA.** Watch for Trinity Lutheran Church and pull into the parking lot. This is perhaps the finest remaining example of the "Big Woods" (named "Bois Grand" by early French explorers) left in Minnesota. Do not even think of bicycling in here! In spring — when wild flowers brighten the forest floor — or for fall colors, it is definitely worth locking up your bike and taking a stroll. Red oaks over 200 years old and near-record-size sugar maples are your reward.

6.6 mi Enter **BAKER PARK RESERVE** on the paved trail off County Road 6. The park was donated by Morris T. Baker in 1957 and was first in the long line of

great Hennepin County Parks. Most activity is focused on Lake Independence. Biking around Lake Katrina and the surrounding marsh showcases the natural beauty of Baker Park. Watch for trumpeter swans on the lake as you bike along the southern and western portion of the loop.

9.4 mi If you're in the mood you can exit the park and catch a cone at the **DAIRY QUEEN** on the northeast corner of County Road 29 and Highway 12.

11 mi Main entrance to **BAKER PARK** is on the left. Bicycle rental, swimming, camping, picnic facilities — and a mess of summer people — can be found here. If the lines are short, I highly recommend a glide on the cable ride at the creative play area.

19.4 mi Follow the scenic contours of County Roads 19, 201 and 24 around the northern edge of Baker and over to scenic **HOLY NAME LAKE**. The quaint Italianate-style Holy Name Church is a landmark signalling your reentry to suburbia.

23.8 mi BACK TO *GO!*

ON THE ROAD TO FREEDOM

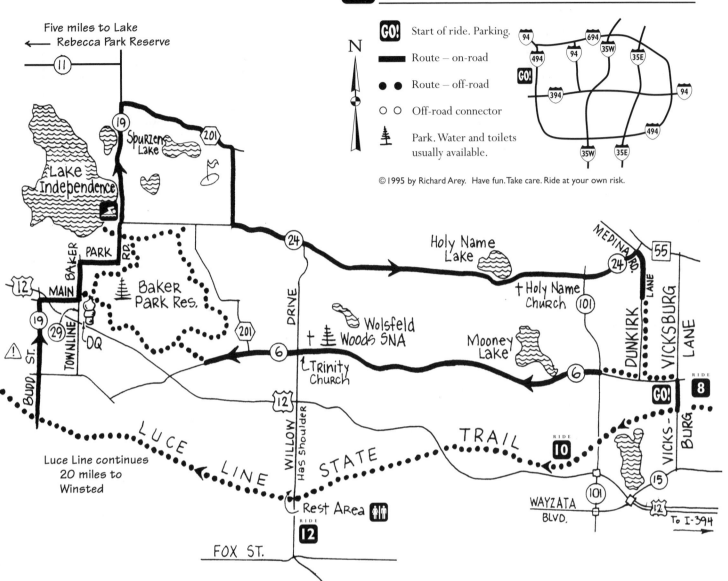

LAKE REBECCA REGIONAL PARK

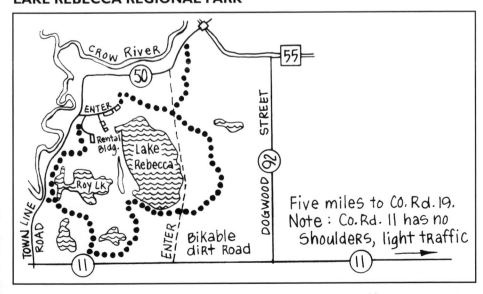

LUCE LINE STATE TRAIL

Hennepin, Carver, McLeod, Meeker. Connects with the Cosmos (Minnesota, that is).

LENGTH RATING

- 69.8 miles – Entire Luce Line Trail, one way
- 29.0 miles – One way, Vicksburg Lane to Winsted (packed gravel)
- 38.0 miles – One way, Winsted to Thompson Lake (ballast, rough)
- 2.8 miles – One way, Vicksburg <u>east</u> to Medicine Lake Road (paved)

Flat as a pancake and easy as pie to Winsted, mountain bikes with some walking necessary (due to rough trail surface) west of Winsted to Cosmos.

CAUTION Be careful at all road crossings. You will need to ford the Crow River near Cosmos.

PHONE DNR Trails and Waterways, 772-7935 or 832-6170.

Although this trail leads to the Cosmos, it was built on the broken dreams of W.L. Luce. In 1902 Mr. Luce began construction on a 1,000-mile rail service from Minneapolis to Brookings, South Dakota. By 1915 or so, an electric train was carrying city folks out to dances at the Stubbs Bay Hotel and Pavilion. But financial difficulties ensued and the line was terminated at Glueck, Minnesota, in 1927. The railway was abandoned in 1971. Through the efforts of the Luce Line Trail Association, the trail was authorized for construction in 1973 and built starting in 1976.

The Luce Line State Trail is said to follow a route used by the Dakota Indians nearly two centuries ago. It provides an excellent escape from the ever-expanding suburbs. The landscape is rolling and wooded at first, becoming level farm-land west of Watertown. In August, watch for the many native prairie flowers blooming along the way. If you bike west of Winsted, you'll be one of the first. A new Luce Line Trail Association (612-587-3368) has formed to improve this last stretch of trail.

2.8 mi The 2.8 mile path <u>east</u> of the trailhead to **MEDICINE LAKE ROAD** is scheduled to be paved in 1995. There is already an underpass at I-494 and a scenic stretch of trail along Parkers Lake.

GO! **TRAILHEAD** with parking and toilets is located at Vicksburg Lane just south of County Road 6. Mile posts below are heading <u>west</u>.

5.4 mi This first stretch to **WILLOW DRIVE** is one of the prettiest and easily the most heavily used. The trail traverses an area of lakes, marsh and hardwood forested moraines just north of Lake Minnetonka. The **REST AREA** just west of Willow Drive has picnic tables, water and outdoor toilets.

7.0 mi A small parking lot is located on the west side of **STUBBS BAY ROAD**.

19.0 mi **WATERTOWN** rests on the banks of the South Fork Crow River. The trail leading here is still quite pretty with occasional canopies of trees and nice views over **OAK LAKE**. A short detour on the quiet streets of Watertown can include a water stop at **VETERANS MEMORIAL PARK** downtown.

29.0 mi Pastures and fields are broken by small knolls covered with oak trees on your way to **WINSTED**. Thrushes, killdeer, finches and pheasant will be your most likely trail companions this far out. A beautiful curving path around Winsted Lake takes you into the quiet old town founded in 1887.

38.0 mi **SILVER LAKE**. The packed limestone path ends at Winsted and the surface is considerably rougher from here on west.

42.0 mi **HUTCHINSON** has a fine 2-mile, packed gravel path through town and along Otter Lake and the Crow River. Hutchinson may some day be the small town bike capitol of the Midwest. A cooperative project between MN DOT and the country of Finland is using the town for a case study on bike-friendly development.

64.0 mi Negotiate several miles of rough trail, ford the Crow River once, and finally, you have entered the **COSMOS**. This tiny town was organized in 1870 under the ancient Greek name for the universe as an orderly and harmonious system.

66.0 mi A pleasant stretch of path leads to the **TRAIL'S END** at Cosmos County Park on Thompson Lake.

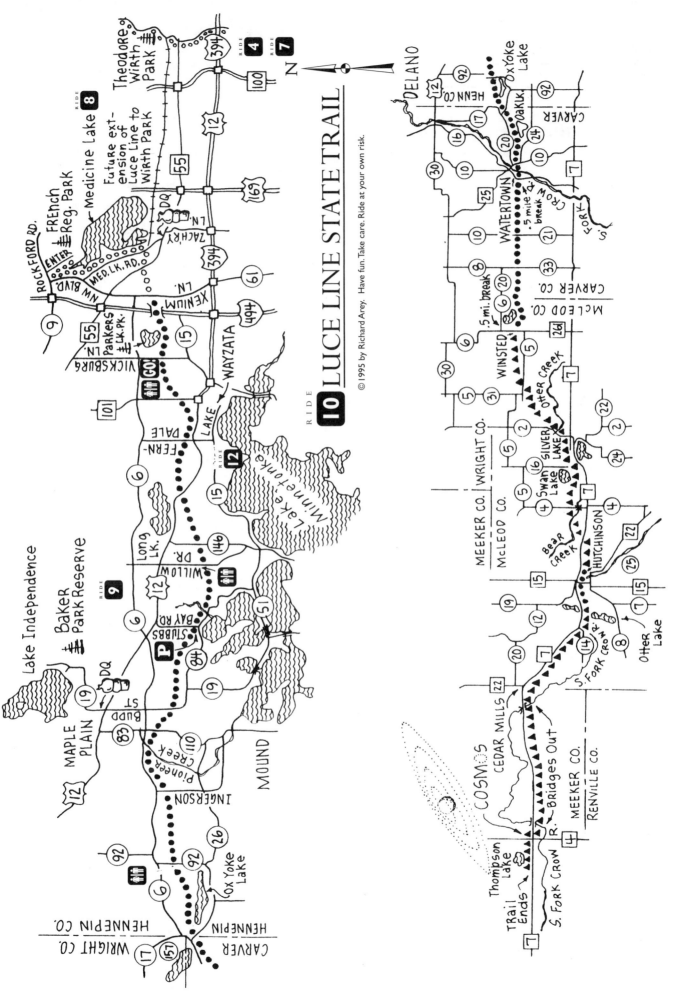

RIDE **10** LUCE LINE STATE TRAIL

©1995 by Richard Arey. Have fun. Take care. Ride at your own risk.

BLOOMINGTON OR BUST

Hennepin County. Connects with RIDES 4, 6, 14, 17, 19, B and C.

LENGTH 19.2 miles – Loop around Hyland Lake Park Reserve described below
RATING 5.0 miles – Paved path in Hyland Lake Park Reserve
TO HYLAND LAKE PARK RESERVE VISITOR CENTER
11.7 miles – From 50th and Minnehaha Parkway in Minneapolis
12.2 miles – From Excelsior and 8th Avenue in Hopkins
7.2 miles – From Staring Lake Park in Eden Prairie

CAUTION Shady Oak Road has a shoulder and some traffic. Watch directions and street signs closely on routes into Bloomington.

Many people heading for Bloomington end up at the Mall of America and come out a little poorer, if not busted. I recommend a different target, the natural center of town being the 1,000 acres of lakes, woods and wildlife that comprise Hyland Lake Park Reserve. (See RIDE B) This oasis in the middle of Minnesota's third largest city is deservedly popular. A creative play area, fishing, picnicking and pleasure boats are yours to enjoy. You can even rent a bike on the premises if necessary. Pack up your tire patch kit and head on down.

GO! Start at the main parking lot in **HYLAND LAKE PARK RESERVE** (941-4362). Park entrance is reached by taking Highway 100 (Normandale Blvd.) south from I-494 to 84th Street. Turn right (west) and follow 84th to East Bush Lake Road. Go south to entrance on left. Of course, if you had biked down you would have saved yourself the car parking fee.

1.8 mi Head up and over to the paved path that follows the west side of **BUSH LAKE** along Bush Lake Road to Veness Road. There are some nice picnic grounds here.

A 3.5 mile side trip (not included in following mileage) up to the virgin stands of oak, maple and basswood in **TIERNEY WOODS** is well worth it and mountain bicycling in Tierney is allowed. Or lock up your bike, take a stroll and imagine the 300 square miles of Big Woods that once swept from Faribault up to St. Cloud.

10.8 mi Retrace your steps to Veness Road and then head south along Bloomington Ferry Road. You skirt the bluffs along Auto Club Road and are teased by a couple nice views across the Minnesota River Valley. Normandale and 98th take you to **MARSH LAKE PARK**. A 100-foot-long earth dam preserves a wildlife refuge and controls the flow of flood waters. I spotted a loon diving for fish here one August afternoon.

11.8 mi Watch closely for a service access road off France Avenue (on the north edge of campus) that takes you to the **NORMANDALE JAPANESE GARDEN**. This small contemplative place was exquisitely designed by Takao Watanabe, a landscape artist from Tokyo.

18 mi **MT. NORMANDALE LAKE** shimmers in the reflection of the sleek office towers that rise above 84th Street. Look cool as you do a lap around these popular paths.

17.1 mi The only on-street biking on this route is the hard uphill on East Bush Lake Road. (This could explain the ski jump you bike past.) There is a shoulder, but sadly, no elevator. Eventually you reach the entrance to **RICHARDSON NATURE CENTER** (941-7993). Bluebirds and deer herds are just part of the attraction. Stop back some time when you can take a stroll as bikes are not allowed inside.

17.3 mi The City of Bloomington has just finished a million dollar renovation of **BUSH LAKE SWIMMING BEACH**. Check it out.

19.2 mi BACK TO *GO!*

RIDE 11 BLOOMINGTON OR BUST

© 1995 by Richard Arey. Have fun. Take care. Ride at your own risk.

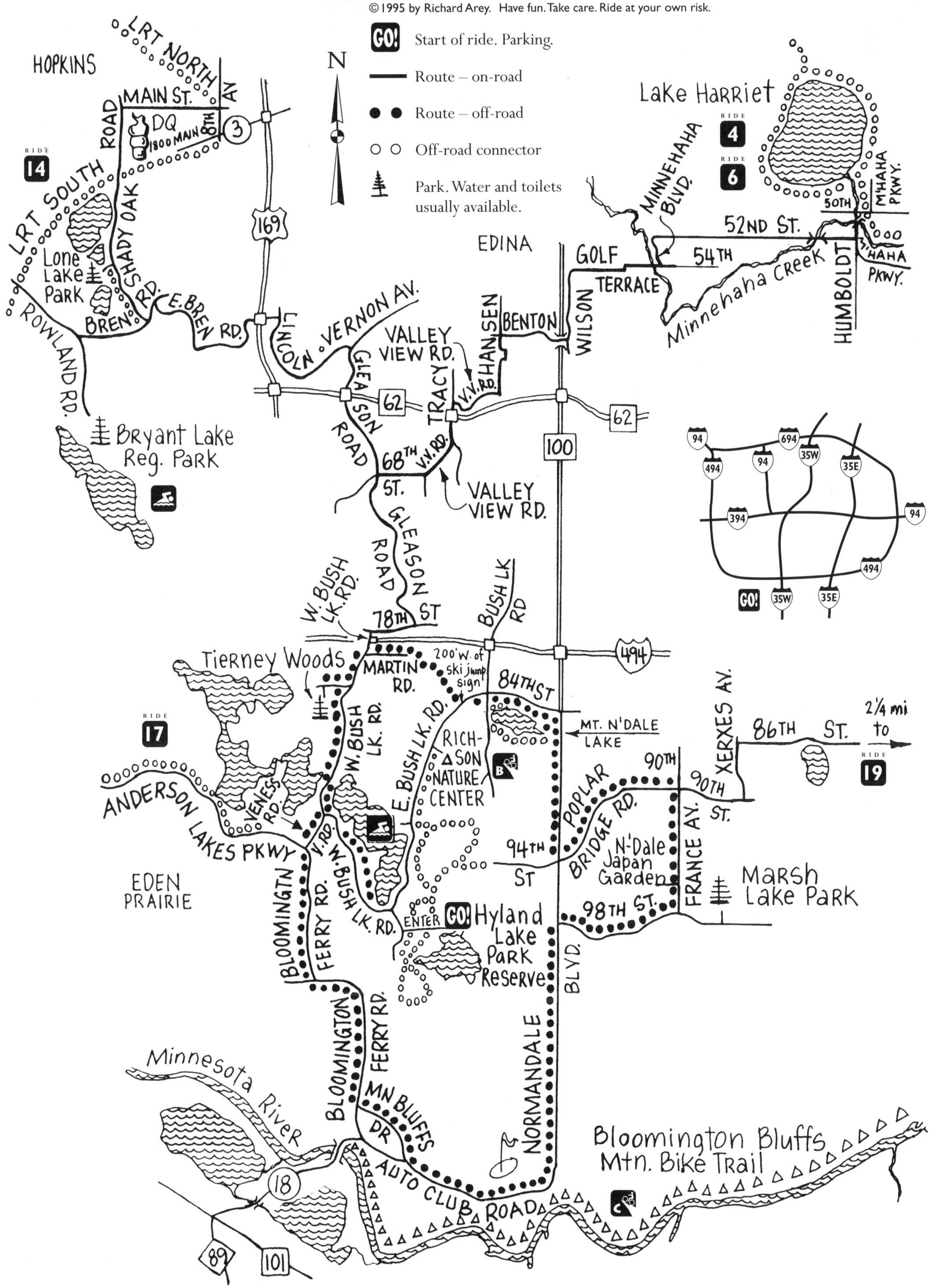

GO!   Start of ride. Parking.

———   Route – on-road

●●●   Route – off-road

○○○   Off-road connector

🌲   Park. Water and toilets usually available.

N

HOPKINS

LRT NORTH

MAIN ST.
DQ
1800 MAIN ST.
8TH AV.
3

LRT SOUTH ROAD

RIDE 14

Lone Lake Park

SHADY OAK ROAD

BREN RD.

E. BREN RD.

ROWLAND RD.

169

LINCOLN

Bryant Lake Reg. Park

VERNON AV.

VALLEY VIEW RD.

GLEASON

62

TRACY

HANSEN

V.V. RD.

BENTON

WILSON

EDINA

GOLF TERRACE

52ND ST.

54TH

Minnehaha Creek

MINNEHAHA BLVD.

Lake Harriet

RIDE 4
RIDE 6

50TH

M'HAHA PKWY.

HUMBOLDT

M'HAHA PKWY.

100

62

94
694
494
94
35W
35E
394
94
494
GO!
35W
35E

68TH
ST.
V.V. RD.

VALLEY VIEW RD.

GLEASON ROAD

W. BUSH LK. RD.

78TH ST.

BUSH LK RD.

Tierney Woods

MARTIN RD.

200'W. of ski jump sign

494

84TH ST.

MT. N'DALE LAKE

XERXES AV.

86TH ST.

2¼ mi to
RIDE 19

RIDE 17

ANDERSON LAKES PKWY

YENES RD.

W. BUSH LK. RD.

V. RD.

W. BUSH LK. RD.

E. BUSH LK. RD.

RICHSON NATURE CENTER

B

POPLAR BRIDGE RD.

90TH
90TH ST.

FRANCE AV.

Marsh Lake Park

EDEN PRAIRIE

BLOOMINGTON FERRY RD.

94TH ST

N'Dale Japan Garden

98TH ST.

ENTER **GO!** Hyland Lake Park Reserve

NORMANDALE BLVD.

Minnesota River

18

BLOOMINGTON FERRY RD.

MN BLUFFS DR.

AUTO CLUB ROAD

Bloomington Bluffs Mtn. Bike Trail

89
101

- 47 -

SWIM ROUND LAKE MINNETONKA

Hennepin County. Connects with RIDES 9, 10 and 13.

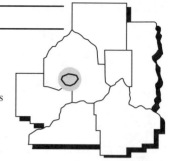

LENGTH   29.2 miles to stop at each beach

RATING   Experienced riders only. LRT route is flat and easy.

CAUTION   County Road 19 and North Shore Drive get busy. Shoulder disappears
on North Shore Drive just before reaching Noerenberg Park.

More than just a guide to all the public swimming beaches on Lake Minnetonka—this is a great bike route for experienced riders in any season. Fall colors make the route especially memorable and the springtime flower displays at Noerenberg Park are well worth stopping for. History buffs should note that the Dakota names "minne" - water, and "tonka" - big, were combined by Territorial Governor Alexander Ramsey after a visit in 1852 and that the Native American name for the lake has been lost in time.

GO! Start at the **MINNETONKA CITY HALL** (939-8200) parking lot just west of I-494 on Minnetonka Boulevard. This lot is always open to the public.

1.7 mi Minnetonka Boulevard is a little rushed (an off-road trail is planned) so you'll be glad to see the Lake Shore Boulevard turn. Take this to Park Lane and **LIBB'S LAKE BEACH**. Start swimming.

5.0 mi Follow the quiet, winding streets over to the **DEEPHAVEN SWIMMING BEACH**. Dip your front tire into the lake while you ponder where **PRINCE** christened his lady friend in the movie *Purple Rain*.

10.1 mi **EXCELSIOR PARK** has a fine beach and bathhouse. With all the people milling about you'll want to be doing your best breaststroke as you round the point.

12.8 mi Watch your directions coming through Excelsior as you head to **CRESCENT BEACH**. This tiny beach

holds a panoramic view. Sunsets must be great here but time's a wasting.

14.7 mi **TONKA BAY BEACH** (alias Wekota Beach Park) is hidden back amidst the big houses. Float awhile as you consider what it would be like to be wealthy.

19.4 mi Stop and smell the roses at **NOERENBERG MEMORIAL PARK.** Fred Noerenberg came here from Berlin in the 1880s and established the brewery that became Grain Belt. Today 10,000 flowers are planted here each year, including some bulbs from the original European stock.

24.6 mi You are almost certainly ready for a swim by now. **WAYZATA BAY BEACH** is a first-class operation with changing rooms and showers. Show off the sidestroke you've been practicing.

29.2 mi **BACK TO GO!** Take McGinty Road or the shortcut across Minnehaha Creek. I'm sure you'll want to towel off and head to **DAIRY QUEEN**, about a mile east of City Hall on Minnetonka Boulevard.

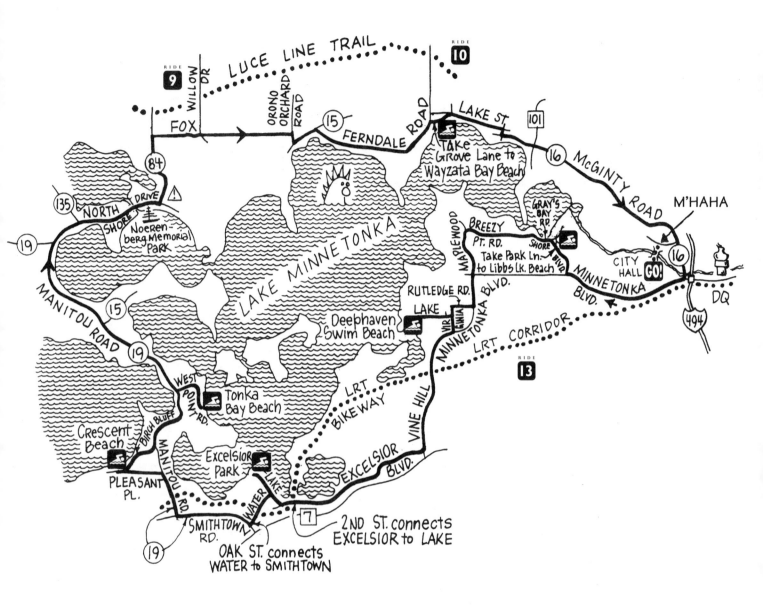

RIDE 12 SWIM ROUND LAKE MINNETONKA

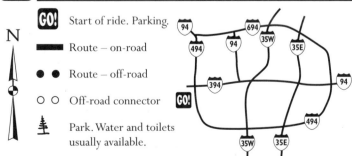

N

GO! Start of ride. Parking.

—— Route – on-road

• • Route – off-road

○ ○ Off-road connector

🌲 Park. Water and toilets usually available.

©1995 by Richard Arey. Have fun. Take care. Ride at your own risk.

13 LRT TRAIL NORTH

Hennepin and Carver County. Connects with Rides 8, 12, and 14

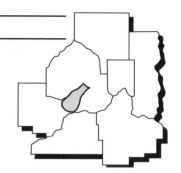

LENGTH
RATING

- 16.0 miles – One way as described to Victoria
- 8.2 miles – Additional paved path in Carver Park Reserve
- 37.4 miles – Loop using County Road 11 and LRT South

Path is packed limestone. Trail is open 5 a.m. to sunset.

CAUTION Be careful crossing all roads along path and on County Road 11 if connecting with LRT Trail South.

This is a very attractive and popular off-road path. LRT Trail North follows the abandoned railroad bed of the Chicago and North Western (C&NW) Railway and traverses beautiful woodlands, skirts the shores of Lake Minnetonka and goes by some very nice real estate before delivering you to Carver Park Reserve (Phone 472-4911). Carver alone has a half days worth of biking and other diversions so some folks may wish to drive out and spend the day here.

GO! Start in downtown **HOPKINS.** The trail begins at 8th Avenue just north of Main Street.

2.4 mi Follow the paved path through the quiet backyards of residential Hopkins. Cross over Highway 7 and into a more natural setting. **DAIRY QUEEN** is across the street at 12940 Minnetonka Boulevard.

3.6 mi The Minnetonka **CIVIC CENTER** has parking and washrooms available on weekdays.

9.5 mi A couple short but tasty stretches of lakeside path take you to the bustling village of **EXCELSIOR**.

14.5 mi **CARVER PARK RESERVE** contains 3,300 acres, 8.2 miles of bike paths and six lakes (Lake Auburn has camping and a swimming beach). These abundant natural resources are the focus of programming at the **LOWRY NATURE CENTER**.

16.0 mi Or, continue on through the town of Victoria to the **DQ** at the corner of County Roads 5 and 11.

14 LRT TRAIL SOUTH

Hennepin and Carver County. Connects with RIDES 11, 13, 15, 16 and 17

LENGTH
RATING

- 12.2 miles – One way off-road limestone path as described
- 17.2 miles – One way to Minnesota Valley Trail

SEE MAP ABOVE

CAUTION Follow the marked signs as you zig-zag across 62nd Street, Valley View Road and Highway 5. There is a 5-foot shoulder and traffic on Highway 212 going <u>into</u> Chaska but shoulder is not continuous coming back.

Dedicated on June 3, 1995, this is the latest — and one of the greatest — rail-to-trail conversions in Minnesota. Employing the old rail bed of the C&NW Railway, this limestone path provides safe and scenic passage from Hopkins to Chaska. Those with a mountain bike and a yen for adventure can bike through Chaska (RIDE 15) and on to the Minnesota Valley State Trail (RIDE 16) that goes all the way to Belle Plaine, a 39.2 mile (one way) off-road trip! Hennepin Parks Trail Hotline is 559-6778.

GO! Start at the **PARK AND RIDE** lot at Excelsior and 8th Avenue in Hopkins, (just west of Highway 169).

6.0 mi The trail winds past a series of lakes and wetlands before taking you up, over and under the bridge at Highway 62. Soon you reach **EDENVALE PARK** at Valley View Road.

8.5 mi The shores of **LAKE RILEY** make a nice rest stop, though there are no facilities.

9.5 mi **A SWEEPING PANORAMA** of the Minnesota River Valley is gained from the overlook marking the trail's long gradual descent to the valley floor.

10.5 mi **BLUFF CREEK RAVINE** is located just past Highway 101. Car parking is available where the trail intersects Bluff Creek Drive.

12.2 mi The path traverses a wide marsh before reaching Highway 212 and **TRAIL'S END**. There is a path or shoulder on 212 that goes into Chaska.

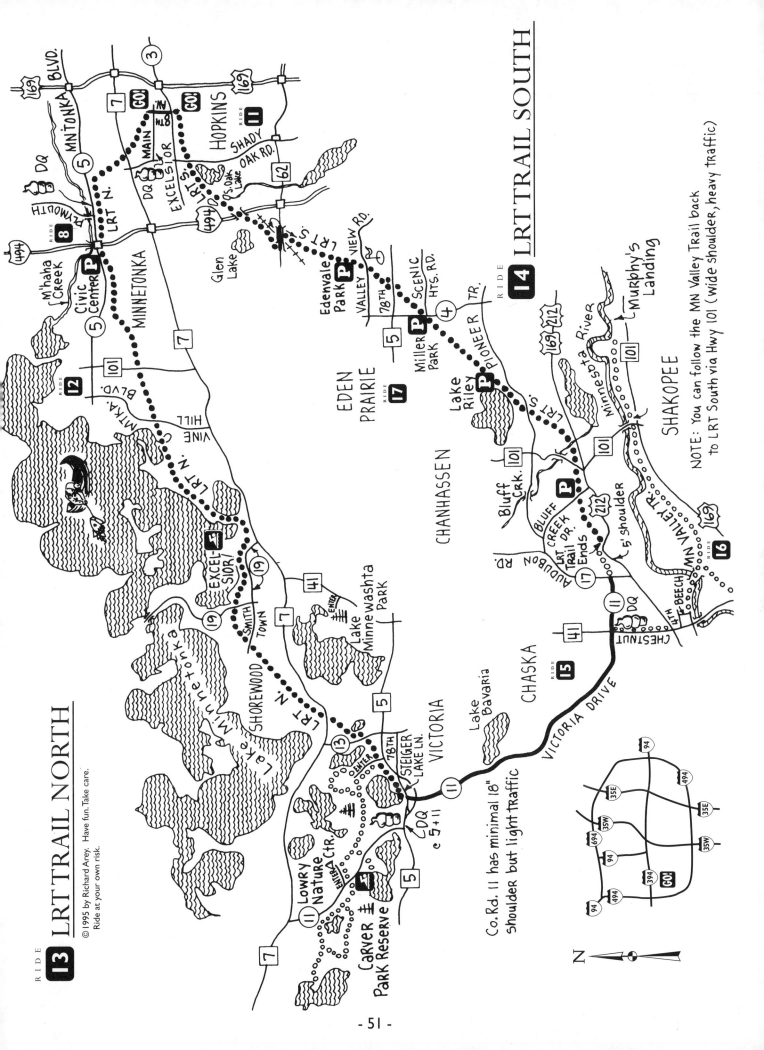

15 CHASKA CHASER

Carver County. Connects with RIDES 14 and 16.

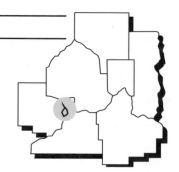

LENGTH   13.2 miles – Route as described below (mostly gravel)
RATING   8 miles – City Square to Shakopee and back (paved)

23 miles – Total miles of path shown on map

⬤ All trails are rated easier but there are some hills.

CAUTION   Watch out for pedestrians along the paths and cars at road crossings.
PHONE   City of Chaska, 448-2851.

> *These are some of the prettiest off-road city paths in the metro area and well worth a visit even if you live as far away as St. Paul. The paved path from Shakopee (See RIDE 16) glides over the vast wetlands of the Minnesota River and an ancient iron swing bridge before cruising into Chaska. The rest of the trails fan north through the old river town, up wooded ravines, past lakes and into the new town of Jonathan. Along the way, there are songbirds and soybeans, modern architecture and monkey bars. There is a bit of everything along these trails that can easily take the better part of a day to explore. Be courteous while sharing the trail and then head for a DQ with a view. That's right. The Dairy Queen at 1095 Chestnut Street North is perched on a bluff with a vista that just doesn't quit. There are several other choices for food and refreshments in downtown Chaska.*

GO!   Start your tour at the **CITY SQUARE** in downtown Chaska on the corner of Walnut and 4th Street. The old fashioned square looks one step removed from the set of *The Music Man* and also features a couple of ancient **INDIAN MOUNDS**. Chaska comes from the Dakota name that was generally given to a first born son.

0.6 mi   Cross over Highway 212 and find the trail going east (right) along the lake. This will take you to the start of the **WOODED RAVINE**.

1.4 mi   **LIONS PARK** is a short way up the path and has ballfields, tennis courts, toilets and a picnic shelter. The **SMALL BROOK** running through the ravine looks innocent enough, but my last trip here in 1992 was shortly after the engorged stream had tossed footbridges around like matchbooks. Exit the ravine up the paved path to the south near the school. Turn right and go north along Highway 41 past the top of the ravine you were just in. (A Highway 41 underpass will connect the ravine in the fall of 1996.)

3.4 mi   Carefully cross **HIGHWAY 41** and look for the connecting path about 50 yards to the north. Continue up the ravine.

4.2 mi   Cross under Hundertmark Road and enter **JONATHAN**. While Chaska is the quintessential river town with roots going back to the mid-1800s, Jonathan is the original new town, developed as a

MODEL COMMUNITY back in the late 1960s. This brainchild of State Senator Henry McKnight has fallen far short of its original goal for a town of 50,000, but the modern architecture, separated path system and lakeside community center are a testament to his dream. Jonathan was named after Jonathan Carver, who journeyed up the Minnesota River in 1766–67 in search of a route to the **PACIFIC OCEAN**.

4.7 mi   **JONATHAN BEACH** is located on the southeast corner of Lake Grace. Swimming is allowed on summer afternoons, and there are changing rooms, toilets, a volleyball court and picnic facilities.

5.5 mi   Follow the **CHAIN OF LAKES** north to McKnight Park. Parking and picnicking are located here. Continue north along the lakes by walking your bike across the railroad tracks.

7.7 mi   The **TRAIL ENDS** at 82nd Street just shy of the Minnesota Landscape Arboretum.

12.4 mi   Retrace your path back to Highway 41 and then follow the paved path along the west side of 41 to **DAIRY QUEEN**. You know what's good for you.

NOTE: A longer return trip can be enjoyed by following the paths west to Community Park. You can then return along the creek to Engler Boulevard and Highway 41. This adds about 4 miles.

13.2 mi   Coast on **BACK TO GO!** Add 8 miles for round trip to Shakopee.

15 CHASKA CHASER

© 1995 by Richard Arey. Have fun. Take care. Ride at your own risk.

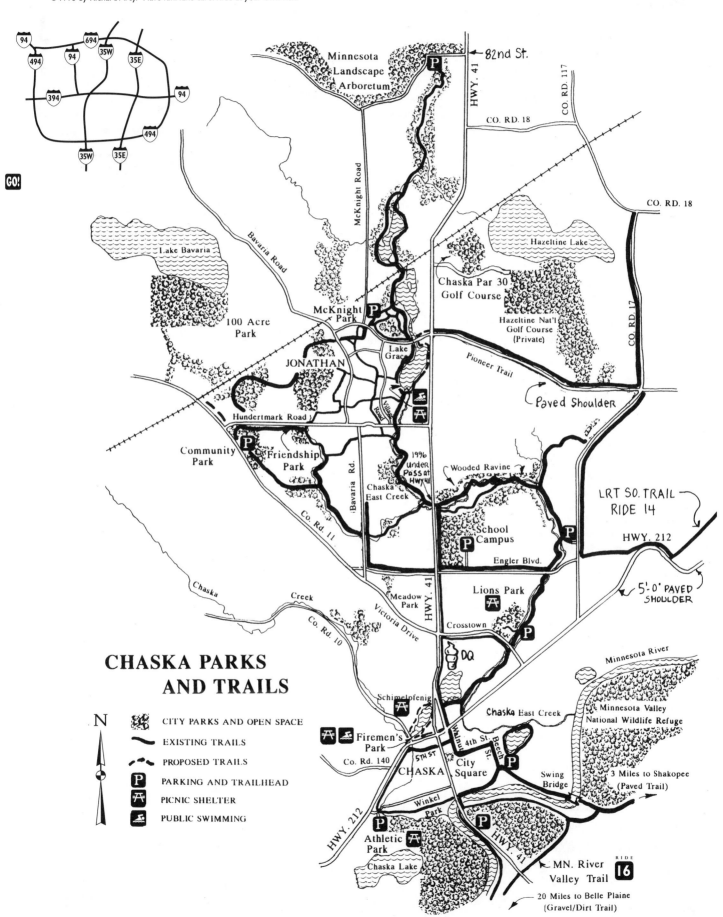

GO!

CHASKA PARKS AND TRAILS

N

🌳 CITY PARKS AND OPEN SPACE

〰 EXISTING TRAILS

⌒ PROPOSED TRAILS

P PARKING AND TRAILHEAD

🏕 PICNIC SHELTER

🏊 PUBLIC SWIMMING

Minnesota Landscape Arboretum

← 82nd St.

HWY. 41

CO. RD. 117

CO. RD. 18

CO. RD. 18

Hazeltine Lake

Chaska Par 30 Golf Course

Hazeltine Nat'l Golf Course (Private)

CO. RD. 17

McKnight Road

Lake Bavaria

Bavaria Road

100 Acre Park

McKnight Park

JONATHAN

Lake Grace

Pioneer Trail

← Paved Shoulder

Hundertmark Road

Community Park

Friendship Park

Bavaria Rd.

Village Road

1996 under pass at Hwy 41

Chaska East Creek

Wooded Ravine

LRT SO. TRAIL RIDE 14

HWY. 212

Co. Rd. 11

School Campus

Engler Blvd.

5'-0" PAVED SHOULDER

Chaska Creek

Co. Rd. 10

Meadow Park

Victoria Drive

HWY. 41

Lions Park

Crosstown

Minnesota River

DQ

Schimelpfenig

Chaska East Creek

Minnesota Valley National Wildlife Refuge

Firemen's Park

Co. Rd. 140

5TH ST

Walnut

4th St.

Beech St.

City Square

Swing Bridge

3 Miles to Shakopee (Paved Trail)

CHASKA

Winkel Park

HWY. 212

Athletic Park

Chaska Lake

HWY. 41

← MN. River Valley Trail

RIDE 16

→ 20 Miles to Belle Plaine (Gravel/Dirt Trail)

MINNESOTA VALLEY STATE TRAIL

Scott and Carver County. Connects with RIDES 15 and G.

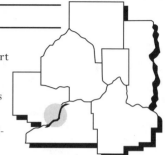

LENGTH ✹ RIDE 16 – 22 miles (one way) Belle Plain to Chaska. Rough, expert
RATING ◐ RIDE 16A – 8 miles (round trip) Shakopee to Chaska. Paved, easier
CAUTION RIDE 16 is long, isolated, and sometimes under water. Mountain bikes work best on the flat dirt and sand trail. Bring extra water and a friend. Mosquitoes are bad in summer. Phone Trail Headquarters (492-6400) in advance to check on trail conditions.

I know this isn't Montana, but I've always thought of the Minnesota River Valley as Big Sky Country. Certainly it is an immense valley — over 3 miles from bluff to bluff — carved by the powerful, glacial River Warren some 10,000 years ago. It is only when the Minnesota River is in a major flood, like the summer of 1993, that you get a hint of the River Warren's size. Floods like this were the impetus for creating the Minnesota Valley National Wildlife Refuge in 1976. It is one of only a handful of urban wildlife refuges in the country. A place where wild coyotes, bald eagles, badgers and beavers live comfortably within minutes of 2 million people.

The Refuge consists of several units strung along the river from Fort Snelling to Belle Plain. Eventually a 75-mile trail will join them all together and extend up the river to Le Sueur. Stop by the Visitor Center (3815 E. 80th Street in Bloomington, or phone 335-2323) for an excellent overview of the Refuge and scheduled activities. RIDES 19, 30, 31 and M visit parts of the Refuge not discussed below.

RIDE 16A: SHAKOPEE TO CHASKA

GO! Trailheads are found at both ends in Chaska and Shakopee. In Shakopee there is free public parking next to the trail one block east of Highway 169 (and at Memorial Park one mile east). This is an extremely popular and beautiful introduction to the Minnesota River Valley. Trail may be flooded during high water.

0.5 mi The path winds through some woods and then breaks into the open where a **GRAND PANORAMA** of the valley unfolds.

3.5 mi The path winds into Chaska and crosses the Minnesota River on an 1870 **RAILROAD SWING BRIDGE** that may be the only one of its kind left in the state.

NOTE: The paved path now extends 2 miles <u>east</u> from Shakopee and will soon go to Murphy's Landing.

RIDE 16: BELLE PLAINE TO CHASKA

GO! Route description begins in Belle Plaine. See map and description for other trailheads. Start where the trail intersects State Highway 25. You will need to park on a side street in **BELLE PLAINE** as there is no trailhead.

4.3 mi **LAWRENCE UNIT** is a **TRAILHEAD** and campground with parking, toilets and picnic facilities.

6.6 mi The 1859 **STAGECOACH STOP** (0.2 miles up from the river) is about all that remains of the pioneer settlement of St. Lawrence.

7.9 mi A small canoe campsite across from **BEVENS CREEK** is the site of a steamboat landing that operated here in the 1850s. This is the trail's most remote section and the path is occasionally sandy, but the opportunity to enjoy a wilderness setting so close to home offsets any drawbacks.

9.7 mi The trail is lifted high above the river to an **OVERLOOK** on a sandy dune.

10.8 mi **THOMPSON FERRY** operated until the 1930s and was the key link between Chaska and Jordan when it began during Minnesota's territorial days. Today, there is a **TRAILHEAD** here with parking.

13.8 mi The **LOUISVILLE SWAMP** area has a **TRAILHEAD** and several miles of mountain bike trails that are described in RIDE G. Take the right fork to enter this area.

16.4 mi The Louisville Swamp trails connect again with the Minnesota Valley Trail at the mouth of **SAND CREEK**.

17.5 mi Shortly after crossing under the railroad tracks the **TRAIL FORKS**. The expansive wetlands impart a feeling of great openness here. In early spring the trail following the river is your best bet, but in drier times the route past Gifford Lake is 1.7 miles shorter and just as scenic.

22 mi The two trails converge, and about a quarter mile later you reach the **PAVED PATH** to Chaska (1 mile) or Shakopee (3 miles). Shakopee was named for the great Dakota Chief Shakopee (**SA-KPE**), meaning six in Dakota, whose village was here.

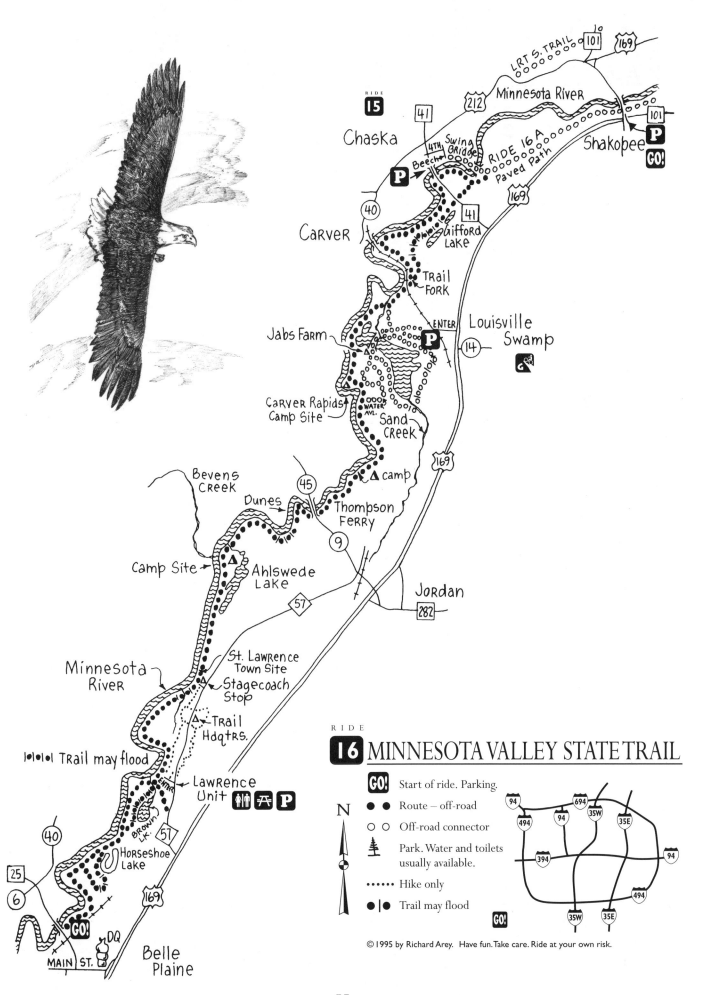

LRT S. TRAIL
101
169
RIDE
15
212 Minnesota River
41
Chaska
4TH Swing Bridge
Beech RIDE 16 A Paved Path
P Shakopee
P
GO!
101
40
41
Carver
Gifford Lake
169
Trail FORK
ENTER
Jabs Farm
P Louisville Swamp
14
Carver Rapids Camp Site
WATER AVL.
Sand CREEK
169
△ camp
Bevens Creek
45
Dunes
Thompson Ferry
9
Camp Site △ Ahlswede Lake
Jordan
57
282
Minnesota River
St. Lawrence Town Site
△ Stagecoach Stop
△ Trail Hdqtrs.
|o|o|o| Trail may flood
ENTER Lawrence Unit 👫 🌲 P
40
57
BROWN LK.
Horseshoe Lake
25
6
169
GO! DQ
MAIN ST.
Belle Plaine

EDEN PRAIRIE – BIKES & BOMBERS

Hennepin County. Connects with RIDES 11 and 14.

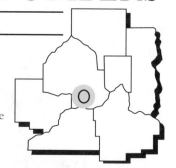

LENGTH
RATING

≈ 20.8 miles – Full loop as described

◐ 2.4 miles – One lap around Staring Lake

◐ 11.1 miles – Short loop, cut across on Anderson Lakes Parkway

CAUTION   Be very careful crossing Pioneer Trail to get to the Air Museum. Please note that Eden Prairie has an excellent map showing their entire park and bikeway system. Phone 949-8300 for information.

The Planes of Fame Air Museum is the marque billing for this route but not the only reason to venture out. The city of Eden Prairie has done an excellent job in providing a network of paths that connect neighborhoods, lakes and office parks. The trail around Staring Lake Park is especially nice as are the views out across the Minnesota River Valley and Anderson Lakes. Eden Prairie was named in 1853 by Mrs. Elizabeth Eliot, an eastern journalist who proclaimed the area a "garden of Eden."

PLANES OF FAME AIR MUSEUM (phone 941-2633). Open Tuesday through Sunday from 11 to 5 p.m. There is a $6.00 charge for adults and $3.00 for kids 7-12, with guided tours on weekends. The beautifully restored planes are a testament to America's World War II airpower. And if you think they are impressive on the ground, then sign up for an open cockpit flight in a Stearman or stop by Memorial Day weekend when your admission charge might get you a free flight on a P38 Lightning.

GO!   Start at **STARING LAKE PARK** parking lot across from the Planes of Fame Air Museum. Park is on the north side of Pioneer Trail one mile west of Highway 169. Families may wish to divide up here. A solid hour or two can be spent doing a couple of laps around Staring Lake and then sliding, swinging and climbing your way around the creative play area. Enjoy the view. **PIONEER TRAIL** follows the track of a major Indian trail later used as a military road from Fort Snelling.

3.4 mi   **RIVER VIEW ROAD** marks the beginning of the major stretch of on-road bicycling. When the leaves are down you can sneak some major views across the Minnesota River Valley. This huge valley was formed over 10,000 years ago when the mighty glacial River Warren flowed through here.

5.5 mi   Enjoy the wooded Purgatory Creek ravine before heading up into the land of big houses. Watch closely for **CANADIAN LANDING** to connect with Franlo Road.

8.1 mi   **ANDERSON LAKES** are a reminder of how this area looked before the suburbs crept in. You can take the shortcut back to Staring Lake Park by continuing across on Anderson Lakes Parkway.

Prairie Center Drive and Valley View Road have paved paths to usher you through the car-centered corporate world. Count the number of **EDEN**s en route and decide if Joni Mitchell was correct when she sang, "they paved paradise and put up a parking lot."

12.7 mi   Hennepin County's **LRT TRAIL CORRIDOR** crosses Valley View Road and offers another shortcut. Save about 2.4 miles if you take it.

13.9 mi   **ROUND LAKE PARK** has a swimming beach and other diversions. A combined path circles the lake.

16.4 mi   You will cross the LRT Trail just before reaching **SCENIC HEIGHTS ROAD**. Take a left and watch your step until you reach the paved path. There is a nice run down Anderson Lake Parkway before reaching the turnoff back to Staring Lake.

20.8 mi   You may want to stop at the **OUTDOOR CENTER** or do an extra lap around the lake before heading **BACK TO** *GO!*

And a special tip-of-the-pencil to my buddy Tim Dunsworth from whom I swiped the name, though not the route, for this ride.

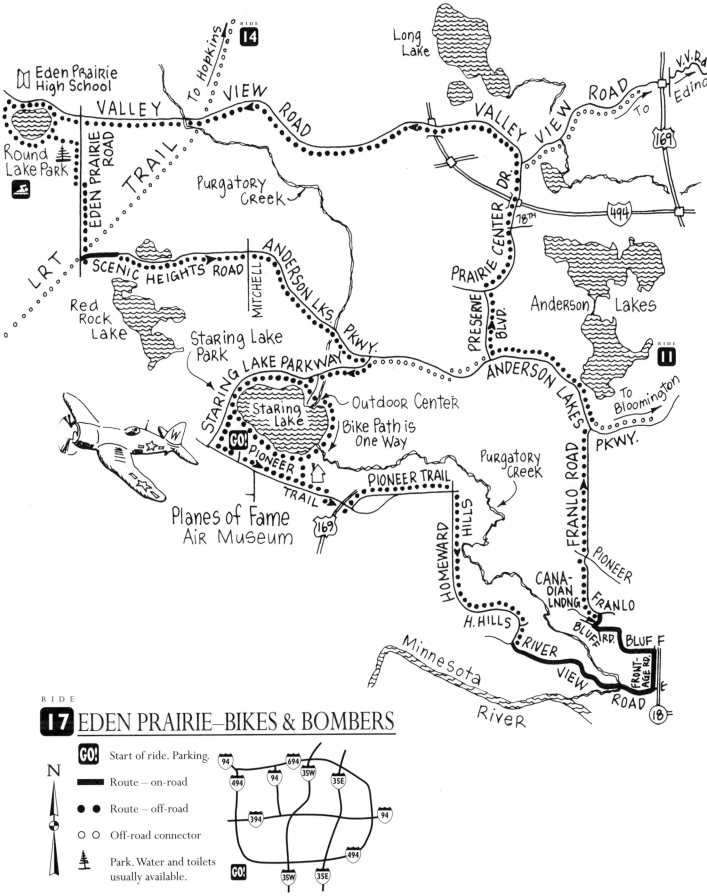

Eden Prairie High School

Round Lake Park

VALLEY VIEW ROAD

To Hopkins

RIDE 14

Long Lake

VALLEY VIEW ROAD

To Edina

V.V. Rd.

169

494

TRAIL

Eden Prairie Road

LRT

Purgatory Creek

SCENIC HEIGHTS ROAD

MITCHELL

ANDERSON LKS. PKWY.

PRAIRIE CENTER DR.

78TH

PRESERVE BLVD.

Anderson Lakes

Red Rock Lake

Staring Lake Park

STARING LAKE PARKWAY

Staring Lake

GO!

Outdoor Center

Bike Path is One Way

ANDERSON LAKES PKWY.

RIDE 11

To Bloomington

PIONEER TRAIL

PIONEER TRAIL

Purgatory Creek

FRANLO ROAD

PIONEER

FRANLO

Planes of Fame Air Museum

169

HOMEWARD HILLS

CANADIAN LNDNG.

H. HILLS

RIVER VIEW ROAD

BLUFF RD.

BLUFF

FRONT- AGE RD.

18

Minnesota River

RIDE

17 EDEN PRAIRIE–BIKES & BOMBERS

N

GO!   Start of ride. Parking.

————   Route – on-road

• •   Route – off-road

○ ○   Off-road connector

🌲   Park. Water and toilets usually available.

94   694

494   94   35W   35E

394   94

494

GO!   35W   35E

© 1995 by Richard Arey. Have fun. Take care. Ride at your own risk.

RIDE 18 — BURNSVILLE BIKE BYWAYS

Scott County. Connects with RIDES 31, D, E and F.

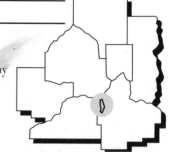

LENGTH ～ 18.4 mile loop

RATING Intermediate – most of route off-road or on shoulders. There are many hills on this route.

CAUTION Highway 13 has wide shoulders but heavy traffic. Avoid it by going back up Parkwood to Burnsville Parkway.

This route circumnavigates the bike-friendly streets and paths of Burnsville. It connects the major parks, winds around beautiful Crystal Lake and directs you to three of the best mountain bike trails in the metro area. (Always call before using. See separate descriptions in the Mountain Biking chapter.) Burnsville has made excellent strides in creating a bicycle-friendly community. Only a portion of their routes are shown on this map. Phone the Burnsville Parks and Recreation Department at 895-4500 to obtain a copy of their map "Going Places — Burnsville Bikeways."

GO! Start at **TERRACE OAKS WEST PARK**. Park is reached by exiting I-35E at County Road 11 and heading north. Go 1 mile and take a right (east) on Burnsville Parkway to entrance on right at Kennelly Road. This is also the starting point for the mountain bike trail. See RIDE D.

3.6 mi **ALIMAGNET PARK** sits above its beautiful namesake lake. There are picnic facilities here complete with bocce ball courts.

5.5 mi Head west (right) at Bluebill Bay Road and watch the street signs closely as you bike through the neighborhood south of **CRYSTAL LAKE**.

7.2 mi The off-road path on the west end of Crystal Lake is the prettiest stretch on this route. Savor it slowly.

8.7 mi Buck Hill Road is the turnoff for the **BUCK HILL MOUNTAIN BIKE AREA**. See Ride E.

11.8 mi Good bike lanes on 150th Street and Judicial Road take you through the suburban office parks and over to **SUNSET PARK**. Add 1.7 miles to your total if you do the loop here.

Head South on Burnsville Parkway about 2 miles to reach **MURPHY-HANREHAN REGIONAL PARK**. See RIDE F.

14.3 mi Burnsville Parkway goes past some nice parks and many homes. Enjoy the **PANORAMIC VIEW TO DOWNTOWN** from Travelers Trail West.

16.3 mi Be bold. Slide down to Highway 13 and order a Nutty Double Fudge at **DAIRY QUEEN**. That burst of sugar will come in handy as you head back up the hill to Terrace Oaks Park.

18.4 mi BACK TO *GO!*

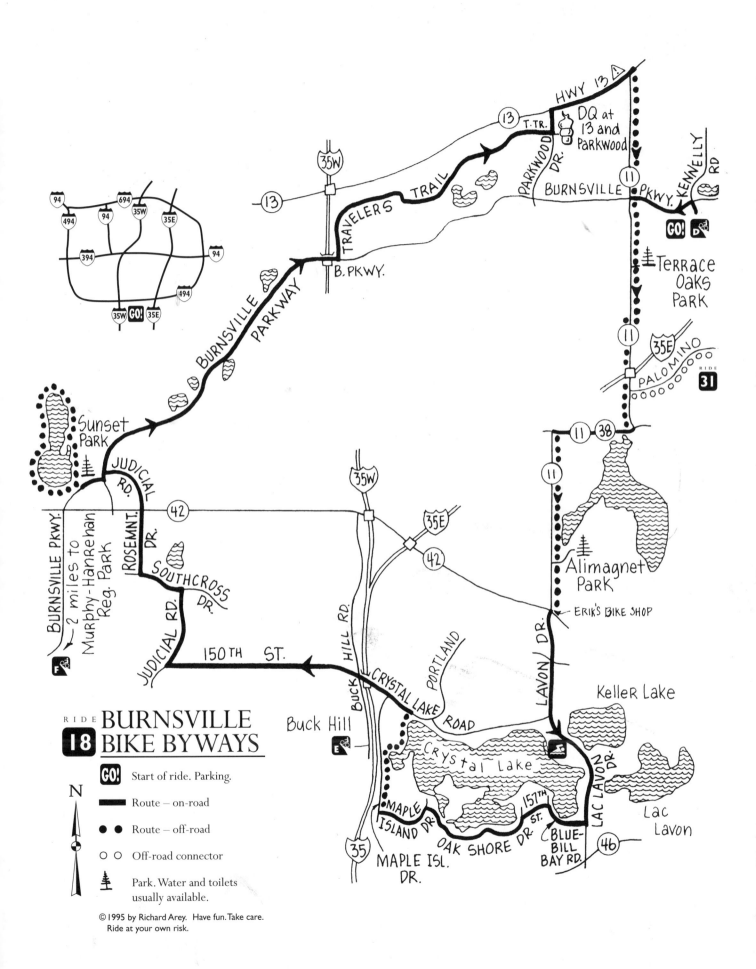

HWY 13

13   T. TR.
DQ at 13 and Parkwood

TRAVELERS TRAIL

35W

13

B. PKWY.

BURNSVILLE   PARKWAY

PARKWOOD DR.
BURNSVILLE PKWY.   KENNELLY RD

11

GO!

Terrace Oaks Park

11   35E
PALOMINO

RIDE 31

Sunset Park

JUDICIAL RD.

11 38

11

Alimagnet Park

Erik's Bike Shop

BURNSVILLE PKWY.
2 miles to Murphy-Hanrehan Reg. Park

ROSEMNT. DR.

42

35W

35E
42

PORTLAND

LAVON DR.

Keller Lake

SOUTHCROSS DR.

JUDICIAL RD.

150TH   ST.

BUCK HILL RD.

CRYSTAL LAKE ROAD

Buck Hill

Crystal Lake

LAC LAVON DR.

Lac Lavon

MAPLE ISLAND DR.

OAK SHORE DR.

157TH ST.

BLUE-BILL BAY RD.

46

35

MAPLE ISL. DR.

RIDE 18 BURNSVILLE BIKE BYWAYS

GO! Start of ride. Parking.

——— Route – on-road

• • Route – off-road

○ ○ Off-road connector

🌲 Park. Water and toilets usually available.

N

BIKING FOR THE BIRDS

19

Hennepin and Dakota County. Connects with RIDES 4, 20 and 31.

LENGTH   29.5 miles – Full loop as described

RATING   10 miles and easier if starting at Old Cedar Avenue Bridge

CAUTION   Two of the places shown can be biked to, but NOT within. Bring a lock and walking shoes. Careful along Lyndale to 66th Street (sidewalk may be best), and when crossing I-494 on 12th Avenue South.

Please note that there are several miles of mountain biking trails shown on the map that are not described in the tour below. These trails can be accessed just below the historic 1836 Sibley House at 55 D Street in Mendota (452-1596) or at the parking lot on Silver Bell Road. Birding is good along this flat dirt route that will be paved in 1996.

Located at the crossroads of three major biomes (northern coniferous forest, eastern deciduous forest, and western tallgrass prairie), and blessed with three major river valleys, the Twin Cities provides plentiful habitat for some of the best birdwatching (birding!) in the Midwest. Over 340 species of birds (out of the 800 possible in North America) have been seen in the seven county area, and this ride takes you to some of the best local places. Bring your binoculars for best results.

Birding is seasonal. Migrants pass through in April (waterfowl, hawks) and May (warblers, shorebirds). Many species are found here all summer and winter. Biking birders in winter will often be rewarded by rarities found on open water near the NSP power plant. Join the Minnesota Ornithologists Union, a local Audubon Society, or call the MOU Birding Hotline (780-8890) for more specific information and trips.

GO!   Start at the parking lot on the north end of **LAKE NOKOMIS** (661-4800) or along the parkway. Hint: Those silver winged creatures flying over the south end of the lake are NOT Canada geese.

3.3 mi   **MOTHER LAKE** is a large, marshy area worth a look. I was startled by a Bald Eagle passing just 40 feet overhead one afternoon.

7.9 mi   This next stretch is a bit boring and a little hectic in places. But consider how much you're helping the environment by bicycling rather than driving to these spots. The **BASS PONDS** are reached by walking your bike down the hill at the end of 86th Street. Look for water birds and warblers in spring.

9.6 mi   A mountain bike trail (shared with hikers!) will take you to the **OLD CEDAR AVENUE BRIDGE**. You can also get there via the sidewalk along Old Shakopee Road or backtrack on 86th Street to Old Cedar Avenue. The off-road paths west of the parking lot are closed to bikers but patience rewards viewing from the bridge. Yellow-headed blackbirds, bitterns, rails and heron are just some of the species that may be observed.

12.2 mi   Continue south and cross over the Minnesota River on the bike/walk bridge. Head upstream on Black Dog Road toward the **NSP POWER PLANT**. Open water in November and December makes this area particularly productive for hardy winter hikers and bikers. Grebes, goldeneyes, gulls and eagles may be spotted. Even if you don't turn up any birds you will enjoy the quiet road next to the river.

23.9 mi   At the end of the road, head back and retrace your steps to 73rd. Cut over to **WOOD LAKE NATURE CENTER** (861-9365) and lock up your bike. Wood Lake is one of the premier birding spots in the state. A migratory hot spot, 21 species of warblers were seen during a single day in early May of 1988. During the summer, check around the boardwalk for rails (sora and yellow) and least bitterns.

26.9 mi   Pick up **MINNEHAHA PARKWAY** at Pleasant Avenue. Keep an eye out for birds along the creek. I once spotted a greenbacked heron wading in some shade.

28.7 mi   You won't even need binoculars to pick out the **DAIRY QUEEN** on Cedar Avenue.

29.5 mi   BACK TO *GO!*

19 BIKING FOR THE BIRDS

©1995 by Richard Arey. Have fun. Take care. Ride at your own risk.

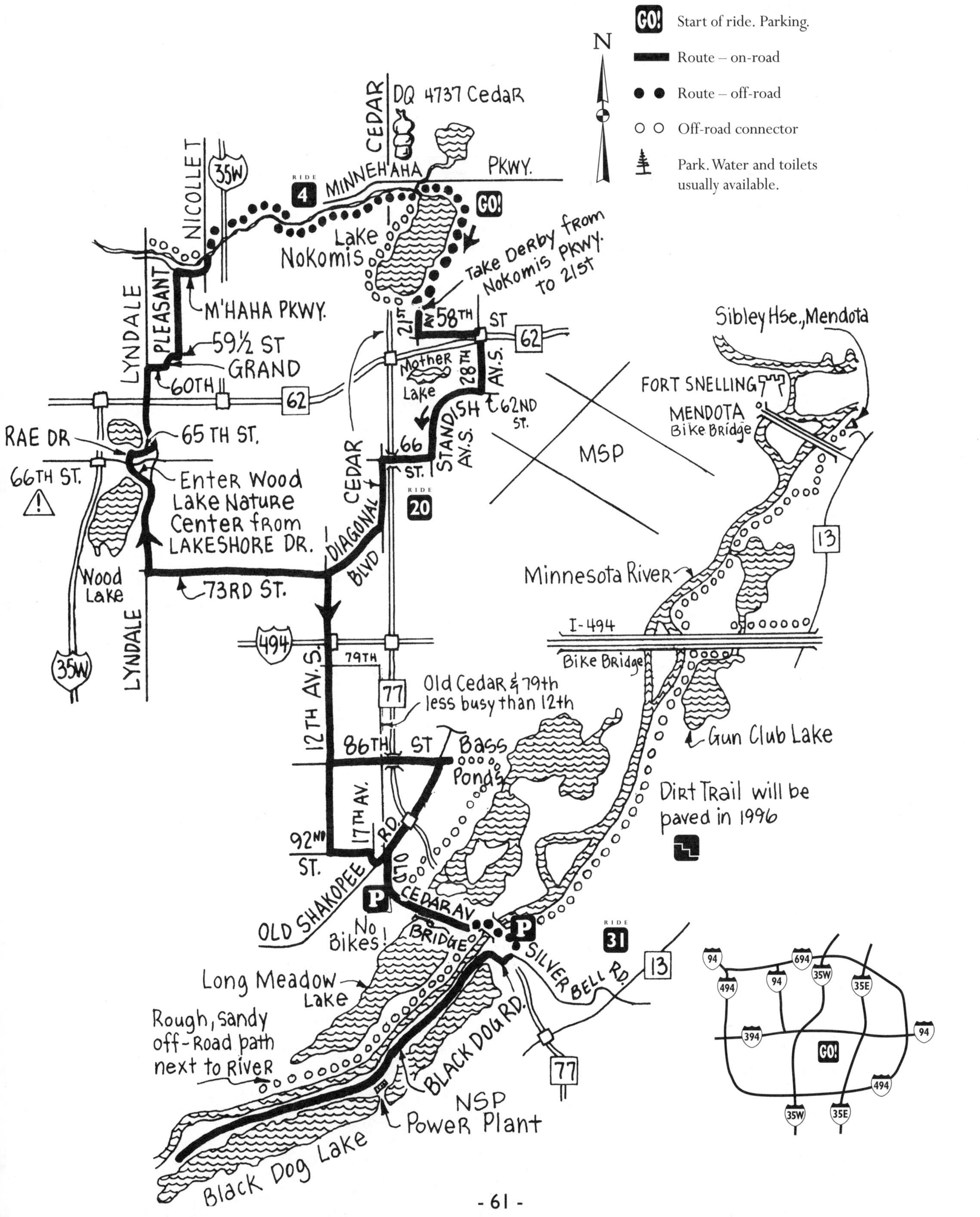

GO! Start of ride. Parking.

●──● Route – on-road

• • Route – off-road

○ ○ Off-road connector

🌲 Park. Water and toilets usually available.

N

DQ 4737 CedaR

CEDAR

MINNEHAHA PKWY.

RIDE 4

Lake Nokomis

GO!

Take Derby from Nokomis Pkwy. to 21st

35W

NICOLLET

LYNDALE

PLEASANT

M'HAHA PKWY.

59½ ST
GRAND

60TH

62

65 TH ST.

RAE DR

66TH ST. ⚠

Enter Wood Lake Nature Center from LAKESHORE DR.

Wood Lake

LYNDALE

73RD ST.

35W

21st

Mother Lake

58TH ST

62

28TH AV. S.

STANDISH AV. S.

62ND ST.

CEDAR

DIAGONAL BLVD

66 ST.

RIDE 20

MSP

Sibley Hse., Mendota

FORT SNELLING

MENDOTA Bike Bridge

13

Minnesota River

I-494 Bike Bridge

494

12TH AV. S.

79TH

77

Old Cedar & 79th less busy than 12th

86TH ST

Bass Pond

17TH AV.

RD.

92ND ST.

OLD SHAKOPEE

P

No Bikes!

OLD CEDAR AV.

BRIDGE

Long Meadow Lake

Rough, sandy off-road path next to River

P

SILVER BELL RD.

RIDE 31

13

BLACK DOG RD.

77

NSP Power Plant

Black Dog Lake

Gun Club Lake

Dirt Trail will be paved in 1996

94
694
35W
35E
494
94
394
GO!
94
35W
35E
494

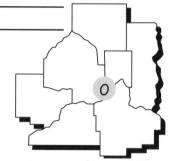

LENGTH   17 miles — Loop as described

RATING   Intermediate, but often used as a training run for racers.

CAUTION   Low flying planes. There is a fair amount of traffic and no longer a shoulder on 34th Avenue.

*This route circles the MSP International Airport. A primary attraction for training is the long stretches of road unencumbered by traffic signals or stop signs on a route that is readily accessible to so many people. The scenic attractions are found between Fort Snelling and Lake Nokomis. The paved path perched above the river on the bluff south of 54th Street is as pretty as you will find anywhere. It runs along an old **TRAIN** line. The **PLANES** are best seen along Post Road and the rush of **AUTOMOBILES** is hard to miss on the Interstate 494 frontage road. Bike safely — you will also be passing the Fort Snelling National Cemetery.*

GO!

Start at **MINNEHAHA PARK** (348-8942). A parking sticker is now required for cars. Minnehaha Park has been a tourist destination for over 150 years thanks to the falls that were immortalized in Henry Longfellow's popular poem, *The Song of Hiawatha*. The name **MI-NI** (water) **HA-HA** (noise of waterfalls or rapids) comes from the Dakota who knew of this place for centuries. The geologic history goes back another 10,000 years and is told on the bronze plaques that are found near the falls. The replica **LONGFELLOW HOUSE** has been relocated into the park and is being renovated for use as a trail center.

Cross Hiawatha and follow **MINNEHAHA PARKWAY**. Serious bicyclists may prefer going straight south on 28th Avenue. The Dakota knew Minnehaha Creek as **WA-KPA** (river) **CI-STIN-NA** (small). The parkway was opened in 1893 and follows an old wagon trail. Today, it is especially pretty in the spring when thousands of daffodils are in bloom and the crab apple trees are bursting with color.

2.1 mi   **LAKE NOKOMIS** has good biking on either the path or adjacent parkway. A small recreation center on the north end of the lake has water and washrooms.

4.8 mi   As **62ND STREET** curves into Standish, you can get some nice views of the planes taking off or landing.

10 mi   This next stretch is where you can pump it up as you race along the perimeter of the airport, eventu-

ally delivering you to **POST ROAD**. Take some time to watch the planes.

11.8 mi   **FORT SNELLING STATE PARK** (725-2390) has a swimming beach (bring your ear plugs), picnic facilities, boat launches, an interpretive center and more. Biking is allowed everywhere except on Pike Island

13.8 mi   Follow the paved path until it starts to climb the bluff along the Mississippi. Rising above you is **HISTORIC FORT SNELLING**. Colonel Josiah Snelling took command of this post in 1820 and the locally quarried limestone walls began to rise in the wilderness. Minnesota did not become a state for 38 more years. The fort was never fired upon and the soldiers were more involved with mediating the fighting between the Dakota and Ojibway than between settlers and Indians until the 1862 Dakota conflict. Duing the winter of 1862 some 1,600 Dakota were confined here and at least 130 died during the long internment.

15.0 mi   There are some informal dirt paths where **MOUNTAIN BIKING** is allowed on the right (east) side of the paved path just before 54th Street. Be careful of hikers.

Follow the trail and service road along the bluff and past the **JOHN H. STEVENS HOUSE** (1849, oldest in Minneapolis) and **PRINCESS DEPOT** (1875) to your real destination — **DAIRY QUEEN**. Forget this training stuff and order a large, dipped ice cream cone.

17 mi   **BACK TO** *GO!*

20 PLANES, TRAINS & AUTOMOBILES

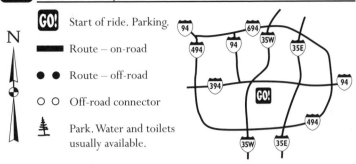

GO! Start of ride. Parking.

N

━━━ Route – on-road

• • • Route – off-road

○ ○ Off-road connector

🌲 Park. Water and toilets usually available.

© 1995 by Richard Arey. Have fun. Take care. Ride at your own risk.

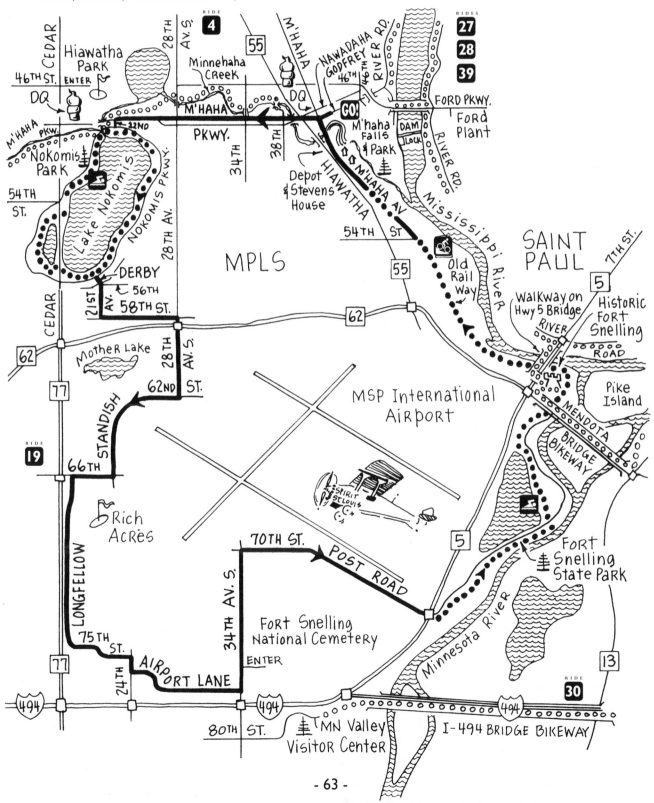

RIDE 21

SCANDIA SOJOURN

Washington County. Connects with RIDE 23.

LENGTH
RATING
◆ 28.8 miles – Full loop using Scandia Trail
● 8 miles – William O'Brien to Marine off-road, round trip
♒ 19.1 miles – Ostrum Trail loop

CAUTION Norell, Olinda and Scandia Trail have light traffic but no shoulders. Use a mirror. Washington or Hennepin Parks parking sticker required at Pine Point.

This is some of the best bicycling to be found in the metro area if you are comfortable on country roads. The oak woods, lakes, marsh and rolling farmland blend harmoniously. The little villages of Scandia and Marine are a delight. This is a landscape — a way of life, really — that has almost disappeared in the Twin Cities area. And to top it off, this ride visits Gammelgarden (site of the first Swedish settlement in Minnesota), beautiful William O'Brien State Park, and the swimming beach on crystal clear Square Lake. Need I mention the award-winning desserts at Crabtree's Kitchen or the Village Scoop?

GO! Start at the parking lot in the **PINE POINT COUNTY PARK** (731-3851) at the end of the Gateway State Trail. Take County Road 55 (Norell Avenue) 3 miles north from County Highway 96 to Pine Point parking lot.

4.1 mi **WARNER NATURE CENTER** (433-2427) is owned and operated by the Science Museum (221-9444) and has a variety of programs available. Habitats for wildlife are exciting and varied and include a beautiful peat bog. Call first to make reservations for programs.

6.2 mi Intersection of County Road 3 and **OSTRUM TRAIL NORTH**. This is a good shortcut over to Marine.

9.1 mi The **HAY LAKE SCHOOL** (1899) and **JOHANNES ERICKSON LOG HOUSE** (1868) anchor this historic corner. An excellent guided tour is available weekend afternoons from 1:30 to 4:30 p.m. for just one dollar.

10.9 mi **SCANDIA**, the oldest Swedish settlement in Minnesota, began in 1850 when three Swedish lads built a log cabin on Hay Lake. **GAMMELGARDEN** houses six structures built between 1850 and 1880 and is open for guided tours (fee charged) on weekend afternoons.

15.1 mi Stop in at **CRABTREE'S KITCHEN** and discover why they won *Mpls. St. Paul* magazine's award for "Best Old-Fashioned Desserts." Try the strawberry shortcake, "made from scratch and as light, sweet and delectable as a summer romance."

15.8 mi **WILLIAM O'BRIEN STATE PARK** offers all the amenities and you can glide on down to the river on the park road. Watch for hawks soaring above the bluffs. Save a couple miles and a 100-foot climb if you do not go down to the river.

20.1 mi Take the off-road paved path down into **MARINE ON ST. CROIX**. Platted in 1839, the downtown is a National Register Historic District. Minnesota's logging era began here and the 1888 Marine Village Hall is still the place for lively weekend dances. Satisfy your ice cream fix at the **VILLAGE SCOOP**.

24.3 mi **SQUARE LAKE PARK** is renowned for the clarity of its water and a dip here is hard to beat on a hot summer day. Those black shiny heads you see are scuba divers, not seals, surfacing. A bath house and picnic facilities overlook the lake.

28.8 mi **BACK TO** *GO!*

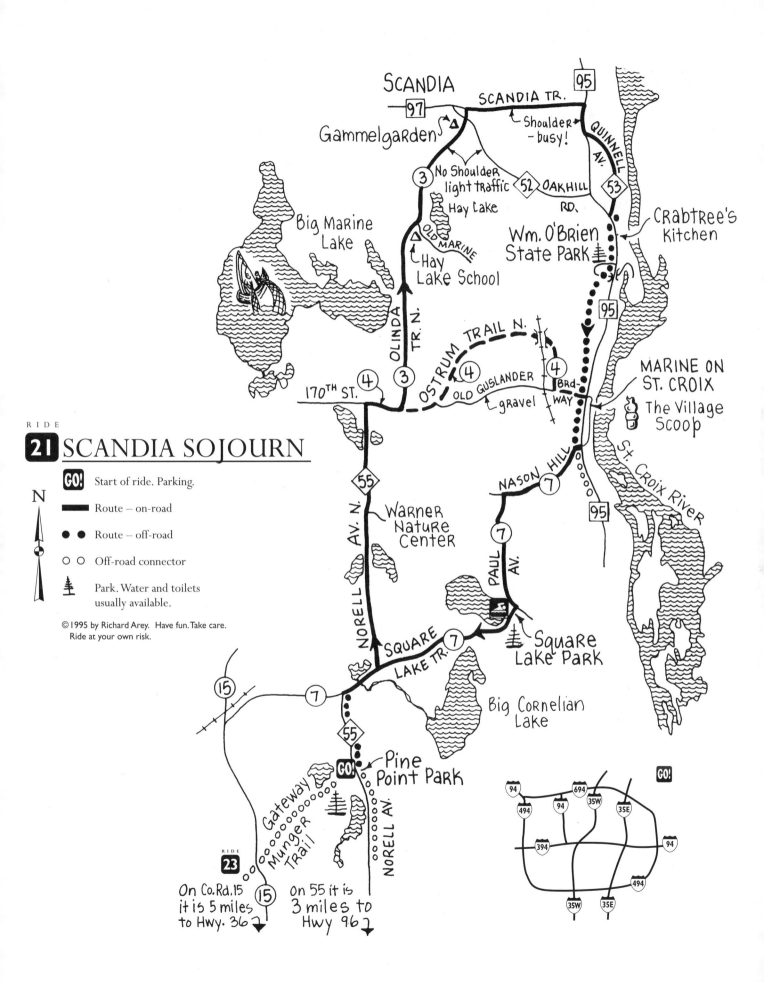

SCANDIA

97

SCANDIA TR.

95

Gammelgarden

Shoulder — busy!

QUINNELL AV.

3

No Shoulder light traffic

52

OAKHILL RD.

53

Hay Lake

Big Marine Lake

OLD MARINE

Wm. O'Brien State Park

Crabtree's Kitchen

Hay Lake School

95

OSTRUM TRAIL N.

OLINDA TR. N.

170TH ST.

4

3

4

OLD GUSLANDER

gravel

4

BRd-WAY

MARINE ON ST. CROIX

The Village Scoop

RIDE
21 SCANDIA SOJOURN

GO!   Start of ride. Parking.

——   Route – on-road

●●   Route – off-road

○○   Off-road connector

🌲   Park. Water and toilets usually available.

N

© 1995 by Richard Arey. Have fun. Take care.
Ride at your own risk.

55

Warner Nature Center

NORELL AV. N.

Nason Hill

7

7

St. Croix River

95

PAUL AV.

Square Lake Park

SQUARE LAKE TR.

7

Big Cornelian Lake

15

7

55

GO! Pine Point Park

NoRELL AV.

Gateway Munger Trail

RIDE
23

15

On Co. Rd. 15 it is 5 miles to Hwy. 36 ⤵

On 55 it is 3 miles to Hwy 96 ⤵

94

494

94

694

35W

35E

GO!

394

94

35W

35E

494

GATEWAY STATE TRAIL

Washington County. Connects with RIDES 23, 26, 27, 28 and 40.

LENGTH
RATING   33.8 miles – Entire Gateway Trail, round trip

21.8 miles – Cathedral to I-694, round trip

14.4 miles – Arlington trailhead to I-694, round trip

Families are fine on the Gateway Trail. It is an intermediate rated street route to get to the trailhead.

CAUTION   There are hills and traffic between the Cathedral and Oakland Cemetery. Sidewalk may be preferable on Rice Street. Be very careful at road crossing.

PHONE   DNR Trails and Waterways, 772-7935.

*T*his is the fastest getaway into the countryside in the east Metro area. The Capitol Route connects Greater St. Paul's two most popular bike routes — Summit Avenue and the Gateway Trail. You can choose either side of the State Capitol to connect with Jackson Street. I'd recommend taking in the view at Cass Gilbert Park on the way out and hitting the Dairy Queen on your return. The Gateway Trail is the southernmost segment of the Willard Munger State Trail that will eventually run from the Minnesota State Capitol to Duluth. State Representative Willard Munger has been a tremendous advocate of conservation and outdoor recreation for years.

GO!   Park on Summit Avenue near the **SAINT PAUL CATHEDRAL.** The trip begins with a long down-hill coast on John Ireland Boulevard, named after the Archbishop who was the force behind the Cathedral's construction (1906-1915).

0.5 mi   Cass Gilbert's impressive **MINNESOTA STATE CAPITOL** was built between 1893 and 1904. Gilbert, a St. Paul native, had originally designed the Capitol's mall to tumble down to the river. Stop back for a free tour some day.

0.8 mi   Go around the right (east) side of the Capitol and up Cedar Street to the fine lookout at **CASS GILBERT MEMORIAL PARK.**

1.8 mi   The historic **OAKLAND CEMETERY** was designed by H.W. S. Cleveland, the godfather of all Twin Cities parks. Famous Minnesotans, including U.S. Senators and St. Paul madams, have come to rest here.

GATEWAY STATE TRAIL

3.7 mi   Begin the Gateway State Trail at the **ARLINGTON TRAILHEAD** located just east of I-35E. (Exit I-35E at either Wheelock Parkway or Maryland Avenue and take side streets to trailhead.) The first

2 miles are paved with asphalt mixed with 3,300 used tires. This is a very pretty introduction to the trail.

NOTE: See map for extension of the Gateway Trail toward the Minnesota State Capitol. This should be complete by 1996.

5.3 mi   **PHALEN PARK.** Take a 3.2 mile lap around the lake if you wish (not included in mileage listed). Just past the park you will cross the unmarked 45th parallel of latitude. You are now halfway between the North Pole and the equator.

7.2 mi   The **GOODRICH GOLF COURSE** is a pleasant interlude as you traverse the suburban landscape.

9.1 mi   The stretch of trail adjacent to Highway 36 is the least appealing, though you will get a kick out of the **GIANT SNOWMAN**. Use great care while crossing the streets.

9.4 mi   Take a break from the traffic with a Dilly Bar at **DAIRY QUEEN** (located at the northwest corner of Highway 36 and 120).

10.9 mi   Trail goes under I-694. See RIDE 23 for map and description of the rest of the **GATEWAY TRAIL.**

21.8 mi   At the I-694 underpass it's time to turn around and head **BACK TO** *GO!*

22 GATEWAY STATE TRAIL

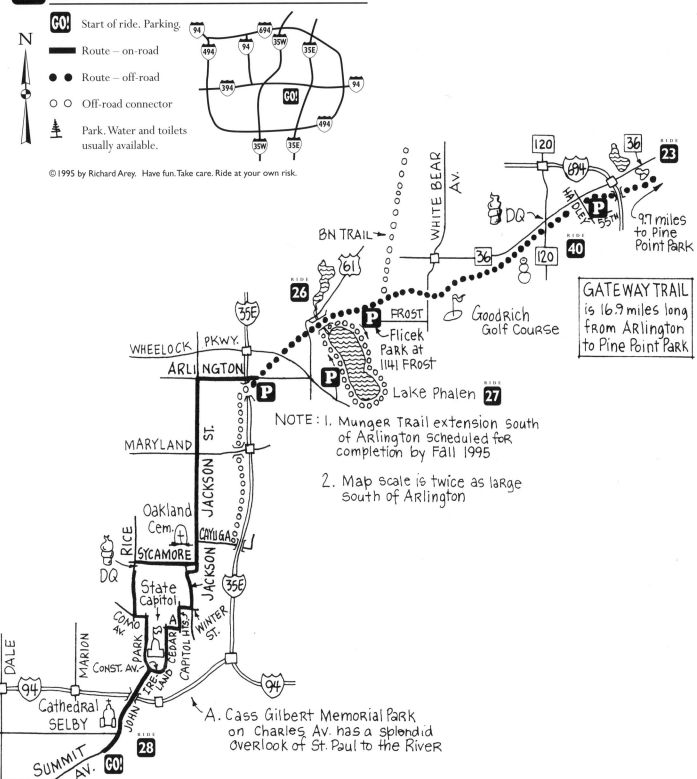

GO! Start of ride. Parking.

■■■ Route – on-road

●●● Route – off-road

○○ Off-road connector

🌲 Park. Water and toilets usually available.

N

© 1995 by Richard Arey. Have fun. Take care. Ride at your own risk.

GATEWAY TRAIL is 16.9 miles long from Arlington to Pine Point Park

9.7 miles to Pine Point Park

BN TRAIL →

FROST

Flicek Park at 1141 FROST

Goodrich Golf Course

Lake Phalen

WHEELOCK PKWY.

ARLINGTON

MARYLAND

JACKSON ST.

CAYUGA

Oakland Cem.

SYCAMORE

DQ

RICE

State Capitol

COMO AV.

CONST. AV.

JOHN IRE.

LAND CEDAR

CAPITOL HTS.

WINTER ST.

Cathedral

DALE

MARION

SELBY

SUMMIT AV.

GO!

NOTE: 1. Munger Trail extension south of Arlington scheduled for completion by Fall 1995

2. Map scale is twice as large south of Arlington

A. Cass Gilbert Memorial Park on Charles Av. has a splendid overlook of St. Paul to the River

WHITE BEAR AV.

DQ

HADLEY

55TH

GATEWAY TRAIL TO STILLWATER

23

Washington County. Connects with 21, 22, 24, and 35.

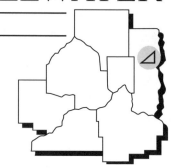

LENGTH   🌓 19.5 miles – Full loop to Pioneer Park
RATING   🌓 15 miles to Pine Point Park and back

Big fun for everyone

CAUTION   Big hill and traffic if you go down into Stillwater. Lots of folks on the Gateway Trail.

PHONE   DNR Trails and Waterways, 772-7935.

It's hard to imagine a better introduction to the scenic wonders of Washington County. This is the prettiest stretch of the Gateway Trail and the view of the St. Croix River from Pioneer Park is as good as it gets in the Midwest. The entire route is off-road or on the broad shoulders of County Road 55. Check out the Outing Lodge at Pine Point or cruise down into Stillwater for lunch and a little antiquing. I have seen deer on more than one occasion leaping across the trail.

GO!   Start at the **MAHTOMEDI HIGH SCHOOL** (426-3281) parking lot. Exit I-694 on Highway 120 and go north 1 mile to Highway 244. Turn right (east) on 244 and go 1.5 miles to Highway 12. Go right (east) on Highway 12 just over half a mile to the high school lot on your left. A paved off-road path leads to the Munger Trail.

0.6 mi   **GATEWAY MUNGER STATE TRAIL** intersects the paved path along Highway 12.

2.8 mi   Rest stop at **MASTERMAN LAKE**. There is parking and a portable toilet here.

6.7 mi   The **OUTING LODGE** is reached from a separate entrance road off County Road 61, about one block north of the trail. The Outing Lodge at Pine Point is well worth a return visit for an overnight getaway

or a special dinner (Phone 439-9747). Built in 1924 as the county poor farm, the brick building has been reborn as a handsome country inn with warm wood paneling and a huge fireplace topped with a ten-foot limestone mantel.

7.5 mi   **PINE POINT COUNTY PARK** is a beauty with maturing pine plantations and ponds filled with the choruses of frogs in spring.

8.7 mi   The off-road path ends but County Road 55 has wide bike-friendly shoulders.

12.5 mi   Laurel Avenue leads to **PIONEER PARK** and a spectacular vista of the St. Croix River Valley. This is a fine place for a picnic.

19.5 mi   Bike the wide shoulders or off-road path on County Highway 12, **BACK TO** *GO!*

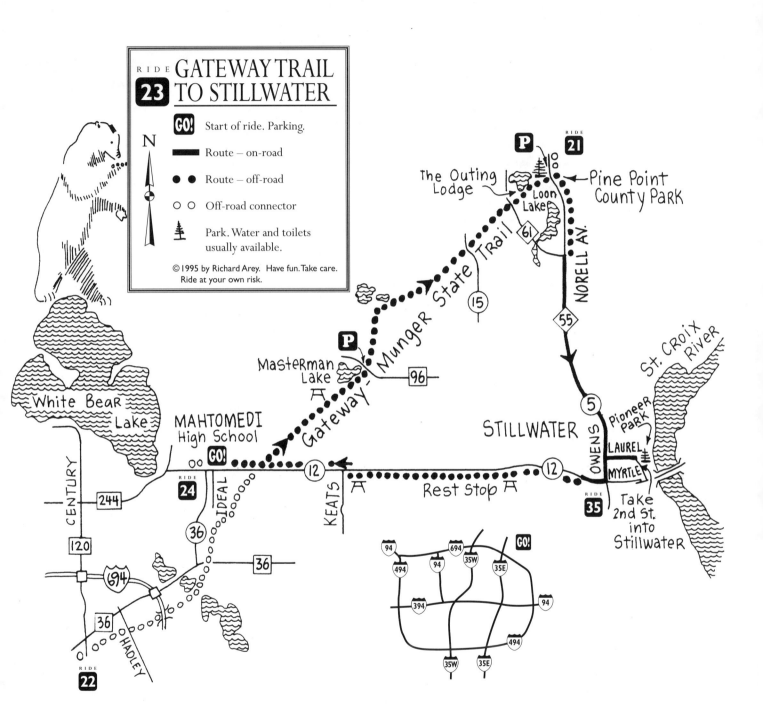

RIDE 23 GATEWAY TRAIL TO STILLWATER

GO! Start of ride. Parking.

Route – on-road

Route – off-road

○ ○ Off-road connector

Park. Water and toilets usually available.

© 1995 by Richard Arey. Have fun. Take care. Ride at your own risk.

N

Pine Point County Park

RIDE 21

The Outing Lodge

Loon Lake

61

NORELL AV.

55

15

Munger State Trail

P

Masterman Lake

96

Gateway –

St. Croix River

5

STILLWATER

OWENS

Pioneer Park

LAUREL

MYRTLE

Take 2nd St. into Stillwater

RIDE 35

White Bear Lake

MAHTOMEDI High School

GO!

RIDE 24

IDEAL

CENTURY

244

120

694

36

36

36

HADLEY

RIDE 22

KEATS

12

Rest Stop

12

94

494

94

694

35W

GO!

35E

394

94

494

35W

35E

24 JERRY'S RIDE

Ramsey and Washington County. Connects with RIDES 22, 23 and 25.

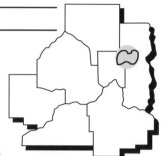

LENGTH ❧ 27 miles – Full loop as described
RATING ◗ 15.6 miles – Bald Eagle Lake loop and back

The Bald Eagle Lake loop is easier and the rest not much more difficult, as traffic is light.

CAUTION There are stretches with only narrow shoulders. Use a mirror. Take the Beach Road to Cedar Street cut-off if you prefer serenity to stopping at Dairy Queen. County Highway 244 (Wildwood Road) is very busy.

*T*his is the Big Lakes ride. White Bear Lake was a resort town for years and has attracted a number of characters in its time — Ma Barker and Machine Gun Kelly, Zelda and F. Scott Fitzgerald, Mark Twain and…my old buddy Jer. As in Jerry Hass. He accompanied me on many of the rides in this book and helped power my first century ride. If you see a couple of funny-looking guys on an old green tandem tooling around Bald Eagle Lake, wave! — that's us. Good views of the lakes, some bona fide historic sites, wide-open spaces (for now) and a Dairy Queen to sweeten the deal are yours for the taking on this ride. And lest we forget. Another Gerry, Gerry Spiess, christened his tiny 10-foot sailboat, Yankee Girl, on White Bear Lake before his World Record (shortest boat) solo voyage across the Atlantic in 1979. But now, let's go biking!

GO! Start your ride at **BELLAIRE PARK** (429-5827). Exit I-694 on Highway 120 and go north one mile, turning left (west) on Highway 244. Go one mile to Bellaire Avenue and take a right (north) on Bellaire to park entrance.

Bellaire Park was originally a streetcar stop on the way to the old Wildwood Amusement Park which ran from 1899 to the mid-1930s.

1.3 mi **JOHNSON BOAT WORKS** is where Iver Johnson designed his class X sailboats, one of which is in the Smithsonian Institute in Washington, D.C. Lake Avenue is one of the bike routes shown on the 1899 St. Paul Cycle Path Association map.

2 mi The wonderfully picturesque **FILLEBROWN HOUSE** sits at Lake and Moorhead. Built in 1879, it is a classic example of Stick Style architecture. It has been restored with Victorian furnishings and is open for tours on summer Sunday afternoons.

3.3 mi Take the paved path, just past the OPTIMIST'S CLUB, that leads to the **WHITE BEAR LAKE COUNTY PARK**. There is a swimming beach, picnic facilities and a boat launch here.

4.1 mi Make a short sprint on Highway 96 and a careful left onto Northwest Avenue. Cross Highway 61 on Buffalo and you will soon be cruising around **BALD EAGLE LAKE**.

10 mi The scenic loop around the lake brings you back to the Highway 61 crossing at 120th Street. Take Hugo back to Buffalo for the **SHORT LOOP**.

16.4 mi The **WITHROW BALLROOM** is a landmark that still holds Saturday night dances. From here you can take County Road 68 to Lansing (gravel) if you want to bike a longer stretch of the Gateway Trail. Or take County Road 9 back to 12.

22.3 mi Intersection of County Highway 12 and the **GATEWAY TRAIL**. Taking 12 to Beach Road to Cedar Street is the more scenic, lower traffic recommendation.

25.1 mi If you simply cannot wait, take the heavily travelled Highway 244 (it does have a good shoulder) to **DAIRY QUEEN**. After boosting your blood sugar level, continue west on County Road E and north on Bellaire.

27 mi **BACK TO GO!** On a hot day you'll wish you had your swimsuit. There is a nice **SWIMMING BEACH** at Bellaire Park.

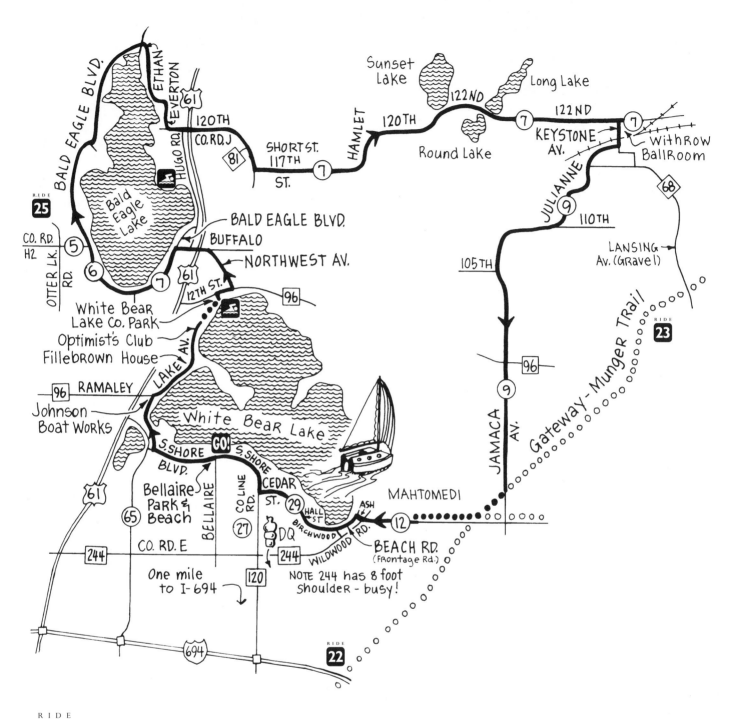

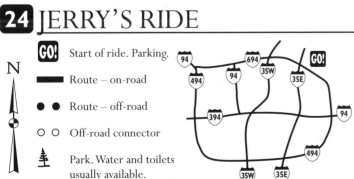

24 JERRY'S RIDE

N

GO!   Start of ride. Parking.

  Route – on-road

●●   Route – off-road

○○   Off-road connector

🌲   Park. Water and toilets usually available.

FORBIDDEN CITY CIRCLE

Ramsey County. Connects with RIDES 24, 26 and 3

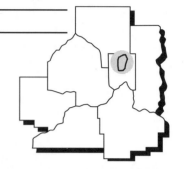

LENGTH 〰 24.1 miles – Full Loop as described

RATING Intermediate, most of route has shoulders, no big hills

CAUTION A ¾ mile stretch on Otter Lake Road has no shoulder.

This is a beautiful countryside ride. Surprisingly rural in places, the road through Lake Vadnais will take you (mentally) far up into the north woods. Ponder the potential of the Arsenal property (being decommissioned) and enjoy the fall colors of the numerous stands of maple-basswood forest. It is, in fact, possible for outsiders to enter the "forbidden city" of North Oaks. All you need to do is get permission from each and every homeowner, as property lines extend to the middle of the street. That done, you will enjoy the off-road trail circling Pleasant Lake. Take some time to enjoy Snail Lake Park and the Tamarack Nature Center.

GO! A small parking lot is found at **VADNAIS LAKE PARK** (484-2020) at the SW corner of Edgerton Road and Vadnais Boulevard. Larger groups may want to start at the big parking lot at Tamarack Nature Center (777-1707). To reach Vadnais Lake Park exit I-694 at Rice Street (Highway 49) and go north, taking the first right onto Vadnais Boulevard. Proceed 1.5 miles to park on right.

1.3 mi Turn right onto Vadnais Lake Road that runs between **LAKE VADNAIS**. This is the last of the chain of lakes that supplies St. Paul's drinking water. Refresh in the pine scented air.

2.8 mi Take a left on County Road F, cross the railroad tracks and take the first right on the unmarked road to **SUCKER LAKE**.

For a 2 mile shorter loop continue west on County Road F to Rice Street. At the end of F is a pretty path through **SNAIL LAKE PARK**. Follow the map.

4.3 mi The palace guard stands watch at the gate house into the **FORBIDDEN CITY**. North Oaks was once the rural retreat and experimental farm of railroad baron James J. Hill. He raised livestock here that he would then donate to farmers along his Great

Northern Railroad line. Three original farm buildings are being renovated. Buy a home here (average cost is $250,000) and you not only get a set of golden keys but the possibility of having someone like Walter Mondale or Kevin McHale as your neighbor.

6.1 mi **GRASS LAKE PARK** is a large wetlands along the south side of Gramsie Road.

10.1 mi A small public park is set into the huge open landscape of the federally owned **ARSENAL**. Public debate will help determine the fate of this land.

14.3 mi Turn right (east) on Ash Street. **FARMS**, marsh and stands of hardwood trees dominate the view — for now, at least.

18.7 mi **TAMARACK NATURE CENTER** (429-7787) is a good place to stretch. Walk over to the interpretive center and spend a little time looking at the natural history exhibits and live animal room. A large tamarack bog once covered this land. Tamarack trees are prized for being rot resistant and this area was clear-cut in 1917 for log home construction.

21.1 mi The last ¾ mile of Otter Lake Road has only a gravel shoulder. Turn right on Goose Lake Road and you pass **GEM LAKE HILLS** golf course.

24.1 mi BACK TO *GO!*

25 FORBIDDEN CITY CIRCLE

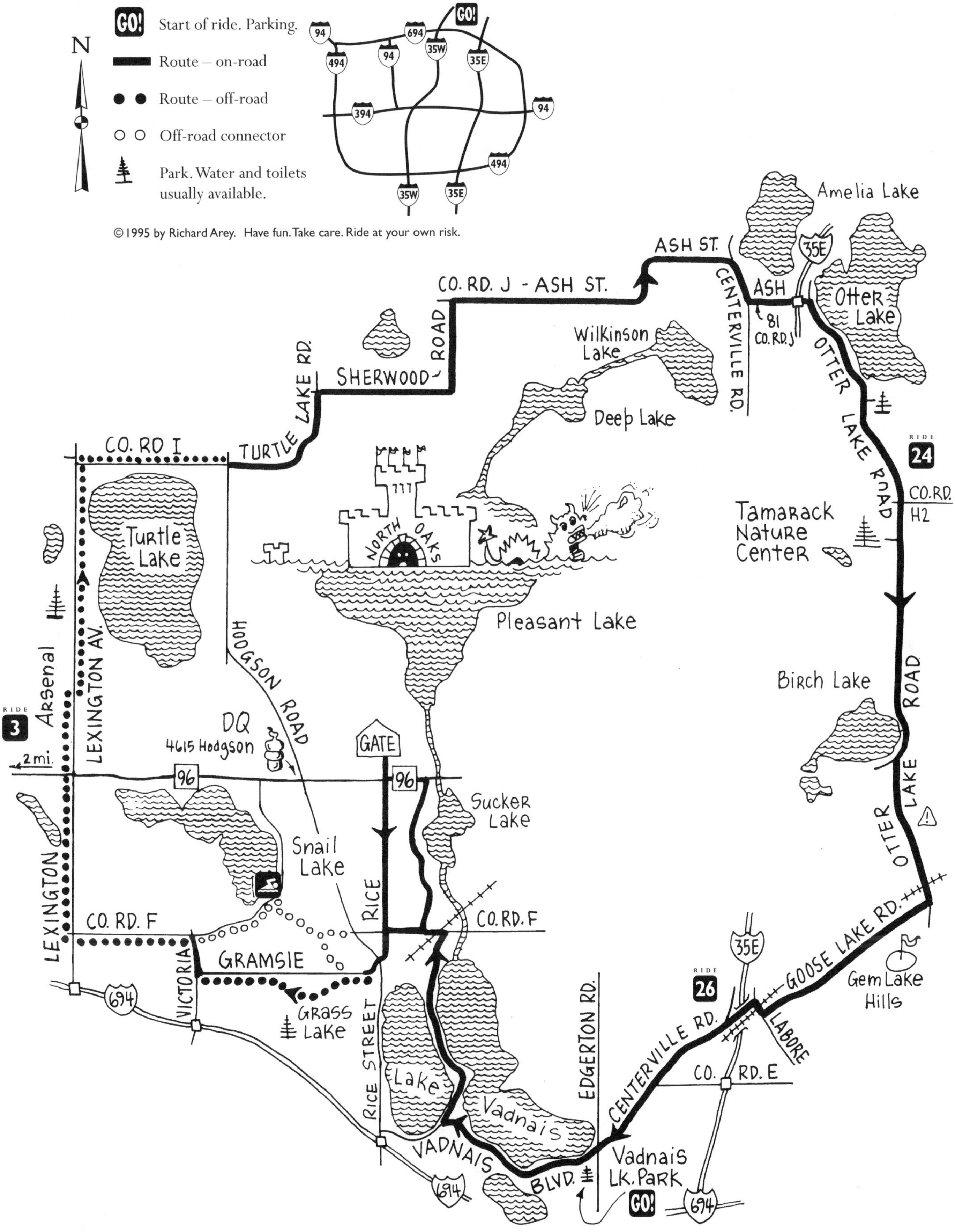

GO! Start of ride. Parking.

N

―――― Route – on-road

● ● ● Route – off-road

○ ○ Off-road connector

🌲 Park. Water and toilets usually available.

94
694
GO!
94
494
694
35W
35E
394
94
494
35W
35E

ASH ST.
CO. RD. J - ASH ST.
Amelia Lake
35E
CENTERVILLE RD.
ASH
81 CO. RD. J
Otter Lake
Wilkinson Lake
Deep Lake
SHERWOOD- ROAD
TURTLE LAKE RD.
CO. RD I
OTTER LAKE ROAD
RIDE 24
CO. RD. H2
Turtle Lake
Tamarack Nature Center
NORTH OAKS
Pleasant Lake
Birch Lake
Arsenal
LEXINGTON AV.
RIDE 3
2 mi.
HODGSON ROAD
DQ
4615 Hodgson
96
GATE
96
Sucker Lake
OTTER LAKE ROAD
⚠
Snail Lake
RICE
LEXINGTON
CO. RD. F
CO. RD. F
Edgerton RD.
35E
RIDE 26
GOOSE LAKE RD.
Gem Lake Hills
GRAMSIE
VICTORIA
694
Grass Lake
RICE STREET
CENTERVILLE RD.
LABORE
CO. RD. E
Lake
Vadnais
VADNAIS
BLVD.
Vadnais Lk. Park
GO!
694

LAND OF LAKES

Ramsey County. Connects with RIDES 22, 25, 27, 28 and 40.

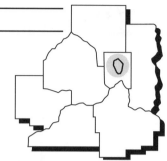

LENGTH
RATING

22 miles – Full loop as described

4.7 miles – Paved path around Lake Phalen and Round Lake

10 miles – Short loop around Gervais Lake plus Lake Phalen loop

17 miles – Medium loop around Lake Owasso

CAUTION
Careful crossing Highway 36 and I-694 on Rice Street. The sidewalk along Rice Street may be preferable.

This is a country cousin to the old AYH favorite Lotsa Lakes route. A great summertime ride with plenty of opportunities to cool off at one of the four swimming beaches. The multitude of lake views are a treat in any season. Geology fans will note that these lakes mark the ancient path of the glacial Mississippi River.

GO! Start at one of the parking lots on the west side of Lake Phalen. **PHALEN REGIONAL PARK** (266-6400) has a swimming beach, oak shaded picnic grounds and small craft for rent. To reach Phalen Park take the Wheelock Parkway exit on I-35E and go east about 2 miles to park entrance on left.

3.2 mi This is one full lap around Lake Phalen.

1.6 mi This is the distance if you go up the west side of Lake Phalen and continue along the creek up and over to the corner of **ARCADE AND ROSELAWN.** Watch for egrets along the creek.

2.8 mi Corner of Keller Parkway (Little Canada) and Edgerton. Go left (south) if you are doing the **SHORT LOOP**.

5.7 mi You've reached the entrance to the **ST. PAUL WATER WORKS**. Beautiful pine groves line the narrow drive between the lakes. Shore fishing along here is excellent. Continue east on Vadnais Boulevard to Rice Street if you are doing the **MEDIUM LOOP**. (Enjoy a swim at Lake Owasso before heading home.)

8.4 mi Another gorgeous stretch along **SUCKER LAKE** takes you to Highway 96.

10.1 mi **SNAIL LAKE REGIONAL PARK** has swimming, boating, picnicking and a great little trail in the woods to the east.

13.6 mi It's hot. It's sunny. It's time for a Misty Freeze at **DAIRY QUEEN**. Or make the scene at **LAKE JOSEPHINE** where you find another beach.

14.8 mi You won't mistake Roseville for New York City but enjoy the ride through **CENTRAL PARK**. Like its big city namesake, you can play a round of bocce ball or feed the ducks on Lake Bennett.

15.9 mi **HARRIET ALEXANDER NATURE CENTER** has a few live amphibians on display and a nice view over a marsh. Phone 482-8266 for program information.

16.9 mi An unmarked trail leads to and through wooded **MATERION PARK**.

20.6 mi After making it across Highway 36 on Rice Street you will have an uphill climb on County Road B followed by a couple nice glides on Edgerton to **WHEELOCK PARKWAY**.

22 mi BACK TO *GO!*

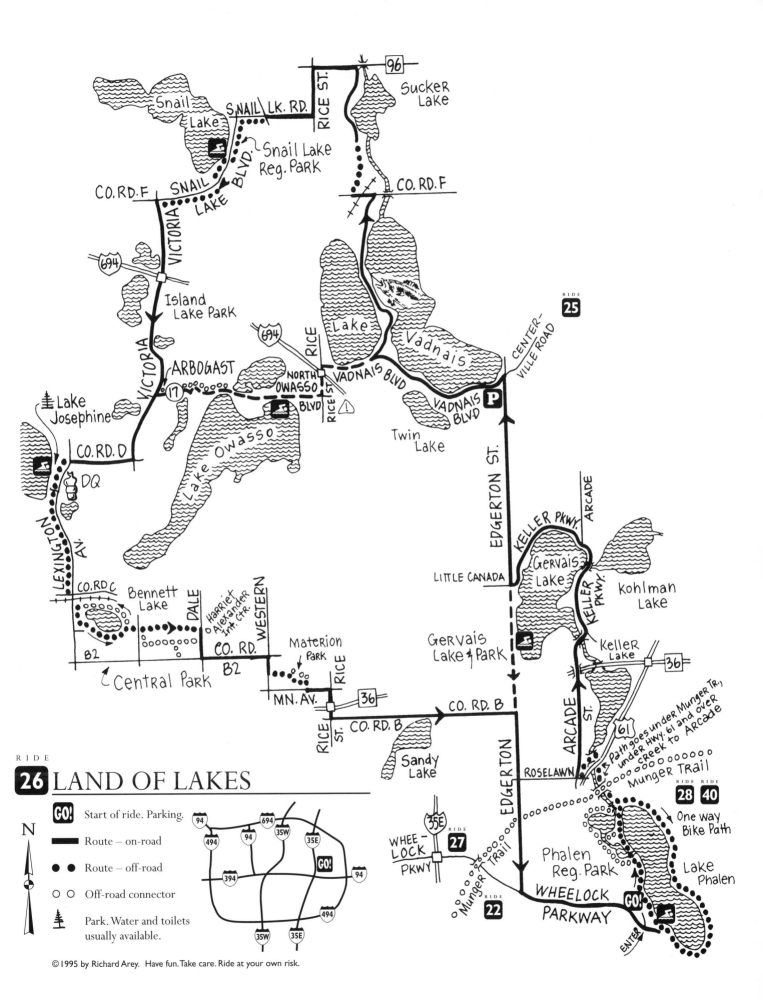

LAND OF LAKES

RIDE **26**

GO! Start of ride. Parking.

N

— Route – on-road

•• Route – off-road

∘∘ Off-road connector

🌲 Park. Water and toilets usually available.

©1995 by Richard Arey. Have fun. Take care. Ride at your own risk.

SAINT PAUL CLASSIC GRAND ROUND

Ramsey County. Connects with RIDES 4, 20, 23, 26, 28, 29, 30, 32, 33, 39 and 40.

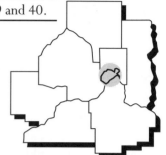

LENGTH
RATING

- 28.2 miles – Full loop as described
- 10.8 miles – Mississippi River Boulevard path, round trip
- 4.1 miles – Como Park paved paths

CAUTION Raymond north of Energy Park Drive is very tight. Use sidewalk as necessary. Shepard and Warner Road bikeway not complete and side-walk on south side is recommended.

This "Grand Round" of St. Paul was conceived and promoted over a century ago by park visionaries such as Horace William Shaler Cleveland and Joseph Wheelock. Today it is nearly complete. The St. Paul Grand Round connects all five of the city's regional parks and features 14 miles of biking along the Mississippi River.

An annual citizen's tour — the Saint Paul Classic Bike Tour — will be held on the loop beginning in 1995. The ride will take place on the Sunday after Labor Day each year. Phone 290-0309 for details.

GO! Start at the overlook where Summit Avenue intersects Mississippi River Boulevard. Enjoy the view over **MISSISSIPPI GORGE REGIONAL PARK**. Head south. Faster bicyclists should use the parkway. Families may prefer the off-road combined path.

2.5 mi Enter **HIDDEN FALLS REGIONAL PARK** (at Magoffin Avenue). Careful on the steep downhill. NOTE: While this park is really quite safe, single bicyclists may prefer to stay on the blufftop path that parallels Mississippi River Boulevard and then Shepard Road. (Saves 0.6 miles).

The riverside paved path enjoys some of the sweetest views of the Mississippi to be found anywhere. Wildlife is abundant and a short stop at the **CROSBY FARM NATURE CENTER** (just past the marina) is worthwhile. Marvel at the immense cottonwoods and take care if a "state endangered" Blanding's turtle should cross your path.

6.3 mi Exit **CROSBY FARM** and head northeast (right) on the paved path along Shepard.

8.1 mi Bike path ends at Randolph. Follow the road and use the sidewalk as necessary to where the new bike path begins.

11.2 mi Follow the bike path along Warner Road. Enjoy the great vista over the river toward the white sandstone cliffs below Indian Mounds Park. The Dakota name for the St. Paul area is **I-MNI-ZA** (ledge) **SKA** (white), or white rocks. Just past Fish Hatchery Road a pedestrian bridge crosses Warner Road and takes you up the bluff.

13.9 mi **JOHNSON PARKWAY** begins. It is definitely worth a short detour over to **INDIAN MOUNDS**

PARK to enjoy the spectacular panorama and the sacred mounds (add 0.8 miles). Johnson Parkway has a wide paved shoulder and was named after Minnesota Governor John Johnson (1905–1909).

16.3 mi **PHALEN REGIONAL PARK** was acquired in 1899 and named after Edward Phalen. Ed distinguished himself by being accused of the city's first murder and later fleeing town. Take a short swim or enjoy a lakeside picnic. A complete loop of Lake Phalen adds 3.2 miles.

WHEELOCK PARKWAY skirts the southern end of Lake Phalen and heads west. It is named after Joseph Wheelock, founder of the St. Paul Pioneer Press (1861) and president of the St. Paul Park Board (1893–1906). Nobody fought harder for establishing St. Paul's parks and a connected parkway system than Wheelock.

21.7 mi Lake Como comes into view and you enter **COMO REGIONAL PARK**. Minnesota's oldest and St. Paul's finest park began as a potato patch farmed by Charles Perry who named the lake after his birthplace, Como, Italy. Enjoy the FREE Zoo, the historic conservatory, Como Pool or a lap around Como Lake (add 1.5 miles).

23.5 mi Take **MIDWAY PARKWAY** to the **STATE FAIR GROUNDS**. NOTE: Como Avenue is the alternative when the fair is in session.

24.6 mi Take a left on Raymond. HEADS UP! This next stretch is busy.

27.1 mi Pelham Boulevard returns you to the **MISSISSIPPI RIVER BOULEVARD**.

28.2 mi BACK TO **GO!**

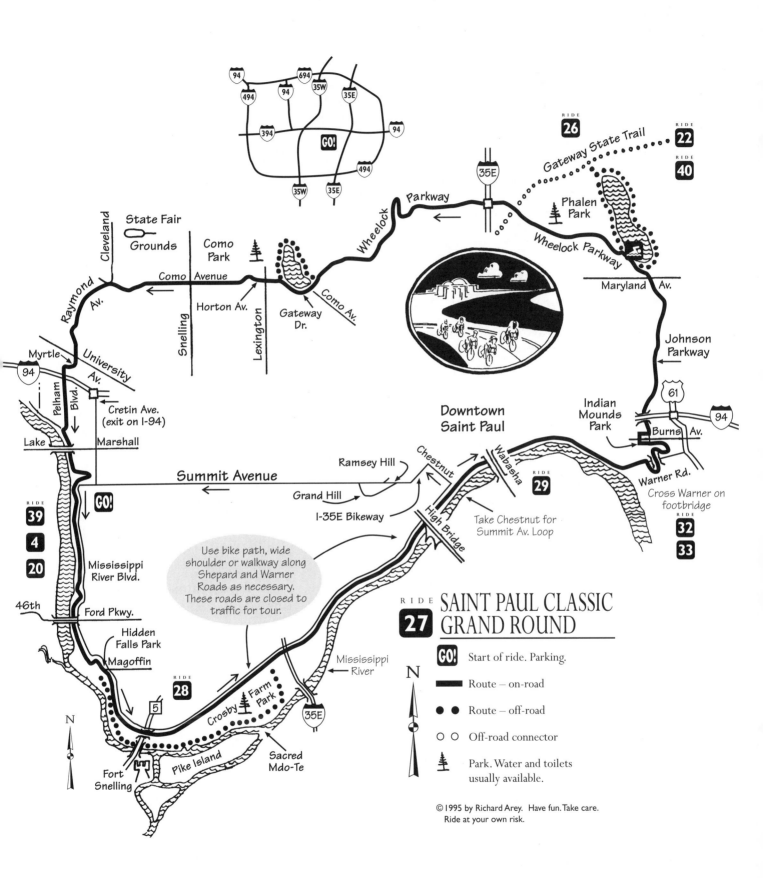

State Fair Grounds

Como Park

Como Avenue

Horton Av.

Gateway Dr.

Como Av.

Cleveland

Raymond Av.

Snelling

Lexington

Wheelock Parkway

Parkway

35E

RIDE 26

Gateway State Trail

RIDE 22

RIDE 40

Phalen Park

Wheelock Parkway

Maryland Av.

Johnson Parkway

Downtown Saint Paul

Indian Mounds Park

61

94

Burns Av.

Warner Rd.

Cross Warner on footbridge

RIDE 32

RIDE 33

Myrtle

University Av.

94

Pelham Blvd.

Cretin Ave. (exit on I-94)

Lake

Marshall

Summit Avenue

Ramsey Hill

Chestnut

Wabasha

RIDE 29

Grand Hill

I-35E Bikeway

High Bridge

Take Chestnut for Summit Av. Loop

GO!

RIDE 39

RIDE 4

RIDE 20

Mississippi River Blvd.

46th

Ford Pkwy.

Hidden Falls Park

Magoffin

Use bike path, wide shoulder or walkway along Shepard and Warner Roads as necessary. These roads are closed to traffic for tour.

Mississippi River

RIDE 28

Crosby Farm Park

35E

5

N

Fort Snelling

Pike Island

Sacred Mdo-Te

RIDE 27 SAINT PAUL CLASSIC GRAND ROUND

GO! Start of ride. Parking.

⸺ Route – on-road

●● Route – off-road

○○ Off-road connector

🌲 Park. Water and toilets usually available.

N

© 1995 by Richard Arey. Have fun. Take care.
Ride at your own risk.

Top freeway diagram: 94, 694, 94, 35W, 35E, 494, 94, 394, GO!, 494, 35W, 35E

SAINT PAUL SAMPLERS

RIDE **28**

Ramsey County. Connects with RIDES 4, 22, 26, 27, 30, 32, 39 and 40.

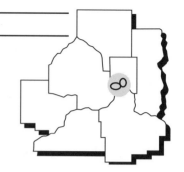

LENGTH RATING

- ⚈ 32.5 miles – Both loops, as described
- ⚆ 9.0 miles to Cathedral and back. Flat with bike lanes.
- ⚈ 21.9 miles – **Gateway Trail – Indian Mounds Loop**.
- ⚈ 14.6 miles – **Mississippi River - I-35E Bikeway Loop**.
- ⚆ 8.0 miles – Hidden Falls-Crosby Farm Park, paved path

CAUTION   The Kellogg – West 7th – Grand Avenue area is very busy.

*S*ummit Avenue is St. Paul's show street and is featured on both of these loop rides. More experienced cyclists are sure to enjoy the GATEWAY TRAIL – INDIAN MOUNDS LOOP, which includes a cruise along Lake Phalen, the eye-popping panorama from Indian Mounds Park and the exhilarating downhill run on Kellogg into downtown St. Paul. A shorter sampler, the MISSISSIPPI RIVER–I-35E BIKEWAY LOOP, goes south along the Mississippi and through beautiful Hidden Falls Park before returning you along the I-35E Bikeway to Summit Avenue.

GATEWAY TRAIL – INDIAN MOUNDS LOOP

GO!   Start at **SUMMIT AVENUE** and Mississippi River Blvd. Take Summit east toward the Cathedral.

2.7 mi   The Governor's mansion is at **1006 SUMMIT AVENUE**. F. Scott Fitzgerald once referred to Summit Avenue as a "museum of American architectural failures," but the fact remains that Summit Avenue is the best preserved monumental residential boulevard in America.

599 Summit • F. Scott Fitzgerald completed *This Side of Paradise* on the 3rd floor and danced in the street when it was accepted by his publisher.

432 Summit • Burbank House (1862), best Minnesota example of an Italian Villa.

240 Summit • J. J. Hill House (1887), take a tour.

4.5 mi   The **ST. PAUL CATHEDRAL** crowns the top of the bluff. Designed by Emmanuel Masqueray and built between 1906 and 1941, the cathedral is a monument to the vision of Archbishop John Ireland.

5.2 mi   Coast to a stop in front of St. Paul native Cass Gilbert's finest effort — the **STATE CAPITOL**. This beautiful Beaux Arts pile (1893-1904) features four gold-gilded horsemen high above the entrance.

8.0 mi   Start of **GATEWAY MUNGER TRAIL** at northeast corner of Arlington and I-35E.

9.8 mi   Watch the left-hand exit and cloverleaf to take you into **PHALEN REGIONAL PARK**.

11.6 mi   Enjoy the lakeside ride, then head south on **JOHNSON PARKWAY**.

14.4 mi   **INDIAN MOUNDS PARK** commands a spectacular view atop historic Carver's Cave and is used by Native Americans in sunrise tobacco ceremonies.

16.7 mi   Whistle into downtown St. Paul and take a peek inside beautifully restored **CITY HALL** (15 Kellogg Boulevard). The 55-ton, 36-foot high God of Peace rules magnificent Memorial Hall.

17.5 mi   Take care as you wind through downtown toward either the **DAIRY QUEEN** (280 W. 7th Street) or **GRAND OLE CREAMERY** (up the hill at 750 Grand Avenue).

21.9 mi   BACK TO *GO.*

MISSISSIPPI RIVER – I-35 BIKEWAY LOOP

GO!   Start at Summit Avenue and **MISSISSIPPI RIVER BOULEVARD.** Head south on Mississippi River Boulevard toward Ford Parkway.

2.5 mi   The waterfall in **HIDDEN FALLS REGIONAL PARK** can be seen from above on the path just past the overlook. Around the bend is the park entrance at Magoffin Avenue. The path along the river is beautiful, with sheer limestone cliffs rising next to you in spots.

4.8 mi   Just past the marina you enter **CROSBY FARM PARK**. This area has an abundance of wildlife and the Nature Center is worth a short visit. I watched a black-billed cuckoo here one fine spring day. The cottonwood trees are huge.

6.9 mi   Exit the park and head up Elway Street. Cross 7th Street on Albion and pick up the **I-35E BIKEWAY**.

10 mi   Follow the I-35E Bikeway back to **GRAND AVENUE**. Depending on how you are feeling take the Ramsey Street hill (very steep) or Grand Avenue hill (moderate) back to Summit Avenue.

14.6 mi   BACK TO *GO!*

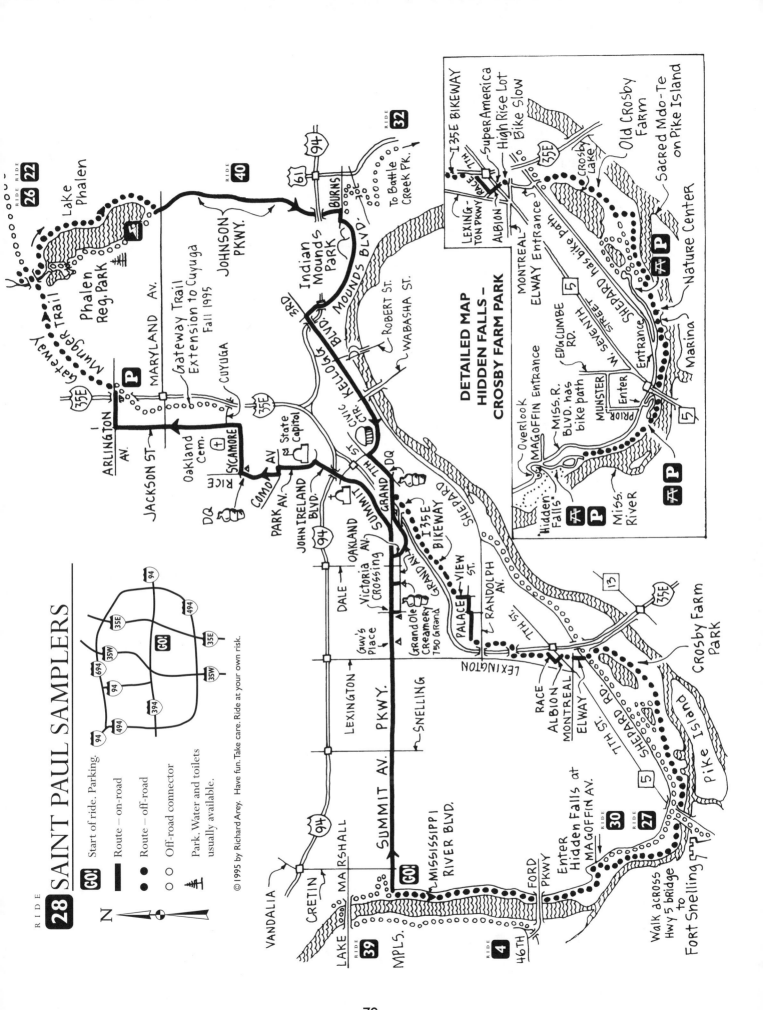

RIDE **28** SAINT PAUL SAMPLERS

GO Start of ride. Parking.
— Route — on-road
∙∙∙ Route — off-road
○○ Off-road connector
☙ Park. Water and toilets usually available.

©1995 by Richard Arey. Have fun. Take care. Ride at your own risk.

DETAILED MAP —
HIDDEN FALLS —
CROSBY FARM PARK

WEST SIDE WINDER

Ramsey and Dakota County. Connects with RIDES 30, 31 and 32

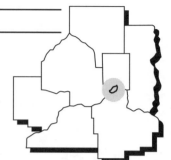

LENGTH   ⚡ 10.8 miles – Full loop as described
RATING   🌀 6.0 miles – Round trip Harriet Island to Lilydale, paved path
CAUTION   Wabasha Bridge construction (1996–97) may cause some access problems to Harriet Island.
NOTE   The Big Rivers Regional Trail will connect Lilydale Regional Park to the Mendota Bridge and Fort Snelling (see maps on pages 81 and 85).

> *B*e the first on your block to test drive the new bike path through Lilydale Park. Check out the fancy new pier at Harriet Island. Ponder the possibilities of outdoor baseball on the riverfront. For those folks who have a hard enough time locating St. Paul, let alone the West Side of the Capitol City, here is a chance to do some exploring. But first, a quick geography primer so you can get your bearings. The West Side is actually on the south side of St. Paul, but the west side of the Mississippi River if you are coming into town on a steamboat. The town of West St. Paul is south of the West Side and South St. Paul is east of West St. Paul. Western Avenue, of course, plows right through up the middle of the city. OK, let's go biking!

GO! Start at **HARRIET ISLAND** in the main parking area near the marina. A good breakfast at the **NO WAKE CAFE** (292-1411) is an excellent way to gear up. The No Wake Cafe is located on the 1946 towboat, *The Covington*, a unique floating bed and breakfast establishment. You'll like it so much you will want to call up Tom Welna and book a couple nights on the Mississippi. Phone 292-1411.

0.2 mi As you head up along the river you quickly reach the **HARRIET ISLAND PICNIC PAVILION**. This distinctive moderne-style building was designed by St. Paul's first black architect, Charles Wigington. It has survived three major river floods since its construction in the 1940s, and the Kasota limestone walls were actually salvaged from the 1886 Industrial Exposition Building. Take a left at the intersection just before you reach the pavilion.

HARRIET BISHOP CREATIVE PLAY AREA. Harriet Bishop came to town on a canoe in 1854 and was St. Paul's first teacher. Since you may still be reeling from your recent geography lesson, you will be glad to know that Harriet Island is no longer an island but is solidly attached to the south bank of the river.

1.0 mi Find the start of the newly separated paved bike path heading southwest. The city disappears as you cross under the High Bridge and into **LILYDALE REGIONAL PARK**. This is a great place for wildlife. In past trips I've seen herds of deer, king-

fishers, pileated woodpeckers and indigo buntings. In early April, scoot over to spring-fed Pickerel Lake and look for migrating loons and other waterfowl.

3.5 mi The **POOL AND YACHT CLUB** marks the end of Lilydale Park and the start of a major uphill ride.

3.8 mi Watch for an unmarked bike path on the south side of the road just below Highway 13. Take it and enter **SCENIC VALLEY PARK**. The paved path through here follows a tiny bubbling brook. The city is still nowhere to be seen, and if it wasn't for the light hum of traffic from I-35E, you would bet you are far out in the countryside.

4.8 mi The underpass at **MARIA AVENUE** is located at the southwest corner of the tennis courts.

5.7 mi The final stretch of path skirts a large wetlands before delivering you back to civilization at **DODD ROAD**.

7.2 mi Ride the broad shoulders of Dodd Road past **SOMERSET COUNTRY CLUB** and back into town.

9.5 mi South side, west side, any side, anytime is good for **DAIRY QUEEN**. Located at Stryker and George Streets.

10.8 mi Take George Street and then the flying curves of Wabasha Street back to Harriet Island and **BACK TO *GO!***

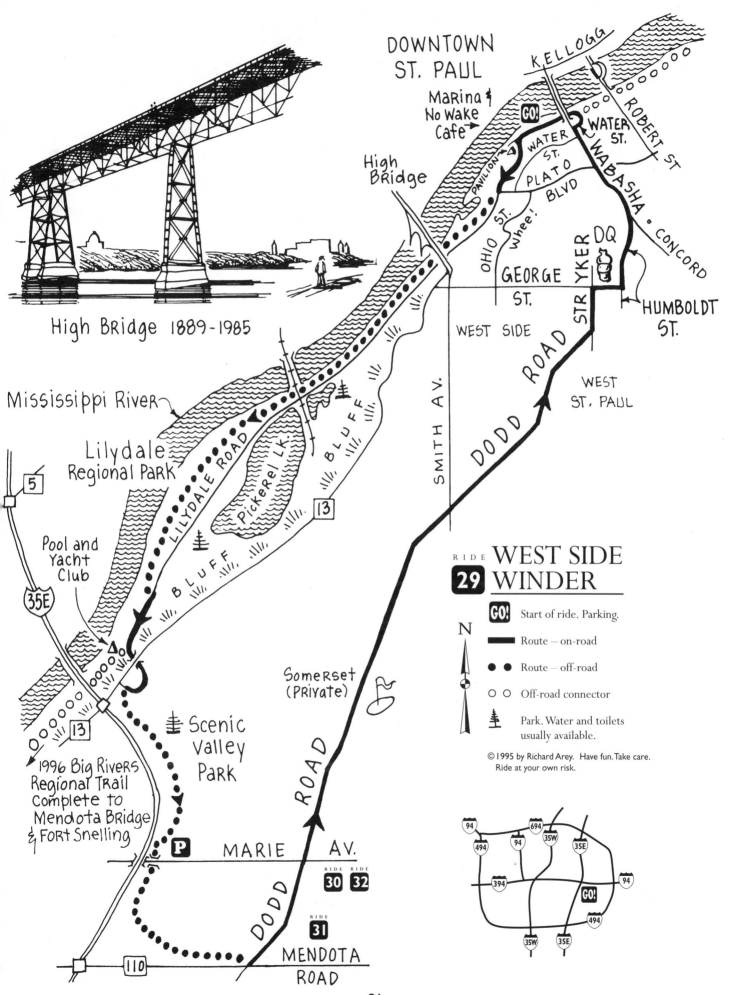

High Bridge 1889-1985

Mississippi River

Lilydale Regional Park

DOWNTOWN ST. PAUL

Marina & No Wake Cafe →

High Bridge

KELLOGG

ROBERT ST

WATER ST.

WABASHA · CONCORD

GO!

WATER ST.

PLATO BLVD

PAVILION

OHIO ST.

Whee! ST.

GEORGE ST.

WEST SIDE

STRYKER

DODD ROAD

DQ

HUMBOLDT ST.

WEST ST. PAUL

SMITH AV.

BLUFF

BLUFF

Pickerel Lk.

Lilydale Road

13

5

Pool and Yacht Club

35E

△

13

1996 Big Rivers Regional Trail Complete to Mendota Bridge & Fort Snelling

Scenic Valley Park

Somerset (Private)

RIDE
29 WEST SIDE WINDER

GO! Start of ride. Parking.

N

——— Route — on-road

• • Route — off-road

○ ○ Off-road connector

🌲 Park. Water and toilets usually available.

© 1995 by Richard Arey. Have fun. Take care. Ride at your own risk.

P

MARIE AV.

ROAD

RIDE **RIDE**
30   32

RIDE
31

DODD

110

MENDOTA ROAD

94

694

494

94

35W

35E

394

94

GO!

494

35W

35E

THREE BRIDGES BIKEWAY

Dakota, Hennepin, Ramsey. Connects with RIDES 4, 20, 27, 28, 29, 31 and 39.

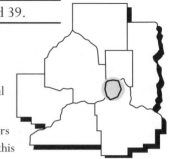

LENGTH 29.3 miles – Full loop as described
RATING 9.6 miles – Minnehaha Falls through Fort Snelling, round trip
CAUTION Bigger hills on Edgcumbe and climbing out of river valleys. Be careful biking along 34th Avenue and Highway 13.
NOTE Completion of the Mendota Bridge Bikeway in 1995 and the Big Rivers Regional Trail in 1996 (see RIDES 29 and 31 for location) will make this a Four Bridges Bikeway.

The Mississippi, Minnesota and St. Croix Rivers provide the main drama in the metro area landscape. This route celebrates two of these three great rivers and includes my favorite downhill run (since giving up the luge), the High Bridge highball that screams across the Mississippi with St. Paul and the State Capitol peering down in the distance. The Ford Parkway Bridge captures a great view of the Mississippi River Gorge, and the 2 mile long I-494 Bike Bridge is a rush.

GO! Start at the parking lot for **LOCK AND DAM NO. 1** (724-2971) located in Minneapolis just below the Ford Bridge: See inset map. A self-guided walking tour (keep your bikes locked) of the lock and dam gives an excellent introduction to these working rivers. The visitor promenade offers a bird's-eye view of boats going through the locks.

0.6 mi Bike down Godfrey Parkway and follow the signs to **MINNEHAHA FALLS**. A tourist trap for nearly two centuries, the falls were immortalized when Alex Hesler took a couple snapshots (daguerreotypes) of the falls in 1852. He brought them back home to Illinois, gave one to a buddy visiting from out East, who in turn showed it to Henry Wadsworth Longfellow. You know the rest.

0.8 mi Or skip the falls and have a cone at **DAIRY QUEEN** (corner of Minnehaha and Nawadaha).

1.9 mi Head south on Minnehaha Parkway past the Princess Depot and on to the start of the **MINNEHAHA TRAIL** at 54th Street. This gorgeous paved path hugging the white cliffs overlooking the Mississippi is a crowd favorite. You're rolling gently downhill on an old railroad grade and soon reach **HISTORIC FORT SNELLING**. The center of white settlement after its erection in the 1820s, this area is also sacred to the Dakota, who called this place **MDO-TE MI-NI-SO-TA**. MDO-TE refers to the confluence of the Minnesota and Mississippi Rivers and the name was later adapted by the town of Mendota.

4.4 mi Follow the paved path over to the **SWIMMING BEACH** in Fort Snelling State Park.

6.1 mi Take the long uphill road out of the State Park and onto **POST ROAD**. Gawk at the planes awhile.

9.1 mi Be careful on 34th Avenue and 80th Street before reaching the **MINNESOTA VALLEY NATIONAL WILDLIFE REFUGE VISITORS CENTER** (335-2323). Find out why this valley is so darned wide and what the timetable is for completing the 80-mile paved path down to LeSeuer. There are superior interpretive displays and you can get maps and program information for future visits.

11.4 mi Cross over the Minnesota River and up to **PILOT KNOB ROAD**.

18.7 mi A quick right on Mendota Heights Road will take you over to Dodd Road, which has a wide shoulder. At Smith Street take a left and head on down. With the State Capitol perfectly aligned in the background, you hit the **HIGH BRIDGE** running.

NOTE: If you want an extra climb on this route, take Wentworth (left), Wachtler (right) and head up Highway 13 to the High Bridge.

19.9 mi Coast to a stop at the **DAIRY QUEEN** (280 W. 7th Street) for a Misty Kiss.

26.3 mi Follow the I-35E Bikeway to Jefferson and up to Edgcumbe Road. Edgcumbe is a scenic, hilly romp through Highland Park. After another fun downhill, take the right on Munster, the left on Prior and you will intersect **MISSISSIPPI RIVER BOULEVARD**.

28.3 mi Take this north to the **FORD PARKWAY BRIDGE**. Stop at one of the beautiful river overlooks along the way.

29.3 mi BACK TO *GO!*

30 THREE BRIDGES BIKEWAY

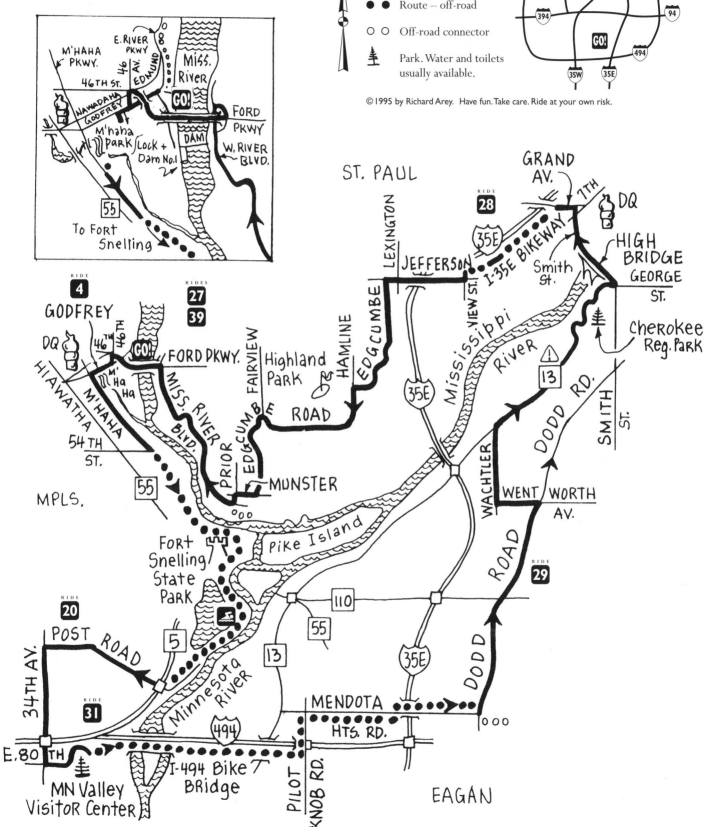

GO! Start of ride. Parking.

──── Route – on-road

•─•─• Route – off-road

○─○─○ Off-road connector

🌲 Park. Water and toilets usually available.

© 1995 by Richard Arey. Have fun. Take care. Ride at your own risk.

RIDE 31

BIKE TO THE ZOO

Dakota County. Connects with RIDES 18, 19, 20, 29, 30, 32, D and J.

LENGTH TO THE ZOO ONE WAY	
12.0 miles	– from Fort Snelling (Complete in 1996)
12.5 miles	– from Marie Avenue and Dodd Road
11.1 miles	– from Minnesota Valley Visitor Center
8.5 miles	– from Old Shakopee Road
6.4 miles	– from Dairy Queen on Highway 13
6.1 miles	– from Patrick Eagan Park

RATING ◐ Virtually every route is on an off-road paved path suitable for all levels of cyclists.

CAUTION Be careful at all intersections. Most routes are hilly.

The Minnesota Zoo (432-9000) is nationally acclaimed for balancing conservation efforts with family entertainment. Why not take this environmental and recreational approach one step further and bike to the zoo! Yes, this is the best place to view wildlife in the Twin Cities. The zoo features over 1,700 animals in specially designed habitats so they feel at home. The Siberian tigers, musk oxen and Tropics Trail are personal favorites. And don't miss the World of Birds show. Biking, of course, is not allowed within the zoo, so bring a lock and some cash to visit.

GO! Since many of the routes overlap, the following descriptions are capsule summaries from each starting point. The mileage listed above uses the most direct route.

FORT SNELLING (725-2390)

Start at the gate of the old stone fort. The path to the **MENDOTA BRIDGE** is about 100 yards due west of here. The bikeway on the bridge is complete and offers a grand panorama that includes both downtowns. This route will be open when the tunnel and connecting path to Pilot Knob Road are finished in 1996.

The entire **BIG RIVERS REGIONAL TRAIL** will be finished in the fall of 1996.

MARIE AVENUE

Dodd Road has a wide shoulder that takes you to the path along Mendota Heights Road. Head south on the rolling hills of Pilot Knob Road. The highest point of land was a landmark known by riverboat pilots as **PILOT HILL**.

MINNESOTA VALLEY VISITOR CENTER

(335-2323)

This striking contemporary structure is the headquarters for the Minnesota River Valley National Wildlife Refuge. Interactive displays, exhibits and handouts introduce you to this incredible resource.

See RIDE 16. The **I-494 BIKE BRIDGE** spans the huge valley carved by the glacial River Warren.

OLD SHAKOPEE ROAD

Take the Old Cedar Avenue Bridge across the Minnesota River (watch for yellow-headed blackbirds) and up to Silver Bell Road. The **HIGHLINE TRAIL** is quite scenic.

DAIRY QUEEN ON HIGHWAY 13

Stoke up on some **STRAWBERRY SHORTCAKE**. Palomino Road is pretty, wooded and steep in spots.

PATRICK EAGAN PARK (681-4660)

A gem of a city park, it is named after the township's first chairman who came here from Tipperary, Ireland, in 1853. Stop in at the privately owned **CAPONI ART PARK** if it is open. **THOMAS LAKE PARK** features a 12-acre native prairie and a picnic pavilion overlooking the lake.

LEBANON HILLS REGIONAL PARK is the premier natural preserve in the area. A beautiful swimming beach and excellent hiking trails are available. There is ample opportunity to find seclusion within the 2,000 acres of lakes, hills and woods, but bicycling is only allowed at the designated mountain bike area west of Johnny Cake Road. See RIDE J.

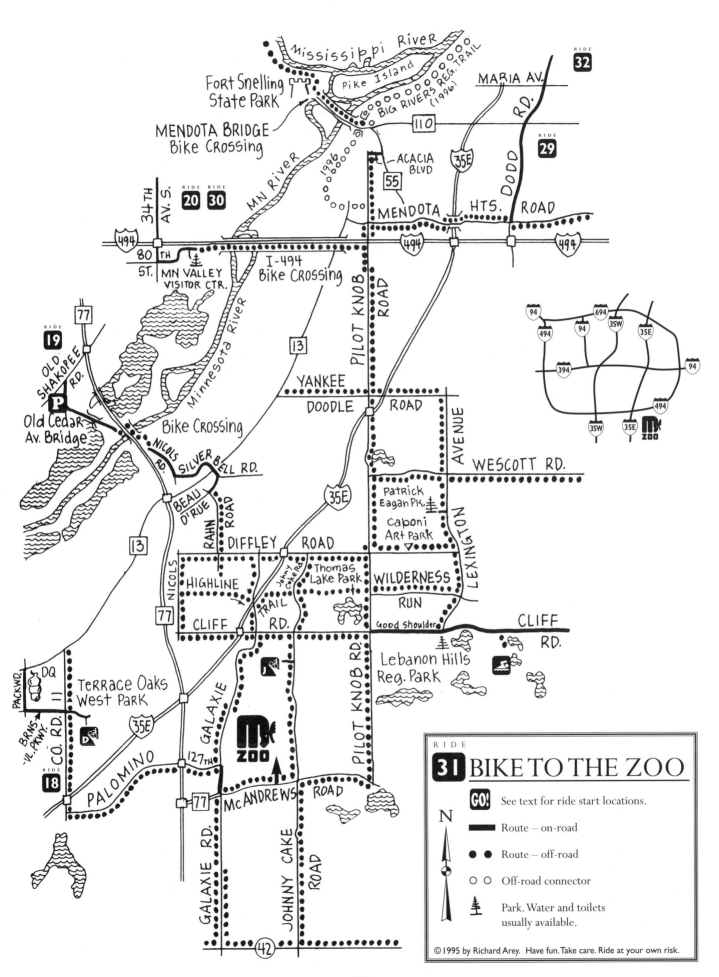

Mississippi River

Pike Island

Fort Snelling State Park

MENDOTA BRIDGE Bike Crossing

Big Rivers Reg. Trail (1996)

MARIA AV.

RIDE 32

110

MN River

ACACIA BLVD

55

35E

DODD ROAD

MENDOTA HTS. ROAD

RIDE 29

34TH AV. S.

RIDE 20 **RIDE 30**

494

80TH ST.

MN VALLEY VISITOR CTR.

I-494 Bike Crossing

494

494

494

77

RIDE 19

OLD SHAKOPEE RD.

P

Old Cedar Av. Bridge

Minnesota River

Bike Crossing

NICOLS RD.

SILVER BELL RD.

13

PILOT KNOB ROAD

YANKEE DOODLE ROAD

AVENUE

WESCOTT RD.

94   694

494   94   35W   35E

394

94

35W   35E

ZOO

494

13

77

BEAU D'RUE

RAHN ROAD

DIFFLEY ROAD

HIGHLINE

Johnny Cake Rd.

Thomas Lake Park

35E

Patrick Eagan Pk.

Caponi Art Park

LEXINGTON

CLIFF   TRAIL RD.

WILDERNESS RUN

Good Shoulder

CLIFF RD.

NICOLS

PACKWD.

DQ

Terrace Oaks West Park

BRNS-VL PKWY.

CO. RD. 11

GALAXIE

PILOT KNOB RD.

Lebanon Hills Reg. Park

D

35E

PALOMINO

RIDE 18

127TH

77

ZOO

McANDREWS ROAD

GALAXIE RD.

JOHNNY CAKE ROAD

42

RIDE 31 BIKE TO THE ZOO

GO! See text for ride start locations.

N

━━━ Route – on-road

• • • Route – off-road

○ ○ Off-road connector

🌲 Park. Water and toilets usually available.

© 1995 by Richard Arey. Have fun. Take care. Ride at your own risk.

RIDE 32 PATTI ROCKS THE RIVER

Ramsey, Washington & Dakota County. Connects with RIDES 27, 28, 29, 30, 33 and 40.

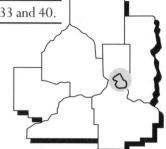

LENGTH ❄ 25.5 miles – Full loop as described
RATING ♠ 5.0 miles – Indian Mounds through Battle Creek, round trip
CAUTION Three major climbs and heavy traffic on Kellogg and Babcock at rush hour. Toll Bridge is open for bicyclists May through October and a 30-cent fee is charged per bicyclist. Bridge phone is 450-0757 and it is worth a call to make sure it's open before riding.

This is a fascinating route that has it all — great scenic vistas, quiet backwoods roads, a bustling downtown (well, St. Paul anyway), a Dairy Queen and a historic 1895 double decker swing bridge. The 1988 movie PATTI ROCKS had a scene featuring this historic toll bridge.

GO! Start at **INDIAN MOUNDS PARK** (266-6400). To reach the park from the west, take the Mounds exit off I-94 and go right (southeast) on Mounds Boulevard. From the east, exit I-94 at Highway 61, go south to Burns Avenue, and right (west) on Burns, forking left on Mounds Boulevard to the park.

Indian Mounds Park offers an unsurpassed view of downtown St. Paul and the Mississippi River. There were 18 mounds when the site was originally surveyed by Edward Neill in 1856. These six mounds are some of the last remaining in Minnesota, where 10,000 had been tallied at the turn of the century. The sacred burial mounds are still used for worship by Native Americans in sunrise tobacco ceremonies. The Dakota knew this place as **WA-KAN TI-PI**, or sacred habitation, referring to Carver's Cave directly below. Picnic areas and restrooms are nearby.

2.5 mi An off-road paved path leads to **BATTLE CREEK REGIONAL PARK**. The entrance is framed by two sandstone cliffs. A creek bubbles out under the white sculpted rocks and if time permits a very scenic side trip can be made on a paved path up the wooded ravine.

8.6 mi Pay your money and bike across the double decker **TOLL BRIDGE**. Imagine a train going overhead. Make a note to rent the video *Patti Rocks* but be sure your kids are in bed as the language is definitely salty.

9.9 mi It is a long uphill climb on 66th Street to reach **SKYVIEW PARK** where you can refill your water bottles and look out over the valley.

11.2 mi Take 70th Street to Cahill if you would like to refuel at **DAIRY QUEEN**. Otherwise, 69th to Clayton to Carmen is less congested.

13.1 mi A couple more hills on 55th Street will take you to the **SALEM METHODIST CHURCH** — a brick landmark since 1854.

15.7 mi Babcock and Oakdale take you to Maria and a modern landmark — the **WATER TOWER**. It is all downhill from here.

18.2 mi Enter scenic **VALLEY PARK** and take the paved path heading north. This will lead you to a curving road exiting the park (go right) headed down toward the river.

19.5 mi Follow Lilydale Road downstream along the Mississippi River and you will soon enter **LILYDALE REGIONAL PARK**. Though you are rapidly approaching a major downtown it feels more like a backwoods road in the bayou. Birdwatching is excellent. Look for wood ducks, kingbirds and common goldeneyes in spring. A new paved path along the river starts at the boat ramp access road. The path (or Lilydale Road) takes you to **PLATO BOULEVARD**.

22.8 mi The **ROBERT STREET BRIDGE** crosses over the Mississippi and provides a dramatic entry into downtown St. Paul. Completed in 1926, the beautiful 264-foot-long rainbow arch was recently refurbished to its original glory.

25.4 mi A long uphill march on Kellogg Boulevard takes you **BACK TO GO!** Enjoy the great view along the way.

- 86 -

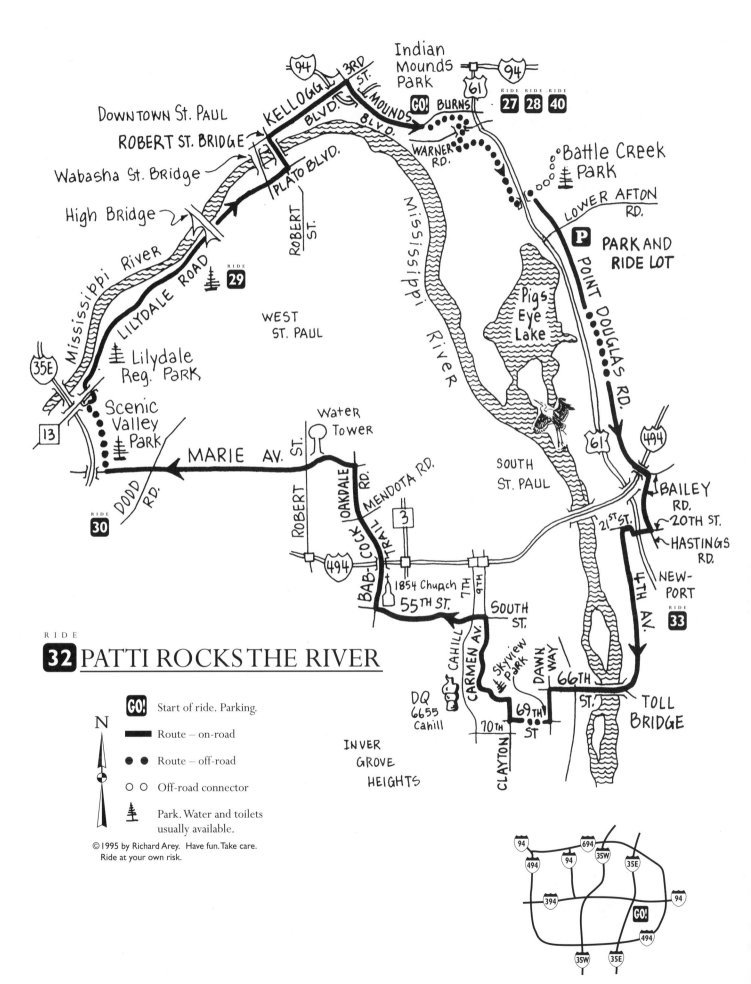

RIDE 32 PATTI ROCKS THE RIVER

N

GO!	Start of ride. Parking.
	Route – on-road
••	Route – off-road
○○	Off-road connector
♣	Park. Water and toilets usually available.

© 1995 by Richard Arey. Have fun. Take care.
Ride at your own risk.

DAKOTA TRAILS

Ramsey & Washington County. Connects with RIDES 27, 28, 32, 34 and 40.

LENGTH ◆ 39.4 miles – Full loop as described
RATING ◆ 21.2 miles – Toll bridge, Red Rock and return   .
            ● 4.0 miles – Battle Creek Park trails

CAUTION Light traffic, except at rush hour, but no shoulder on Grey Cloud
             Island Drive and Bailey Road. Big hills over I-494, on 70th Street and
             Bailey Road.

The place names of the Dakota Indians echo across Minnesota. This tour brings together archaeological sites and features that have been revered for centuries. Red Rock, Indian Mounds Park, Battle Creek and Grey Cloud Island all resonate with storied pasts. The trip begins with a spectacular view over the Mississippi River from Indian Mounds Park. It includes half a dozen more river views along the way. The southern half of the ride is surprisingly rural for now but bicycling over to the Dairy Queen on 80th Street gives an indication of what may lie ahead. Grey Cloud Island is destined to be a tremendous addition to the metropolitan park system. Tell your influential friends and politicians.

GO!

Start at **INDIAN MOUNDS PARK** (266-6400). To reach the park from the west, exit I-94 at Mounds Boulevard and go right (southeast) on Mounds. From the east, exit I-94 at Highway 61, go south to Burns Avenue, then right (west) on Burns, forking left on Mounds Boulevard to the park.

Indian Mounds Park, dating back to 1893, is not simply one of the oldest parks in the region — it is a living link with a time and people that fades into prehistory. The mounds were built as burial sites by various Native American nations commencing with the Hopewell culture some 2,000 years ago. The mounds remain sacred for Indians who honor the dead with sunrise tobacco ceremonies. Picnic grounds with restrooms are located nearby.

2.5 mi Two large shoulders of sandstone guard the entrance to **BATTLE CREEK REGIONAL PARK**. From this ravine in June, 1842, Ojibway Indians attacked the Dakota village of Kaposia across the river. A paved bike path follows the creek up this beautiful wooded ravine and adds about 2 miles to the trip. Otherwise, continue along Bob Dylan's famous Highway 61 — the Point Douglas Bike Route.

4.8 mi **FISH CREEK OPEN SPACE** lies hidden just past Carver Avenue. Take a short walk to a tiny waterfall.

8.6 mi If it is still open, pay your money and bike across the historic **1895 TOLL BRIDGE**. This double decker swing bridge was featured in the 1988 movie *Patti Rocks*.

13.9 mi Cross the bridge onto **GREY CLOUD ISLAND**. If good sense prevails this will eventually be one of the gems of the Mississippi National River and Recreation Area. The 1,400-acre park reserve will include trails, camping and an interpretive center. There is certainly a wealth of material to interpret. There are ancient habitation sites here that date back long before the time of the Dakota woman, **MA-HPI-YA** (clouds) **HO-TA** (grey) **WIN** (woman), for whom the island is named.

16.0 mi **END OF THE ROAD.**

21.5 mi Take Hadley Avenue and Grange to the **DAIRY QUEEN** at 7175 S. 80th Street. Stoke up for the big hill on 70th Street.

27.4 mi Cross Highway 61 twice more and head up 11th Avenue to the Newport United Methodist Church and the historic **RED ROCK**. The rock is smaller than expected and was moved here from its original location on the banks of the Mississippi River. Known by the Dakota as **IN-YAN** (stone) **SA** (red), it has been revered for generations and the ancient painted red stripes are still barely visible.

33.5 mi If traffic is light and you have the energy, take Bailey Road up the big bluff and then over on Sterling and Carver to McKnight Road. Enter **BATTLE CREEK PARK** from Lower Afton Road and take a lap before heading over to glide down through beautiful Battle Creek Ravine.

39.4 mi One more hill and it is **BACK TO GO!**

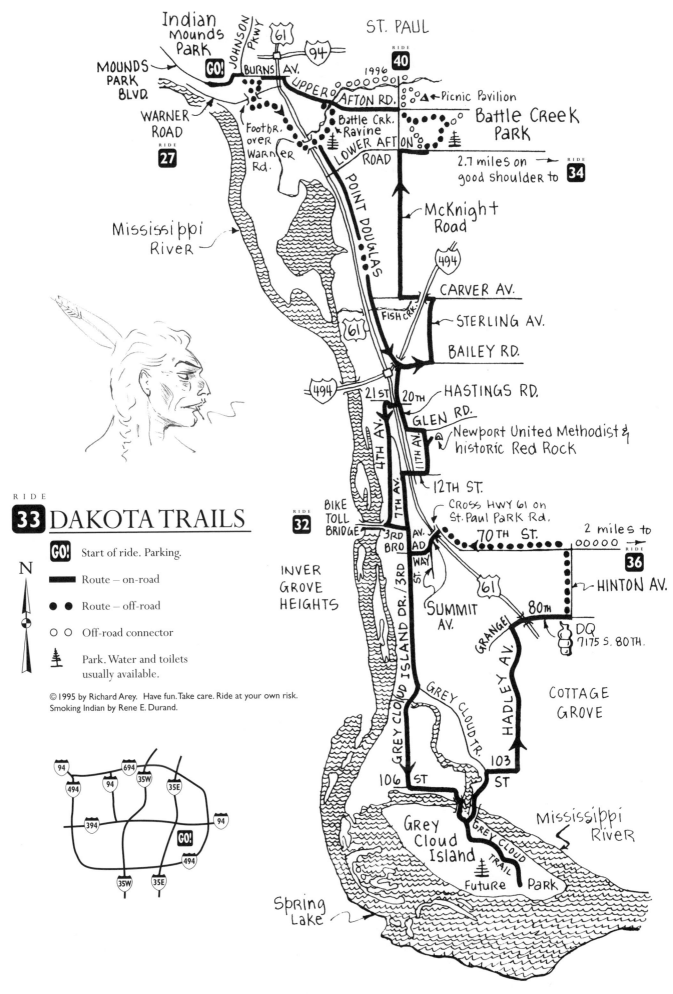

Indian Mounds Park

MOUNDS PARK BLVD.

JOHNSON PKWY

61

94

ST. PAUL

RIDE 40

1996

GO!

BURNS AV.

UPPER AFTON RD.

Picnic Pavilion

Battle Creek Park

WARNER ROAD

RIDE 27

Footbr. over Warner Rd.

Battle Crk. Ravine

LOWER AFTON ROAD

2.7 miles on good shoulder to

RIDE 34

Mississippi River

POINT DOUGLAS

McKnight Road

494

CARVER AV.

61

FISH CRK.

STERLING AV.

BAILEY RD.

494

21ST

20TH

HASTINGS RD.

4TH AV.

11TH AV.

GLEN RD.

Newport United Methodist & historic Red Rock

7TH AV.

12TH ST.

Cross Hwy 61 on St. Paul Park Rd.

70TH ST.

2 miles to

RIDE 36

BIKE TOLL BRIDGE

RIDE 32

3RD BRO

AV. AD

3RD/3RD

WAY ST.

INVER GROVE HEIGHTS

00000

HINTON AV.

61

SUMMIT AV.

80TH

DQ 7175 S. 80TH.

GRANGE!

HADLEY AV.

COTTAGE GROVE

RIDE 33 DAKOTA TRAILS

GO! Start of ride. Parking.

N

—— Route – on-road

● ● Route – off-road

○ ○ Off-road connector

🌲 Park. Water and toilets usually available.

© 1995 by Richard Arey. Have fun. Take care. Ride at your own risk.
Smoking Indian by Rene E. Durand.

GREY CLOUD ISLAND DR./3RD

GREY CLOUD TR.

103 ST.

106 ST.

Grey Cloud Island

GREY CLOUD TRAIL

Future

Park

Mississippi River

Spring Lake

94

694

494

94

35W

35E

394

94

GO!

494

35W

35E

WONDERFUL WOODBURY

Washington County. Connects with RIDES 32, 33, 35, 36, H and I.

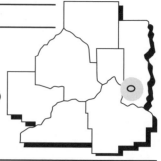

LENGTH ⬣ 14.2 miles - Full loop as described
RATING ⬣ 10.0 miles - Half loop
CAUTION Route is tricky to navigate the first time around. Woodbury (739-5972) has an excellent map of its parks and bikeway system.

*W*oodbury township was named in honor of Judge Levi Woodbury in 1858 — the same year Minnesota became a state. Levi was a New Hampshire resident and an old buddy of the local chair of the county commission. It is not known if Woodbury ever even visited here, but if you're in the neighborhood, definitely stop by. This route bends and twists to capture every inch of natural beauty it can muster. Colby and Wilmes Lakes are treats. Get off your bike to explore a bit of the Tamarack Nature Preserve. Here is a wild chunk of the far north settled in the suburbs.

The key to Woodbury's beautiful trail system is the city's farsighted public policy that requires developers to dedicate 150-foot-wide strips of land around their lakes for public trails. This policy is unique in Minnesota and bodes well for future trail development as the progressive community continues to grow.

GO! Start your tour in **OJIBWAY PARK**, Woodbury's recreational hub. The park entrance is reached by exiting I-494 at Valley Creek Road and heading east. Take the first right (south) on Woodlane Drive to Courtly Road. Go left (east) on Courtly and right on Ojibway Drive one block to entrance.

Water, washrooms, play areas and a host of other recreational opportunities are available.

Take the path directly east of the recreation center for 0.4 miles.

0.4 mi Take the right fork at the "T" intersection and proceed along the creek 0.4 miles to Tower Drive.

3.0 mi **COLBY LAKE** is the centerpiece of the town's biggest park. It is a beauty. Follow the paved path north up the short chain of lakes.

5.4 mi A thin wooded ravine follows a tiny creek up to **SEASONS PARK**. Check out the action on the soccer fields.

6.3 mi Exit the ravine, cross a street and proceed past the parking lot and along the creek.

6.6 mi Take the left fork in the path at the pond.

6.7 mi Take a sharp left toward the tennis courts after passing the baseball fields.

7.8 mi After negotiating the small residential maze take the bike paths along Radio Drive and Valley Creek Road to **TAMARACK NATURE PRESERVE**. This is a bog, not for bikes, but worth the short walk in. Tamaracks (larch trees) have soft needle-like leaves that turn golden yellow in fall. Tamarack bogs are much more comfortable in the wilds of central Canada. They are growing here at the southern edge of their range.

9.0 mi One block north of Valley Creek Road on Bielenberg Drive is — you guessed it — a **DAIRY QUEEN**.

If the path is not completed to Bielenberg Drive, you will want to backtrack to Valley Creek Road.

9.5 mi Wind your way over to the historic limestone **BISCHOSLICHE METHODISTEN CHURCH** built in 1868. On Steeple View Road, you know.

10.0 mi Head south, back into Ojibway Park and soon you will **PASS GO!** Collect $200 and head for Carver Lake.

11.8 mi Uh oh! **CARVER LAKE** has a resort hotel on it, pay $300. Enjoy the view before heading......

14.2 mi BACK TO *GO!*

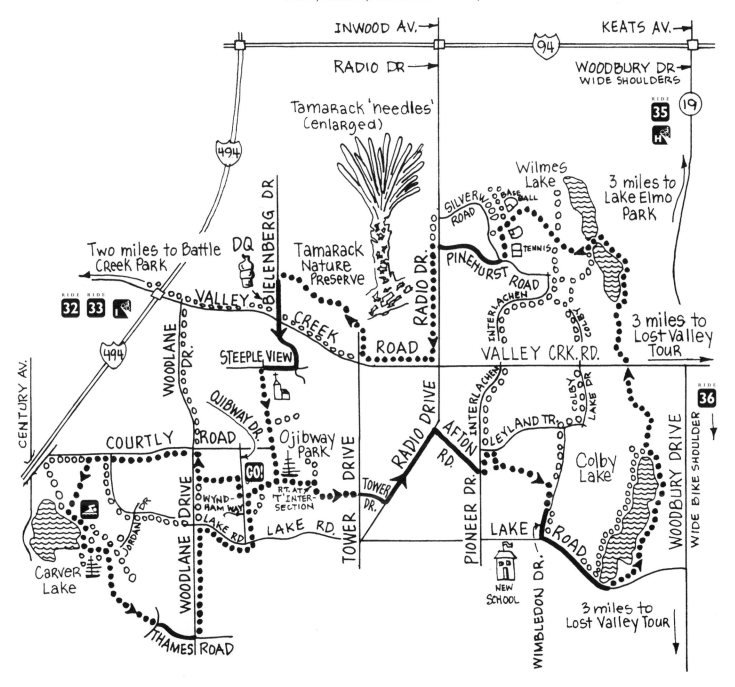

RIDE
34 WONDERFUL WOODBURY

N

GO! Start of ride. Parking.

━━━ Route – on-road

●●● Route – off-road

○ ○ Off-road connector

🌲 Park. Water and toilets usually available.

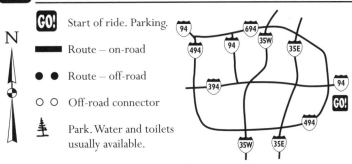

© 1995 by Richard Arey. Have fun. Take care. Ride at your own risk.

INWOOD AV. →

KEATS AV. →

94

RADIO DR →

WOODBURY DR
WIDE SHOULDERS

RIDE 35

19

Tamarack 'needles'
(enlarged)

Wilmes Lake

3 miles to Lake Elmo Park

494

SILVERWOOD ROAD
BASE BALL

Two miles to Battle Creek Park

DQ

Tamarack Nature Preserve

PINEHURST ROAD

TENNIS

RIDE 32 RIDE 33

BIELENBERG DR.

VALLEY

CREEK

ROAD

RADIO DR.

INTERLACHEN

COLBY

3 miles to Lost Valley Tour

494

STEEPLE VIEW

VALLEY CRK. RD.

CENTURY AV.

WOODLANE DR.

QIBWAY DR.

Ojibway Park

TOWER DRIVE

RADIO DRIVE

AFTON RD.

INTERLACHEN

OLEYLAND TR.

COLBY LAKE DR.

RIDE 36

COURTLY ROAD

GO!

R.T. AT 'T' INTER-SECTION

TOWER DR.

Colby Lake

WOODBURY DRIVE
WIDE BIKE SHOULDER

WYND-HAM WAY

JORDAN DR.

WOODLANE DRIVE

LAKE RD.

LAKE RD.

PIONEER DR.

LAKE ROAD

Carver Lake

NEW SCHOOL

WIMBLEDON DR.

3 miles to Lost Valley Tour

THAMES ROAD

35 STAGECOACH TO STILLWATER

Washington County. Connects with RIDES 23, 36 and H.

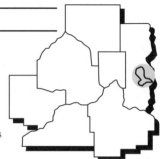

LENGTH ⬆ 43.9 miles – Longest loop as described
RATING ⬆ 5.5 miles – Lake Elmo Park Reserve paved path
⬆ 25.4 miles – Shortest loop to Stillwater
⬆ 30.4 miles – Afton and Hudson (but not Stillwater) and back

CAUTION Car parking fee at Lake Elmo (free with Washington or Hennepin Parks sticker). Stagecoach Trail has no shoulder south of Hudson Road. Big hills and traffic in Stillwater.

*S*teamboating the scenic St. Croix river towns would be a good subtitle for this ride. Afton, Hudson, Lake Elmo and Stillwater are all quite charming. You may wish you had brought a trailer along if you enjoy antiquing. Stop in one of the excellent used book stores in Hudson or Stillwater — or the Afton Toy Shop — for a more portable treasure. If nothing else, you're sure to return with some memorable images of quaint villages, unspoiled countryside and the wide pristine waters of the St. Croix River.

GO! Start at **LAKE ELMO PARK RESERVE** (731-3851). Take Keats Avenue (County Road 19) north 1 mile from I-94 to park entrance. Lake Elmo offers 3½ square miles of recreational opportunities. As a *Park Reserve*, 80 percent of the land will remain in a natural state. Besides the paved paths there is an 8-mile mountain bike course (See RIDE H) and horseback riding. Boating, camping, picnicking and a wonderful 2-acre swimming pond are all part of the mix.

3.8 mi Follow County Roads 10 and 15 to the **HUDSON ROAD BIKE ROUTE.** (An off-road path along County Road 19 also leads there but is less scenic.)

NOTE: Another interesting way to get to Afton is to cross I-94 at County Road 71 and take Hudson Boulevard east to **INDIAN TRAIL.** This leads you down to Stagecoach Trail.

6.0 mi **ST. CROIX TRAVEL INFORMATION CENTER** has all the requisite traveler's needs and is the geographic center of I-94. A paved path behind the rest area leads to a secluded overlook of the farmstead site where three generations of the Splinter family tended the land from 1883 to 1976.

7.4 mi Intersection of I-94 and **STAGECOACH TRAIL.** You will save 14.1 miles if you skip the side trips to Afton and Hudson.

11.6 mi Scenic Stagecoach Trail winds down to **AFTON.** Pick up an ice cream cone at **SELMA'S** and stroll down to the river.

15.4 mi An off-road paved path leads up to 8th Street (I-94 and 95).

17.6 mi Follow 8th Street until it ends and goes below the I-94 bridge. A ramp on the north side takes you to the bikeway over the St. Croix River and into **HUDSON.** Time for a **DAIRY QUEEN.**

21.5 mi Back to I-94 and Stagecoach Trail. Head north on the broad shoulders of this historic route.

29.5 mi A long fast downhill on 3rd Street takes you into the heart of **STILLWATER.** It is just a couple blocks down Chestnut or Myrtle to the main business district or the river. Award-winning **SEBASTIAN JOE'S** ice cream has a shop at 215 Main Street. Climb the 2nd Street hill up to **PIONEER PARK** and a wonderful vista.

30.4 mi Owens and Myrtle Street. Decision time. The quickest way back is to continue two more blocks to Olive Street and take Highway 5. This busy route has a wide shoulder and saves 4.5 miles. **HIGHWAY 5** is one of the oldest travel routes in Minnesota and even appeared on the 1899 St. Paul Cycle Path Association Route Map of the Twin Cities.

39.5 mi Take the paved path or wide shoulder of Highway 12 to Keats Avenue and head south into the town of **LAKE ELMO.** The stamped metal siding of the Lake Elmo mill is particularly striking on a sunny day.

43.9 mi Enjoy the beautiful stretch of County Road 17 along Lake Elmo before heading **BACK TO** *GO!*

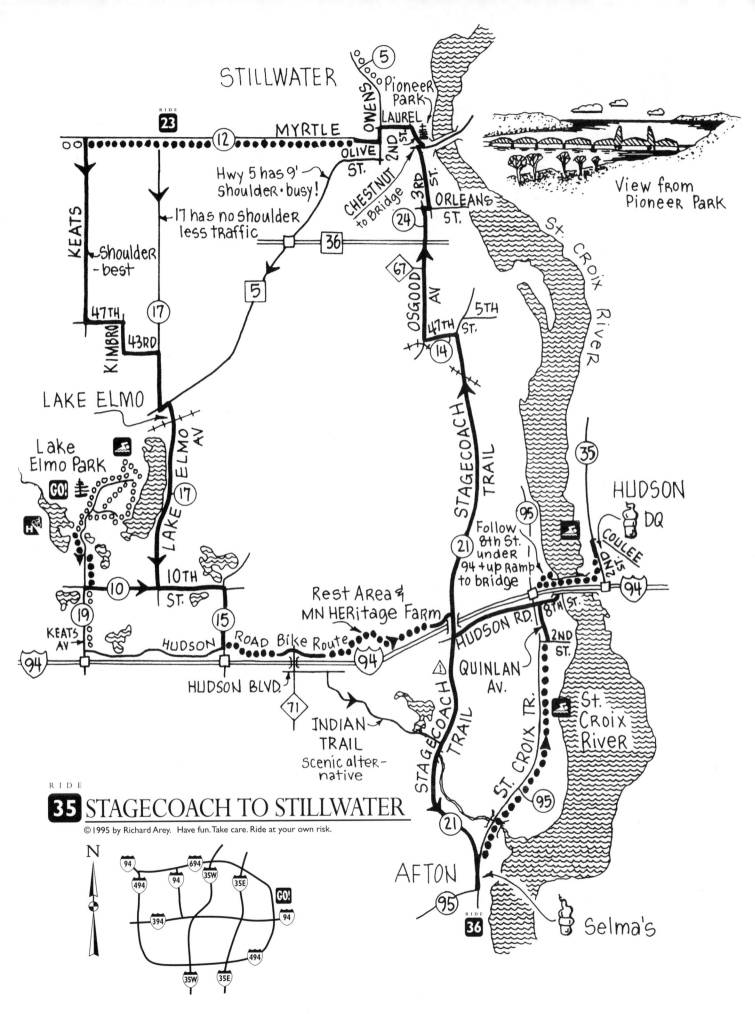

STILLWATER

RIDE
23

MYRTLE

Pioneer Park

5

OWENS

LAUREL

2ND ST.

OLIVE ST.

Hwy 5 has 9' shoulder · busy!

CHESTNUT to Bridge

3RD ST.

ORLEANS ST.

St. Croix River

View from Pioneer Park

12

17 has no shoulder less traffic

36

24

KEATS

Shoulder - best

5

67

OSGOOD AV.

5TH ST.

47TH

17

47TH

14

KIMBRO

43RD

LAKE ELMO

LAKE ELMO AV.

STAGECOACH TRAIL

35

HUDSON DQ

Lake Elmo Park

GO!

17

95

Follow 8th St. under I 94 + up Ramp to bridge

COULEE

CO. 15

21

H

10

10TH ST.

94

19

15

Rest Area & MN HERitage Farm

Road Bike Route

94

HUDSON RD.

8TH ST.

2ND ST.

KEATS AV.

94

HUDSON

QUINLAN AV.

St. Croix River

HUDSON BLVD.

71

INDIAN TRAIL scenic alternative

STAGECOACH TRAIL

ST. CROIX TR.

95

RIDE
35 STAGECOACH TO STILLWATER

©1995 by Richard Arey. Have fun. Take care. Ride at your own risk.

N

94

494

94

694

35W

35E

GO!

94

394

AFTON

95

RIDE
36

Selma's

21

35W

35E

494

LOST VALLEY TOUR

Washington County. Connects with RIDES 33, 34 AND 35.

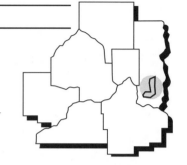

LENGTH
RATING

◈ 41.1 miles – Full loop as described below

◈ 32.7 miles – Valley Creek Cutoff, without Afton Park

◤ 19.6 miles – Half Lost Loop using Co. Hwy. 20 shortcut

🚲 ◈ 7.0 miles – **Afton Alps Mountain Bike Area**, see below

CAUTION Light traffic except in and near Afton on weekends when roads get busy. Parts of Co. Rd. 21 and Co. Rd. 71 have no shoulder. Hilly!

*T*his delightful tour of Southern Washington County features ice cream at Selma's (try the cookie cones!) and views of the distinctive Bissell Mound. Scenic solitude can be found on the gravel Trading Post Trail. And if you have the time (and energy), the trip down into Afton State Park is well worth it.

GO!
Start at **COTTAGE GROVE RAVINE REGIONAL PARK** (731-3851). Watch for the County Road 19 (Chemolite Road) exit off Highway 61, south of Cottage Grove. Parks sticker or fee required. Cottage Grove Ravine is a handsome park centered around a picturesque pond. There are some great hiking and skiing trails in the 4-mile-long ravine but these are closed to bicyclists. The ravine is believed to have been carved by a former channel of the glacial St. Croix River.

5.3 mi **LOST VALLEY PRAIRIE STATE NATURAL AREA** is a ½ mile detour up Nyberg. Rare prairie plants can be found (with the help of a naturalist) on the rocky hilltops.

10.3 mi **AFTON STATE PARK** (436-5391) is classified a "natural" park to preserve and perpetuate presettlement landscape features of the St. Croix River Valley. A scenic 3.2 mile (one way, 300-foot drop) paved bike path winds down through restored prairie, a wooded ravine and along the St. Croix River. Stop at the Interpretive Center to see the excellent displays. A secluded swimming beach and picnic area is found on the river.

🚲 AFTON ALPS MOUNTAIN BIKE AREA

Afton Alps (436-1320) has just opened an exciting and demanding seven mile mountain bike course. The area features the longest climbs (and descents!) around, some tough single-track riding, plus a unique 30-foot bridge spanning one of the deep wooded ravines. Deer abound. The area will be open seven days a week, till dusk, through late October. Admission is $5.

15.3 mi **SELMA'S ICE CREAM PARLOR** in downtown Afton is a must stop. Stroll on down to the river or check out the wondrous Afton Toy Shop.

VALLEY CREEK CUTOFF

Take a left from County Road 21 directly on to Valley Creek Trail and then another left on Trading Post Trail to Oakgren.

19 mi **BISSELL MOUND** is a natural formation that looks like either a miniature Midwestern volcano or an ancient Native American Indian Mound. Use your imagination.

19.7 mi The scenic, hilly, gravel **TRADING POST TRAIL** is a fine getaway. Neal Avenue is a paved (without shoulders) alternative that shortens the trip 3 miles.

27.3 mi County Highway 20 (70th Street) has a paved shoulder.

34.7 mi **BACK TO** *GO!*

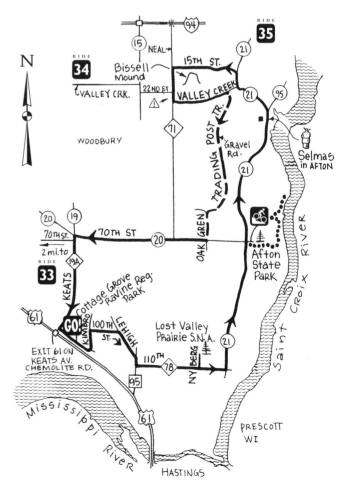

37 CHIMNEY ROCK RAMBLE

Dakota County.

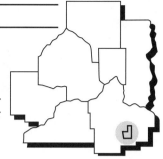

LENGTH 🚲 24 miles

RATING Not too tough a mountain bike, gravel road route.

CAUTION There is almost no traffic except near Miesville and a short dash on 61. This is one of the most rural rides in this book and I did notice a rather large dog on 210th Street. It did not give chase.

*T*his route is for all you folks that have been riding your mountain bikes on city streets and paved paths. Here's a chance to get out into the country and eat up some gravel roads. Your bike is ready — are you?

Chimney Rock Ramble explores a small corner of the Twin Cities metropolitan area that was never scoured by the last glacial advance. Proof lies in the 25-foot high pillar called Chimney Rock. This sandstone kingpin would certainly have been bowled over had the huge sheets of ice pushed through here. The southeast leg of this ride passes through the rugged undeveloped Miesville Ravine Park Reserve. Then it's back to civilization and the little town of Miesville.

GO!

Start at **MARSHAN TOWN HALL**. There is a small parking lot at 205th Street on the west side of Highway 61. (See inset map.)

2.8 mi **CHIMNEY ROCK** rises above the surrounding farmscape. It is on private land so admire it from the road.

6.3 mi Go straight across Highway 50 and onto the **MINIMUM MAINTENANCE ROAD**. The sign says, "Travel at your own risk," but you are on your mountain bike, so no problem.

14.2 mi You haven't entered an Appalachian hollow but you are in the "driftless area." **MIESVILLE RAVINE REGIONAL PARK** was never filled with glacial drift (rock material deposited as a result of glaciation). Instead the ravine has enlarged and deepened over time. Park Reserve development is still a number of years off.

18 mi If you time your trip just right you'll be able to catch the **MIESVILLE MUDHENS** in action at Jack Ruhr Field. These boys play a solid brand of town ball that has earned them state championships in 1978, 1989, 1992 and 1993. You can always pick up a schedule, a King burger and a cold cola at **KING'S PLACE** across the street.

22.2 mi You bike past a **STATE GAME REFUGE** and the **BELLWOOD OAKS** golf course on 210th Street East. Check out which place has the most birdies.

24 mi A half mile dash on Highway 61 takes you **BACK TO GO!** Traffic can be heavy but there is a wide shoulder.

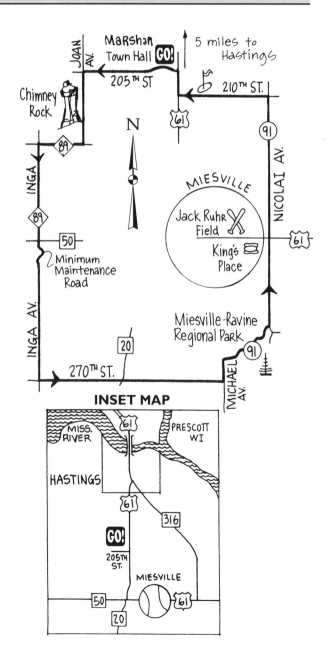

INSET MAP

CANNON VALLEY TRAIL

Goodhue County. Connects with RIDE K.

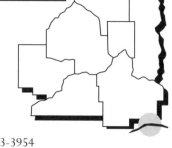

LENGTH
RATING

⬮ 40.0 miles – Cannon Falls to Red Wing, round trip

⬮ 20 miles – Welch to Cannon Falls, round trip (best intro)

⬮ 20 miles – Welch to Red Wing, round trip

Easy, flat paved off-road trail. There is a slight downhill incline from Cannon Falls to Welch.

CAUTION   Trail gets busy on weekends. No pets are allowed.

FEE   1995 Wheel Pass is $2/day or $10/year   **PHONE** (507) 263-3954

*T*he Cannon Valley Trail runs through secluded and spectacular scenery on a former Chicago North Western Railroad line. This rail trail was named one of the best in the country by Bicycle magazine and it is easy to see why. The landscape, history, wildlife and natural features are outstanding and unique.

While most of the Twin Cities area was scoured flat by glaciers, the Cannon River Valley is part of the "driftless area." Rugged, almost Appalachian in feel, this valley was never filled with glacial drift (rock material) and has enlarged and deepened over time. Fragile sandstone peaks crown the surrounding bluffs in many places. The Dakota knew the Cannon River as IN-YAN BO-SDA-TA WA-KPA or "River-of-the-standing-rock." Human activity in the valley dates back to nearly the time of the glaciers — almost 10,000 years — the oldest documented sites of people living in Minnesota.

Today, the trail undulates gently as it follows the state designated "Wild and Scenic" Cannon River. Anchored by the picturesque towns of Red Wing and Cannon Falls, the trail offers bicyclists three seasons of fun. In spring, enjoy the wildflowers and a rich passel of migrating warblers and waterfowl. Summer cyclists enjoy the long stretches of shaded

GO!   Start at the city trail in downtown **CANNON FALLS** on Highway 19 one block west of the stoplight. Old concrete railroad posts marking the mileage out of Mankato are found on the trail (and used in parentheses here).

2.0 mi
(75.5)   **PRAIRIE REMNANT** with pasque flowers that bloom around Easter, as well as monarda, coneflowers, and fall-blooming asters.

2.8 mi
(76.3)   The trail hugs a rock cut carved high above the river that provides a **SCENIC OVERLOOK**.

3.8 mi
(77.3)   The **ANDERSON MEMORIAL REST AREA** is a popular spot for picnicking and splashing in the spring-fed waters.

6.5 mi
(80)   The rough-cut granite block displayed here is from a **1912 TRAIN WRECK**. The 500-pound block has only been stolen once.

9.5 mi
(83)   **HIDDEN VALLEY CAMPGROUND** is privately owned and operated. The campground can get rambunctious on weekends.

10.0 mi
(83.5)   Water, portable toilets, picnic tables and parking are found at **WELCH STATION**. The tiny town of

Welch is just a few blocks north and presents the difficult choice of frosty beers or hand scooped **ICE CREAM**. There is mountain biking available at Welch Village. See RIDE K.

11.5 mi
(85)   A 150-foot long bridge crosses **BELLE CREEK**. Look for warblers, woodpeckers, wild turkeys and deer here.

15.3 mi
(88.8)   The **RAILROAD FLYCATCHER** you pass under was once used to establish the height of a train that could pass under an upcoming bridge or tunnel.

18.0 mi
(91.5)   The large **MARSH** is a productive habitat for migrant and resident birds, while the nearby **BLUFFTOPS** are home to ancient archaeological sites.

19.7 mi
(93.2)   The trail ends just short of the historic **RED WING POTTERY** shopping district, but a signed bike route will take you there.

20.0 mi   The charming town of Red Wing is just a few blocks away. Follow the signs to **BAY POINT PARK** overlooking the Mississippi.

40.0 MI   BACK TO *GO!*

CANNON VALLEY TRAIL

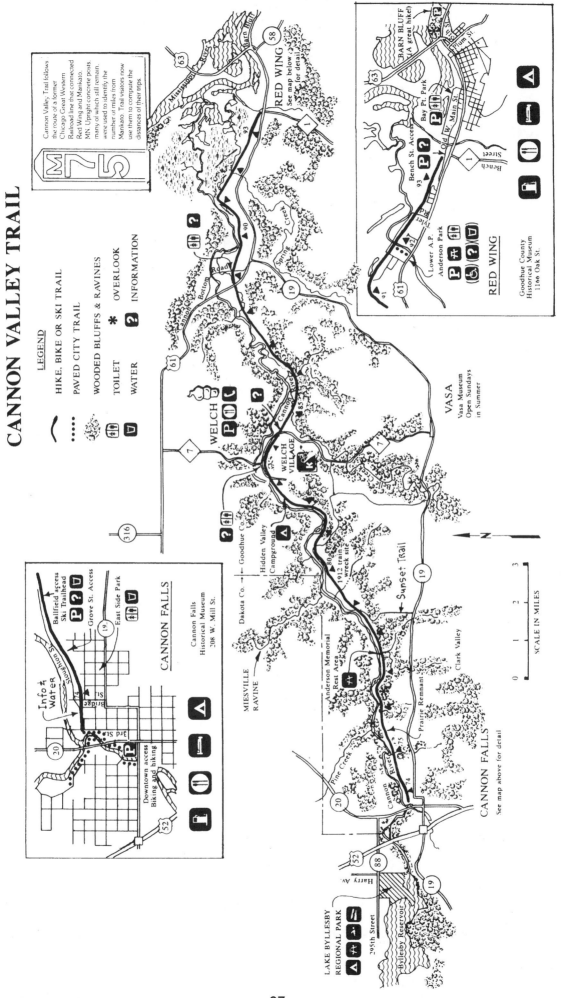

LEGEND

—— HIKE, BIKE OR SKI TRAIL

······ PAVED CITY TRAIL

🌲 WOODED BLUFFS & RAVINES

🚻 TOILET

▣ WATER

✳ OVERLOOK

❓ INFORMATION

Cannon Valley Trail follows the route of a former Chicago Great Western Railroad line that connected Red Wing and Mankato. MN. Upright concrete posts, many of which still remain, were used to identify the number of miles from Mankato. Trail visitors now use them to compute the distances of their trips.

RED WING

Goodhue County Historical Museum 1166 Oak St.

CANNON FALLS

Cannon Falls Historical Museum 208 W. Mill St.

VASA
Vasa Museum Open Sundays in Summer

MIESVILLE RAVINE

CANNON FALLS
See map above for detail

LAKE BYLLESBY REGIONAL PARK

SCALE IN MILES

0 1 2 3

N

MISSISSIPPI RIVER GORGE RIDE

Ramsey and Hennepin County. Connects with RIDES 4, 5, 20, 27, 28 and 30.

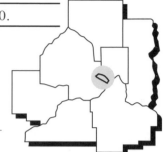

LENGTH ⬔ 19.4 miles – Full loop as described
RATING ⬒ 8.5 miles – Ford Parkway to Washington Avenue Loop
CAUTION Downtown and the University have quite a bit of traffic at rush hour. Bring a lock as you will need to walk to some of the falls. Cross the Mississippi on the Ford Parkway Bridge to avoid the stairs on the Highway 5 walkway.

A beautiful loop around the mighty Mississippi. This ride features the legendary St. Anthony and Minnehaha Falls as well as lesser known cascades such as Hidden Falls, Shadow Falls and Bridal Veil Falls. Early spring, or after a heavy rain, are the best times to visit these ephemeral beauties. Spring (or later in fall) is also best because much of the river gorge becomes obscured once the trees have leafed out. And if you're touring in very early spring, you will certainly enjoy the curtains of ice clinging to the cliffs below the University's West Bank.

GO! Start your tour where Summit Avenue intersects **MISSISSIPPI RIVER BOULEVARD**. There is a small parking lot or use the street. Head south.

1.8 mi **LOCK AND DAM NO. 1 FALLS** can be observed from the overlook just south of the Ford Parkway Bridge (cross here for the short loop).

2.4 mi Just down the road a piece is a nice overlook of the Mississippi. Park your bike and take the stone staircase down into the ravine. Admire the beautiful WPA-era stonework, and in short order, **HIDDEN FALLS** will be revealed.

3.75 mi Continue south on Mississippi River Boulevard and watch for the **HIGHWAY 5 BRIDGE** down below. Find the unmarked stairway that leads to a walkway on the bridge across the river.

3.9 mi Walking up the stairs on the Minneapolis side of the river takes you right into **FORT SNELLING STATE PARK**. Proceed counterclockwise around the old stone fort. On the south side of the fort take the long ramp down until you intersect the paved path and take this left, heading upstream, under the Highway 5 Bridge you just crossed.

6.9 mi A lovely stretch of trail hugs the bluff and provides some nice river views, eventually taking you to **MINNEHAHA FALLS**. There are concessions, washrooms, picnic facilities and, of course, the laughing, leaping waters. Take the time to read the geological markers that point out an **ABANDONED WATERFALL**.

11.6 mi Godfrey Parkway becomes West River Parkway as you head north. Just north of Franklin Avenue (cross the Mississippi here for the short loop) the path and road make a long exciting descent to the river. The **ICE FALLS** on the cliffs often last into April.

12.9 mi Now comes the tricky part. Take 4th Street out of the river valley. Jog over to 6th Street and you will soon see **THE DOME** looming ahead. It was here on the night of October 25, 1987, that the Minnesota Twins beat the St. Louis Cardinals to become World Champions. A brilliant, defining moment in Minnesota history.

14 mi Follow the striped bike lanes to another Minnesota landmark. The James J. Hill **STONE ARCH BRIDGE** (1883) is an engineering masterpiece that echoes the great roman aqueducts. The new walking and biking paths lead to a terrific view of **ST. ANTHONY FALLS**, "the most abrupt drop in the 2,200 mile course of the Mississippi River." The Ojibway called this cataract **KITCHI KAKABIKA**, "The Great Falls," or literally, "The Great Severed Rock."

15.3 mi Second Street curves up to the bike lane on University Avenue. Take a right (southwest) where the big overhead sign says 14th Avenue SE and you will be on **EAST RIVER ROAD.**

16.7 mi The next tourist attraction also requires a bit of a hike. **BRIDAL VEIL FALLS** is best appreciated from below. Walking paths that start just south of Franklin Avenue will take you there.

19 mi **SHADOW FALLS** Lock your bike at the top of the ravine near Cretin and follow the tiny walking path down for a view of this delicate, moss covered drop.

19.4 mi BACK TO *GO!*

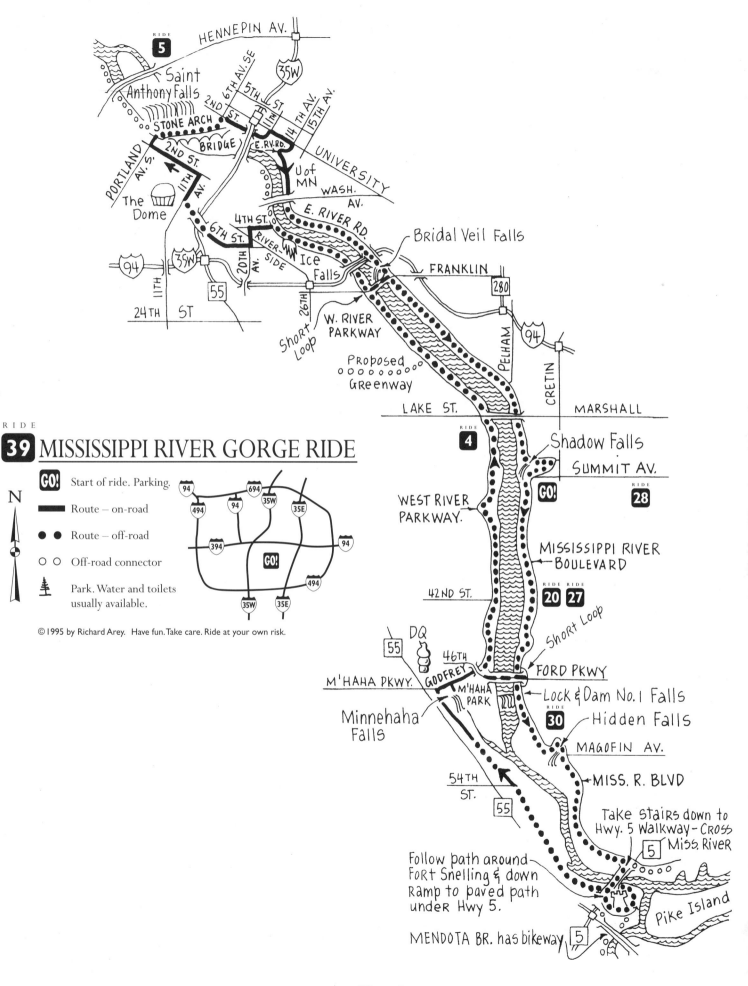

RIDE 5

HENNEPIN AV.

35W

Saint Anthony Falls

6TH AV. SE

5TH ST.

2ND ST.

STONE ARCH

11TH

4TH AV.

15TH AV.

BRIDGE

E. RV. RD.

U of MN

UNIVERSITY

WASH. AV.

PORTLAND AV. S.

2ND ST.

11TH AV.

The Dome

E. RIVER RD.

4TH ST.

6TH ST.

RIVER-SIDE

20TH AV.

Ice Falls

Bridal Veil Falls

FRANKLIN

280

94

35W

11TH

55

24TH ST

26TH

Short Loop

W. RIVER PARKWAY

Proposed Greenway

PELHAM

CRETIN

94

LAKE ST.

MARSHALL

RIDE 39 — MISSISSIPPI RIVER GORGE RIDE

GO! Start of ride. Parking.

N

——— Route – on-road

●● Route – off-road

○○ Off-road connector

🌲 Park. Water and toilets usually available.

94   694

494   94   35W   35E

394

GO!

94

494

35W   35E

© 1995 by Richard Arey. Have fun. Take care. Ride at your own risk.

RIDE 4

Shadow Falls

SUMMIT AV.

GO!

RIDE 28

WEST RIVER PARKWAY.

MISSISSIPPI RIVER BOULEVARD

RIDE 20 RIDE 27

42ND ST.

Short Loop

DQ

55

46TH

GODFREY

M'HAHA PKWY.

M'HAHA PARK

Minnehaha Falls

FORD PKWY

Lock & Dam No.1 Falls

RIDE 30

Hidden Falls

MAGOFIN AV.

MISS. R. BLVD

54TH ST.

55

Take stairs down to Hwy. 5 Walkway – Cross Miss. River

5

Follow path around Fort Snelling & down Ramp to paved path under Hwy 5.

MENDOTA BR. has bikeway

5

Pike Island

RAGS TO RICHES RIDE

Ramsey County. Connects with RIDES 22, 26, 27, 28, 32, 33 and I.

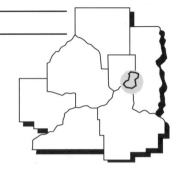

LENGTH   〰 22.8 miles – Full loop as described

RATING   ◐ 14.4 miles – Short loop around Silver Lake

CAUTION   Hilly in spots. Swede Hollow Trail opens late 1995. Mounds Boulevard - 7th Street connection to Swede Hollow can have heavy traffic.

*F*or over a century the shanty town of Swede Hollow welcomed the poorest newcomers to St. Paul. In 1850 it was home to the Swedes, followed by the Irish, Poles, Italians, and finally, Mexican Americans, before the shacks were razed in the 1950s. Not so far, but a world away, McKnight Road is named after William McKnight, who began his tenure at 3M as an assistant bookkeeper. Rising through the ranks, McKnight led the Minnesota Mining and Manufacturing Company to the top of the heap as an international business concern. The gleaming 3M corporate campus you pass by on McKnight Road is a far cry from the 18th century industrial relics along upper Swede Hollow.

This ride capitalizes on the recently built Swede Hollow Trail and Burlington Northern (BN) Regional Trail. A less than stellar path along Beam Road leads to a pleasant circuit of Silver Lake and the always difficult summertime choices of ice cream or a cool swim. Beaver Lake is a fine addition to the crowd pleasing paths along Battle Creek, Indian Mounds and Lake Phalen.

GO!   **LAKE PHALEN REGIONAL PARK** (266-6400).
To reach Phalen Park exit I-35E at Wheelock Parkway and head east 1.7 miles to park entrance on
left. Phalen is a wonderful full-service facility with
a swimming beach, picnicking, washrooms, boat
rental and golf course. Many folks remember the
magical ice palace built here in 1986.

1.4 mi   The **GATEWAY STATE TRAIL** is reached via a
short ramp just past the stone arch underpass north
of Lake Phalen. Head east. In about 1 mile you
reach one of Minnesota's newest paved rail-trails,
the **BURLINGTON NORTHERN REGIONAL
TRAIL**. This makes a beeline north and affords
some nice views as it approaches Beam Avenue.

4.8 mi   If you always wanted to bicycle to **MAPLEWOOD
MALL** you can now check that off your list. The
paved path only gets you so close. You will still need
to cross a vast moat of cars.

7.8 mi   **SILVER LAKE** is a delight with three parks sprin-
kled around the perimeter. Take a right on 20th
Street to the swimming beach, picnic area and small
playground.

7.7 mi   Or, continue south on County Highway 120 to
DAIRY QUEEN. The Banana Supreme always
works for me.

8.3 mi   Either route returns you to the Gateway Trail and
the **BIG SNOWMAN**.

9.2 mi   **McKNIGHT ROAD** is the next decision point.
After crossing the long steel bridge you can con-
tinue along the Gateway Trail back to Lake Phalen.
This is the **SHORT LOOP**. Or cloverleaf off the
Gateway and head south on McKnight.

13.3 mi   Just past **3M** is the potentially dangerous I-94
underpass. You may opt for crossing to the west
side of McKnight at the stoplight and using the sidewalk until you can cross safely back to the path.

13.9 mi   **BATTLE CREEK REGIONAL PARK** (777-1707)
has a modern picnic pavilion and trails that will all
be connected in 1996 via a ravine trail.

17.9 mi   Follow Upper Afton Road or the Highway 61 paved
path over to **INDIAN MOUNDS PARK**. Break
out a picnic and enjoy the spectacular view over the
Mississippi River and downtown St. Paul.

19.6 mi   The **SWEDE HOLLOW TRAIL** is a little tough to
connect with. It begins at the busy 7th Street-Payne
Avenue intersection. Your reward for persevering is
an impressive stone arch underpass leading to a
most unexpected scene. The wooded hollow is cool
and green. And dancing down a limestone stairway
is **PHALEN CREEK**. Mostly buried now, it makes
the most of its brief moment in the sun. Further
on, the old **HAMMS BREWERY** is a historical
highlight dating back to 1856.

22.8 mi   Follow the trail to Lake Phalen and **BACK TO** *GO!*

40 RAGS TO RICHES RIDE

© 1995 by Richard Arey. Have fun. Take care. Ride at your own risk.

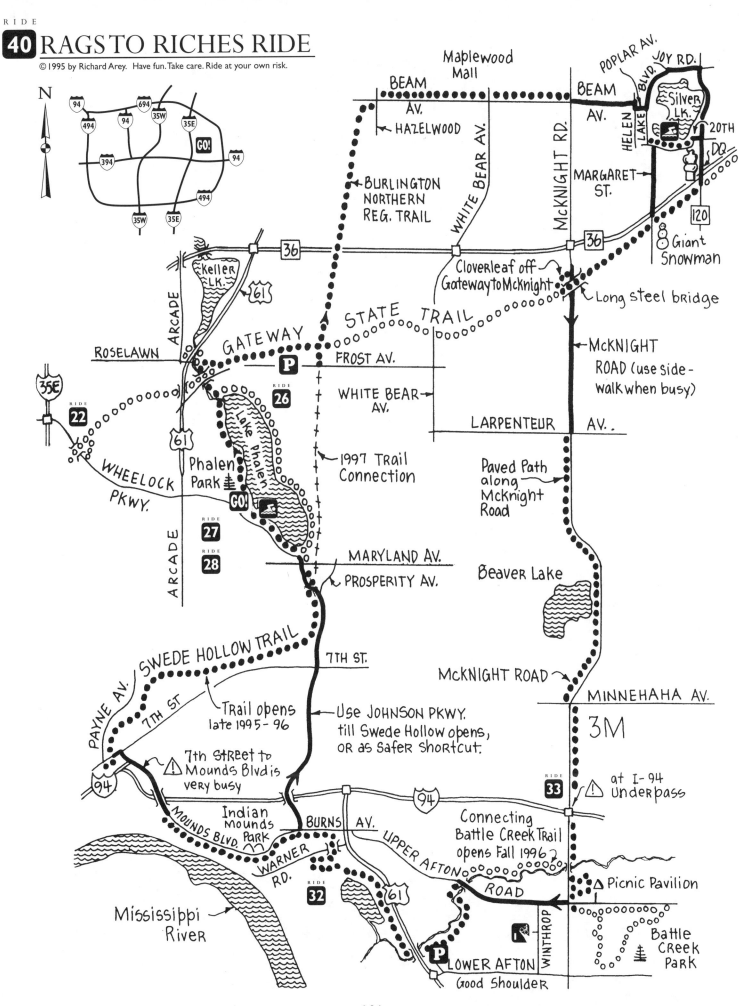

N

94 694 94 35W 35E
494 94 35W 35E GO!
394 94
494
35W 35E

Maplewood Mall

POPLAR AV. JOY RD.

BEAM AV.

BEAM AV.

HELEN

LAKE BLVD.

Silver Lk.

HAZELWOOD

WHITE BEAR AV.

McKNIGHT RD.

MARGARET ST.

20TH

DQ

120

BURLINGTON NORTHERN REG. TRAIL

36

36

Giant Snowman

Keller Lk.

61

Cloverleaf off Gateway to McKnight

Long steel bridge

ARCADE

GATEWAY STATE TRAIL

McKNIGHT ROAD (use sidewalk when busy)

ROSELAWN

P

FROST AV.

RIDE 26

WHITE BEAR AV.

LARPENTEUR AV.

35E

RIDE 22

61

Lake Phalen

1997 Trail Connection

Paved Path along McKnight Road

WHEELOCK PKWY.

Phalen Park

GO!

ARCADE

RIDE 27

RIDE 28

MARYLAND AV.

Beaver Lake

PROSPERITY AV.

SWEDE HOLLOW TRAIL

7TH ST.

McKNIGHT ROAD

PAYNE AV.

7TH ST

Trail opens late 1995-96

Use JOHNSON PKWY. till Swede Hollow opens, or as safer shortcut.

MINNEHAHA AV.

3M

7th Street to Mounds Blvd is very busy

94

94

RIDE 33

at I-94 Underpass

Indian Mounds Park

BURNS AV.

Connecting Battle Creek Trail opens Fall 1996

MOUNDS BLVD.

WARNER RD.

UPPER AFTON ROAD

Picnic Pavilion

RIDE 32

61

WINTHROP

Battle Creek Park

Mississippi River

P

LOWER AFTON Good Shoulder

Scott Hebel "catching some air" as he flies across the finish line to win the Tour de Buck at Buck Hill in 1991. Scott came in second to Greg LeMond at Chequemegon in 1990 and 1991. While mountain biking satisfies the most adventurous athletes, it also accommodates the average cyclist looking to explore new (and often quite level) territory.

MOUNTAIN BIKE RIDES

Mountain biking is a blast. It is enjoyed by families and friends as well as more athletic types. Mountain biking can simply be a quicker way to escape into the woods on a level dirt path or it can be a vigorous workout on the steepest hills imaginable in Minnesota. While bird watchers at **Murphy–Hanrehan Regional Park** battled with mountain bikers over trail access, other bird watchers from the St. Paul Audubon Society rode their mountain bikes to observe 50 different species of birds, including a bald eagle, on the trails at **Lake Elmo Park Reserve.**

Mountain biking continues to be controversial because it is a relatively new sport and trails are already crowded. Almost every trail in this book (and thus in the metro area) is open only on an experimental basis and could be closed at any time. Always call first to confirm that a trail is open and do your part in following the rules of the trail.

Contact the **North Central Mountain Bike Group** at 452-0907 to find out about how you can help keep trails open and which rides are currently available. If they do not know about a ride or area it is probably illegal to ride there.

See the BICYCLE ORGANIZATIONS chapter for information on mountain bike and cyclocross (even more challenging!) racing clubs. There are regular mountain bike racing events throughout the year including Bike on Ice races, the Tour de Bump, and the one and only Chequamegon Fat Tire Festival. See the ANNUAL BIKE EVENTS chapter.

RULES OF THE TRAIL

1. Ride on open trails only. Call first to confirm.
2. Yield to pedestrians (and horses, pets and other bikers).
3. Control your bicycle speed.
4. Leave no trace. Stay off wet trails.
5. Never spook animals.
6. Be prepared.

Now is the time to give the great sport of mountain biking a try. You probably own one (about 90% of all bicycles sold these days are mountain bikes) and yet you probably have never taken it out onto a trail. Here's how to get started.

BASIC EQUIPMENT

I have biked the entire length of the **Minnesota Valley Trail** on an old Schwinn 10- speed with skinny tires. The easier routes listed below can be enjoyed with virtually any bike, though mountain bikes will give you more traction, more stability and greater enjoyment.

The most challenging routes will require a bona fide mountain bike in good repair. And there is truth to the saying that better equipment will increase your skills, interest and adrenalin level. I never had so much fun mountain biking

as the day I borrowed a buddy's bike with front suspension. While I'd always appreciated the scenery and solitude of a mountain bike trail, it became crystal clear how a really good mountain bike could turn a quiet backwoods adventure on the **Bloomington Bluff Trail** into a creek splashing, brush crashing romp. Here are some places where you can rent good mountain bikes.

MOUNTAIN BIKE RENTAL

Buck Hill (435–7174) and Afton Alps (436-1320) rent high quality mountain bikes with or without suspension. Retail outlets that rent mountain bikes include:
• Bennett's Cycle, 633–3019
• Calhoun Cycle, 827–8231
• Campus Bike Shop, 331–3442
• Twin City Bike, 729–3534

BE PREPARED

Some of these routes will take you miles away from help, drinkable water and food. Mountain bike trails tend to be open toward fall when days are shorter and temperatures cooler. So bring:

• Helmet, water and food
• Windbreaker, gloves, hat
• Map, compass, flashlight
• Spare tube or patch kit
• Pump, tire irons, wrenches
• First aid kit, bug repellent
• Pocket knife, duct tape, cash

CHOOSING A RIDE

Call first before heading out. Most of these trails are only open for a limited season. Nothing will shut down a trail faster than riding on it when it is closed.

● Easier, Family Fun Rides
• Elm Creek (A)
• Louisville Swamp (G)
• Lake Elmo (H)
• Biking for the Birds — sandy, flat trails along the Minnesota River (19)

⚡ More Challenging Trails
• Bloomington Bluff Trail (C)
• Terrace Oaks (D)
• Battle Creek (I)
• Minnesota Valley Trail—not hilly, but isolated (16)
• Chimney Rock Ramble — gravel roads in Dakota Co. (37)

⚡ Most Challenging Trails
• Hyland Hills (B)
• Buck Hill (E)
• Murphy Hanrehan (F)
• Lebanon Hills (J)
• Welch Village (K)
• Afton Alps (New! See RIDE 36.)

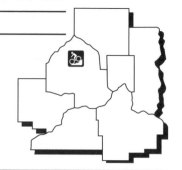

RIDE A — ELM CREEK PARK RESERVE

Hennepin County. Connects with RIDES 2 and 7.

OWNER	Hennepin Parks (424-5511)
FEE	$4 daily or $18 annual
OPEN	April 15 through October 31, 5 a.m. to sunset.
LENGTH	5 miles — turf trail (includes 1 paved mile)
RATING	9.1 miles — paved trail
CAUTION	Trail is bumpy in spots and may be closed if trails are too wet.

Elm Creek is a good place to give mountain biking a first try. The trail is relatively short, easy and quite beautiful in places. Combine some exercise with an educational visit to Eastman Nature Center.

Elm Creek is Hennepin Park's largest preserve. It contains five lakes, three streams, extensive wetlands and mature hardwood forests within the 5,400-acre site. It is easy to look across the wide unbuilt expanses and imagine you have stepped 200 years back in time. Native Americans found good hunting grounds here and wildlife is still plentiful.

To fully enjoy this park, try some of the 9 miles of paved paths. Take a side trip up to **EASTMAN NATURE CENTER** (420-4300) to see the live animal exhibits. Scramble around the creative play area, take a swim or enjoy a picnic.

The mountain bike trail itself is a bit tame but allows you to visit more of the park. There are no really challenging stretches but do not get too complacent. One of the state's better woman mountain bikers took a spill and broke her collarbone in a race here.

And if you get a little tired or long for more rugged terrain as you make your rounds, consider this — a monarch butterfly tagged at Elm Creek in 1986 was later found some 2,000 miles away by a researcher in the Sierra Madre Mountains of Mexico.

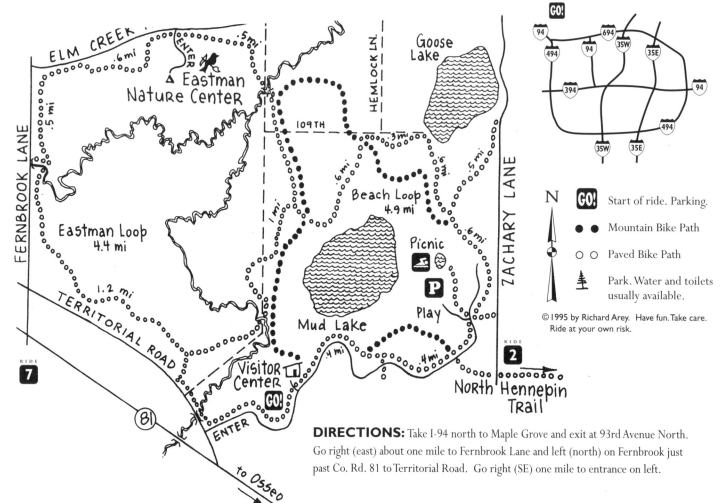

DIRECTIONS: Take I-94 north to Maple Grove and exit at 93rd Avenue North. Go right (east) about one mile to Fernbrook Lane and left (north) on Fernbrook just past Co. Rd. 81 to Territorial Road. Go right (SE) one mile to entrance on left.

HYLAND HILLS SKI AREA

Hennepin County. Connects with RIDE 11.

OWNER	Hennepin Parks Trail Hotline 559-6778 Call first.	**FEE**	$3 daily plus parking permit.
OPEN	Late May through Labor Day. Call first.		
LENGTH	2 miles	**RATING**	Experienced
CAUTION	Big hills — hey, it is a ski area! And please note that mountain biking is allowed only in the ski area.		

Hyland Hills was the first local downhill area to offer mountain biking. It is a natural fit, since followed by Buck Hill and Welch Village. A good workout takes you to the top of Mount Gilboa — second highest point (1,021 feet) in Hennepin County. Enjoy the view of the Minneapolis skyline before hurling downhill.

Hennepin Parks must be applauded for their efforts to keep current with recreation trends and demands. While other park districts hem and haw, they have done their best to give mountain biking a fair shot.

Hyland Hills offers as much elevation as you will find in a midwestern mountain bike course. This translates into heavy uphill pulls and flying descents. By keeping the mountain bikes restricted to the ski area there is no conflict with other trail users and environmental impacts are minimized by alternating trail alignments every year. This bodes well for its continuing operation.

While there are trails listed for all ability levels, it is best for newcomers to start elsewhere or take it easy the first couple times around. Watch for races that are held here and other special events.

N

GO!   Start of ride. Parking.

● ●   Mountain Bike Path

○ ○   Paved Bike Path

🌲   Park. Water and toilets usually available.

© 1995 by Richard Arey. Have fun. Take care. Ride at your own risk.

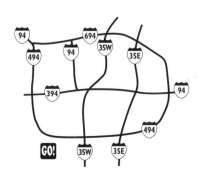

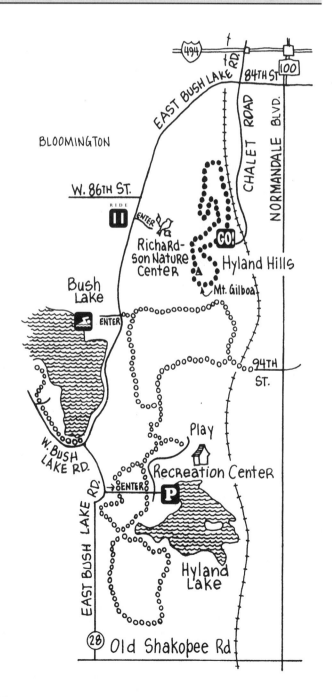

BLOOMINGTON BLUFF TRAIL

Hennepin County. Connects with RIDE 11.

OWNERS City of Bloomington (948-8877)
U.S. Fish and Wildlife Service (854-5900)

LENGTH ☒ – ☒ 10 miles one way

RATING Experienced. Enter only at either end of the trail.

CAUTION Stay on trail and out of closed areas as described and posted. This is an
isolated area so bring along a friend. Mosquitoes are thick in summer.
Trail is narrow, two-way and shared with hikers. Control speed on hills.

> *For my money, this is the best mountain bike trail in the Twin Cities. It has every feature desired in terms of scenery, length, technical challenges, wildlife and remoteness. There is also a rich sense of history and intimate views of the Minnesota River. Most people will cherish this ride as a great stump jumping, creek splashing romp.*

GO! Start at the **INDIAN MOUNDS ELEMENTARY SCHOOL** located 3 blocks east of Old Shakopee Road on 98th Street and 11th Avenue South. The trail begins at the south end of 11th Avenue just before 100th Street.

Follow the trail down to the bottom of the ravine and **GO RIGHT (WEST–SOUTHWEST)** at the intersecting trail near the river. Do not go left (east–northeast) into the wildlife sanctuary that is closed to bicyclists.

The first stretch of trail is the most rugged. Without knowing it you will be passing by some ancient **INDIAN MOUNDS** located on private land on the blufftops. They are now imperceptible rises.

0.4 mi **VALLEY OVERLOOK** and small picnic area. A little past here, and also located on a private blufftop, is **QUINN'S POINT**. This is the site of Peter Quinn's log cabin homestead. The first white man to live in Bloomington, Quinn was commissioned in 1842 to teach Indians how to live by the plow, not the hunt. He later became one of the first casualties of the 1862 Dakota Conflict.

1.0 mi **PARKER'S PICNIC GROUNDS** and overlook, now fallen into disuse, was a popular spot from the 1930s until 1965.

1.3 mi Watch for a marked trail on the right up the bluff that takes you to the **POND – DAKOTA MISSION PARK**. The 1856 brick residence was the first home of Gideon Pond, who established the first white residence in Minneapolis with his brother Samuel in 1834. In 1842, Gideon established a mission for the local Dakota and in 1850 began publish-

ing the *Dakota Friend*, a bilingual paper. The National Register Historic Site is open only by appointment. Phone 948-8878.

2.9 mi A future **TRAIL ACCESS** will be located just east of the I-35W bridge at the end of Lyndale Avenue. This access will open in 1996.

5.3 mi **NINE MILE CREEK** crosses the trail. You better hope the large downed tree (I used it October 28, 1994) is still in place. Crossing will be difficult without it.

The mouth of the creek is the former site of **TI TAN-KA TA-NI-NA** (habitation, large, ancient), the oldest village of the Mdewakantonwan Dakota. The French explorer Nicolas Perrot first noted this village in 1689.

Nine Mile Creek refers to the distance to Fort Snelling, and parts of the trail have surely been trod for centuries.

7.0 mi An old iron **SWING BRIDGE** crosses the river. Twenty-five years ago a narrow driving lane for cars shared space on the railroad bridge.

10.0 mi County Road 18 and the end of the trail. A small **TRAILHEAD** and parking lot is located on the west side of 18. The **OLD BLOOMINGTON FERRY BRIDGE** crosses the Minnesota River here. In 1996 the new Bloomington Ferry Bridge will open and the old bridge reserved just for bicyclists and hikers. The old bridge ended the ferry business that had operated here since 1852. Drifting further back in time one sees Native Americans fording the river shallows on ponies.

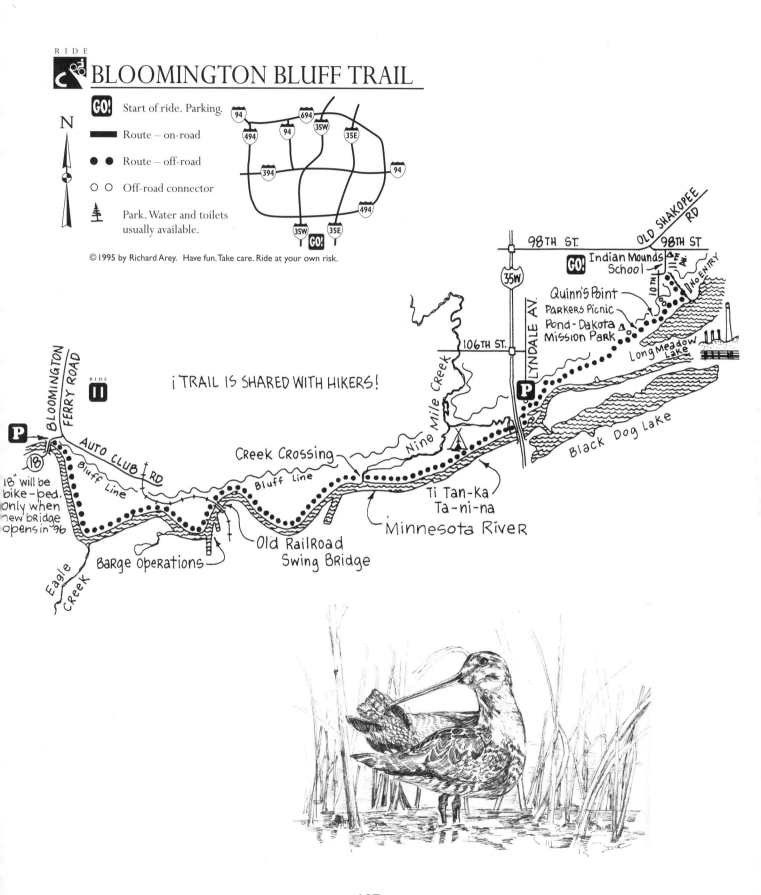

BLOOMINGTON BLUFF TRAIL

GO!   Start of ride. Parking.

————   Route – on-road

• • •   Route – off-road

○ ○   Off-road connector

🌲   Park. Water and toilets usually available.

N

© 1995 by Richard Arey. Have fun. Take care. Ride at your own risk.

94   694

494   94   35W   35E

394   94

35W   494   35E

GO!

98TH ST.   OLD SHAKOPEE RD

35W   **GO!** Indian Mounds School   98TH ST

Quinn's Point

Parkers Picnic

Pond-Dakota Mission Park

LYNDALE AV.

10TH

No ENTRY

106TH ST.

Long Meadow Lake

¡TRAIL IS SHARED WITH HIKERS!

RIDE **II**

BLOOMINGTON FERRY ROAD

P

AUTO CLUB RD

Bluff Line   Bluff Line

Creek Crossing

Nine Mile Creek

Black Dog Lake

18

18" will be bike-ped. only when new bridge opens in '96

Barge Operations

Eagle Creek

Old Railroad Swing Bridge

Ti Tan-ka Ta-ni-na

Minnesota River

RIDE TERRACE OAKS PARK

Dakota County. Connects with RIDE 18.

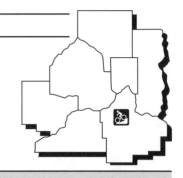

OWNER	City of Burnsville (895-4500)
LENGTH	3.4 miles
RATING	Intermediate and better with some tricky single-track riding
CAUTION	Stay on designated trails and be respectful of hikers. It is easy to get turned around here. Call first to confirm that trails are still open.

Terrace Oaks has a rollicking terrain of hummocks, hills and depressions thanks to the last glacier that pushed through here some 10,000 years ago. Gary Sjoquist has designed an excellent mountain bike experience with some very technical single-track riding through the oak woodlands. Riding amidst the fall colors is a real treat.

Local politics may close this beautiful little mountain bike course (or convert it into a golf course!) at any time so enjoy it while you can. Mountain bike advocate and racer Gary Sjoquist has worked closely with the city in developing and maintaining the trails. Respectful use will help keep it open.

The narrow, twisting single-track (squirrel track?) trail segments are perhaps the most unique aspect of this park. They require some strength and superior bike handling skills. Not to mention that they are a lot of fun.

Signage still needs some attention but this is a great little park that you are sure to enjoy.

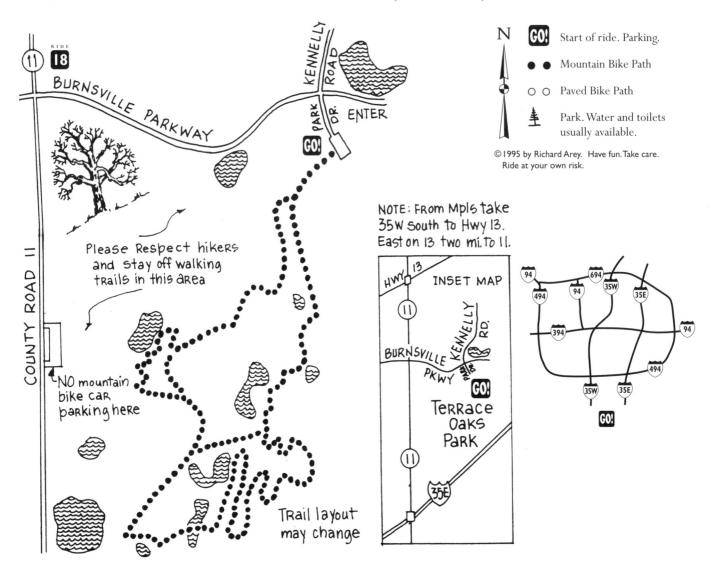

N

GO! — Start of ride. Parking.

● ● — Mountain Bike Path

○ ○ — Paved Bike Path

🌲 — Park. Water and toilets usually available.

RIDE 18

BURNSVILLE PARKWAY

KENNELLY ROAD

PARK DR.

ENTER

GO!

COUNTY ROAD 11

Please Respect hikers and stay off walking trails in this area

NO mountain bike car parking here

Trail layout may change

NOTE: From Mpls take 35W South to Hwy 13. East on 13 two mi. to 11.

HWY 13

INSET MAP

11

BURNSVILLE PKWY

KENNELLY RD.

GO!

Terrace Oaks Park

11

35E

94   694

494   94   35W   35E

394   94

494

35W   35E

GO!

RIDE E BUCK HILL MOUNTAIN BIKE AREA

Dakota County. Connects with RIDE 18.

OWNER	Buck Hill Ski Area (435-7174)
OPEN	May 10 – October 30, Thursday through Sunday
LENGTH	🌊 – ♦ 3 miles **RATING** Intermediate to expert
FEE	$5.00
CAUTION	Casey Jones you better watch your speed.

B uck Hill provides a full-service, first-class mountain bike facility. Beginners in good condition can rent quality mountain bikes for starters, while experienced riders come to train or compete each summer in the mountain bike race series. Not for neophytes.

The 1881 *History of Dakota County* explains, "at the west end of Crystal Lake is a high hill, called by the early settlers, Buck Hill. From the top of this high eminence the Indians would watch the deer as they came to drink from the cool waters of the lake."

You will soon be ready for a cool drink because, as any suit can tell you, it takes hard work to get to the top. This is especially true at Buck Hill where you climb over 200 feet to reach the top. Your reward — burning hamstring muscles and a view of four states. Make that four lakes, and maybe one deer, if you are lucky. In any event, you are guaranteed a good workout.

The "Enchanted Forest" nicely offsets the open slopes of the main ski area. Excellent signage keeps you on track and headed in the right direction. Highlights include a beautiful little single-track trail in the woods just south of the Apex Picnic Area. And thrill seekers can really catch some air at the bottom of Don's Descent.

Sure, there is a lot of climbing here. But as a couple of kids put it, "We're here for the downhills!"

MOUNTAIN BIKE RACES

Buck Hill hosts two of the Midwest's finest mountain bike races each August. The **TOUR DE BUMP** has several race categories and beginners are welcome. Those seeking greater pain should find three buddies and enter **HOIGAARD'S 24 HOURS OF BUCK** marathon mountain bike ride.

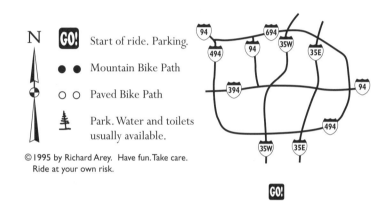

N

🟦GO! Start of ride. Parking.

● ● Mountain Bike Path

○ ○ Paved Bike Path

🌲 Park. Water and toilets usually available.

© 1995 by Richard Arey. Have fun. Take care. Ride at your own risk.

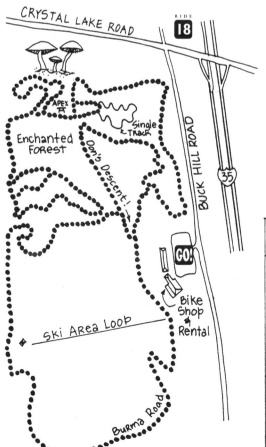

CRYSTAL LAKE ROAD

RIDE 18

Apex

Single Track

Enchanted Forest

Don's Descent!

BUCK HILL ROAD

35

GO!

Bike Shop Rental

Ski Area Loop

Burma Road

GO!

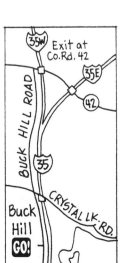

35W   Exit at Co. Rd. 42

35E

BUCK HILL ROAD

42

35

Buck Hill GO!

CRYSTAL LK. RD.

MURPHY - HANREHAN PARK RESERVE

Scott County. Connects with RIDE 18.

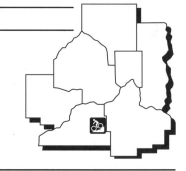

OWNER	Hennepin Parks	**PHONE**	Trail Hotline 559-6778
OPEN	Approximately August 15 through October 31 but CALL FIRST		
FEE	$4 daily parking or $18 annual permit		
LENGTH	6 miles	**RATING**	Intermediate to Expert
CAUTION	Bike here only when open and only on designated trails. Big hills!		

A great, rugged mountain bike trail in a gorgeous setting. As suburban sprawl engulfs the surrounding landscape Murphy-Hanrehan stands out as a big (3,000 acres), beautiful oasis of woods and water. Follow all the rules and keep your fingers crossed that Hennepin Parks keeps Murphy open for mountain bikers a couple months each year.

The local heavyweight champion of mountain bike courses, Murphy's been knocked down a couple of times but never out. A shortened mountain bicycling season is necessary to protect the soil and vegetation, and to prevent erosion on the trail's steep slopes. As a bird watcher, environmental advocate and mountain biker, I hope proper management and due respect by trail users will keep this trail open. It's a beauty.

Murphy-Hanrehan is a rock-and-roller-coaster-of-a-ride. Big climbs followed by plummeting drops keep you busy. This area is a favorite of racers. If the course has a drawback, it is that there is little chance to just spin and enjoy the scenery. On the plus side, if you could only choose one time to be open, then fall would be it. The oaks and maples cast a brilliant glow that is captured perfectly in the park's many ponds and lakes.

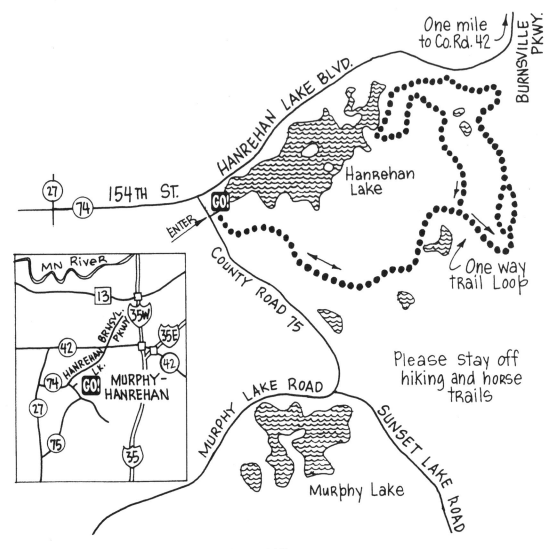

LOUISVILLE SWAMP

Scott County. Connects with RIDE 16.

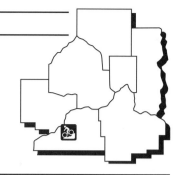

OWNER	U.S. Fish and Wildlife Service, 854-5900 or 492-6400
LENGTH	11.5 miles – Louisville Swamp loops
RATING	Easier, but be prepared if going a distance on the State Trail
CAUTION	Trail floods during high water in spring. Trail is shared with hikers. Mosquitoes are fierce in summer.

Louisville Swamp is one of the great unspoiled retreats in the metro area. A vast land that echoes with the ghosts of Dakota Indians, fur traders and pioneer settlers. Deer and bird life is abundant. People are not. Go now.

A wonderful place with a rich natural and cultural history that can be enjoyed by all bicyclists. The trail is mostly level as it circles the broad wetlands. Short rises take you through restored prairie and oak savanna with some surprising panoramic vistas.

The diverse habitats are home for both Northern Water Snakes (non-poisonous) and prickly pear cactus (which blooms in July). A visit with the Audubon Society yielded over 45 species of birds one morning, and wild turkeys have been introduced.

The sense of wildness belies the fact that humans have lived here for centuries. **WI-YA-KA OTI-DAN** — the "little village of Sand River" — was a thriving Dakota community when Jean Baptiste Faribault built his trading post nearby in 1802.

By the 1860s the fur trade and Indians had moved on and two pioneer families arrived. Frederick Jabs was almost as self-sufficient as the Dakota preceding him. He raised his own vegetables and hunted rabbit, otter and squirrels. The Jabs family made their own sausage using "everything but the squeal." The original stone house now serves as a trail shelter.

The trail surface is mostly packed dirt and gravel. Parts of the Little Prairie Loop are so bumpy as to be unbikeable. You may find some stretches closed or extremely muddy. Elsewhere, huge slabs of exposed granite break the trail surface and tell of this land's ancient past.

DIRECTIONS Take Highway 169 nine miles southwest from I-494 to Shakopee. Continue south on 169 to 145th Street (watch carefully) and turn right (west) on 145th to parking lot on left.

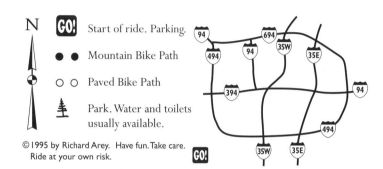

N

GO!   Start of ride. Parking.

● ●   Mountain Bike Path

○ ○   Paved Bike Path

   Park. Water and toilets usually available.

©1995 by Richard Arey. Have fun. Take care. Ride at your own risk. GO!

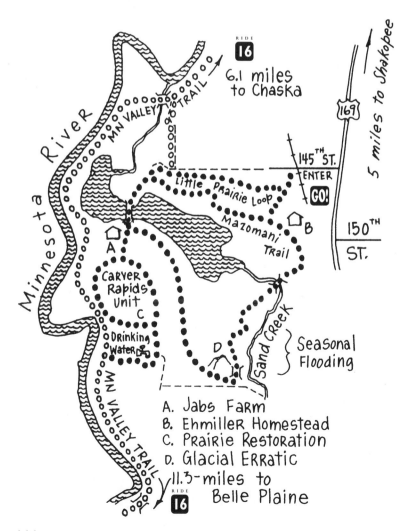

RIDE 16

6.1 miles to Chaska

5 miles to Shakopee

Minnesota River

MN VALLEY TRAIL

Little Prairie Loop

145TH ST. ENTER GO!

Mazomani Trail

150TH ST.

Carver Rapids Unit

Drinking Water

Sand Creek

Seasonal Flooding

A. Jabs Farm
B. Ehmiller Homestead
C. Prairie Restoration
D. Glacial Erratic

11.5 miles to Belle Plaine

RIDE 16

RIDE
H
LAKE ELMO PARK RESERVE

Washington County. Connects with RIDE 35.

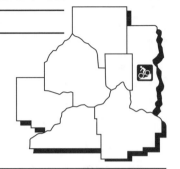

OWNER	Washington County Parks (731-3851)
OPEN	Spring through fall except when very wet
FEE	$3 daily or $14 annual vehicle permit (or Hennepin Parks sticker)
LENGTH	◐–〰12 miles **CAUTION** Horses and hikers share trail.

*L*ake Elmo provides an excellent introduction to mountain biking for folks living in the east metro area. The course is long and scenic as it winds around Eagle Point Lake. The full-service park offers many other diversions — swimming, camping, picnic pavilions, creative play areas, horseback riding, hiking and 7.5 miles of biking on paved paths.

The mountain bike paths at Lake Elmo may seem relatively tame for those who have careened down the hills at Lebanon or Murphy-Hanrehan, but take note. My tour was going quite smoothly when I started descending a small hill toward a pond. Higher water had caused bikers to veer off the main path on a slight detour. I followed, and with no warning, hit a rock the size of a box hidden in some weeds. The bike stopped dead, launching me on a complete somersault over the handlebars. With Dan as my witness I landed in soft grass with nary a bruise.

Your tour is not likely to be as eventful but keep your eyes open. This is the longest mountain bike loop trail in the metro area. It passes through reclaimed farmland, woods and marsh. The trail is generally hard packed dirt in good condition.

Lake Elmo Park Reserve was the site for the St. Paul Audubon Society's first biking for the birds trip. On the morning of October 1, 1994, a small group spotted 50 species including six types of woodpeckers, northern harriers, a Bobwhite and an immature Bald Eagle soaring overhead. Personally, I would recommend coming to a complete stop before getting out the binoculars.

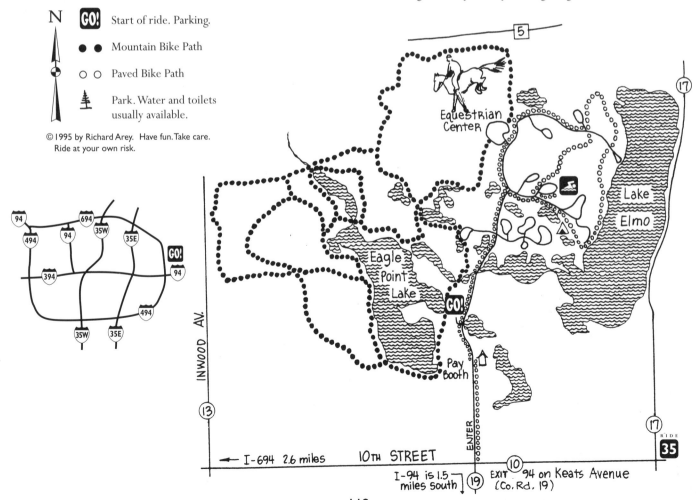

N

GO! Start of ride. Parking.

● ● Mountain Bike Path

○ ○ Paved Bike Path

🌲 Park. Water and toilets usually available.

© 1995 by Richard Arey. Have fun. Take care. Ride at your own risk.

- 112 -

BATTLE CREEK REGIONAL PARK

Ramsey County. Connects with RIDES 30, 32, 33, 34 and 40.

OWNER	Ramsey County Parks Department (777-1707)
OPEN	Daylight hours unless posted otherwise
LENGTH	2.5 miles
RATING	Intermediate
CAUTION	Shared trail with hikers

*T*his is the newest experimental mountain bike trail to open in the metro area. And while it isn't exceptionally long, it is a fine addition. The 147-acre parcel commands high ground overlooking the Mississippi River and includes some nice downhill runs.

Old timers will remember downhill skiing at this very same location. Battle Creek follows the trend of converting ski areas into mountain biking arenas. The park is also blessed with an extensive oak forest on top of the bluff. By changing course you can create a variety of loops that will keep your interest for a good long workout.

The St. Paul Bicycle Club held their Frigid Madness Cyclocross races here on November 20, 1994. This unique event requires that 10 percent of the course must be completed on foot. This includes running straight up the steepest pitch of the old ski runs with your bike slung over your shoulder, and leaping over strategically placed hay bales. And you thought mountain biking was tough.

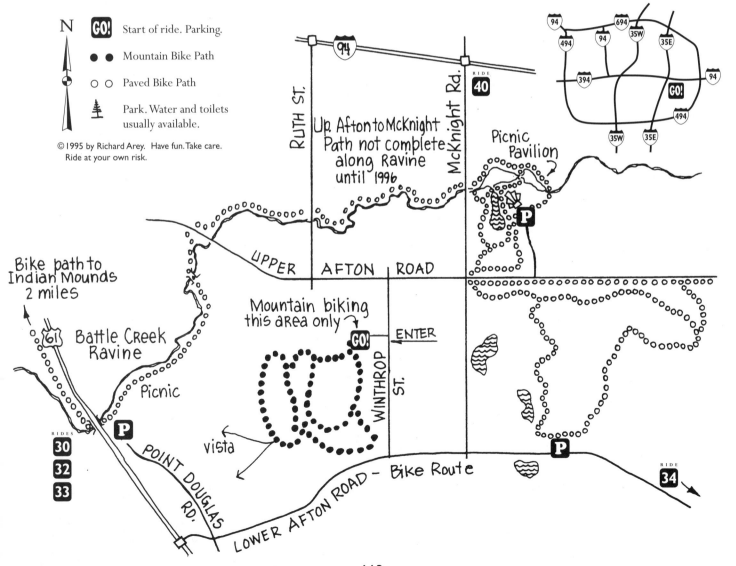

N

GO! Start of ride. Parking.

● ● Mountain Bike Path

○ ○ Paved Bike Path

Park. Water and toilets usually available.

© 1995 by Richard Arey. Have fun. Take care. Ride at your own risk.

LEBANON HILLS REGIONAL PARK

Dakota County. Connects with RIDE 31.

OWNER	Dakota County Parks Department (437-6608)
OPEN	Daylight hours unless posted otherwise
LENGTH	〜 – ⩗ 2.1 miles
RATING	Intermediate to Expert
CAUTION	Steep hills — but that's the point.

Good things come in small packages. This is a compact course with some tough uphill grades and one memorable downhill featuring a flying banked curve. Take some time to enjoy the scenery. The course is completely wooded with a nice overlook on top where you can view the Minneapolis skyline.

This course is short but sweet if you have the right stuff. The fastest riders can do the outside loop in seven minutes flat. That leaves very little time to stop and smell the flowers. You will get a great workout here no matter what your times are.

Thank Dakota County for this small gem and do not be tempted to explore other parts of Lebanon Hills except on foot, skis or horseback.

N

GO!	Start of ride. Parking.
● ●	Mountain Bike Path
○ ○	Paved Bike Path
🌲	Park. Water and toilets usually available.

© 1995 by Richard Arey. Have fun. Take care. Ride at your own risk.

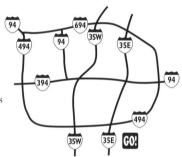

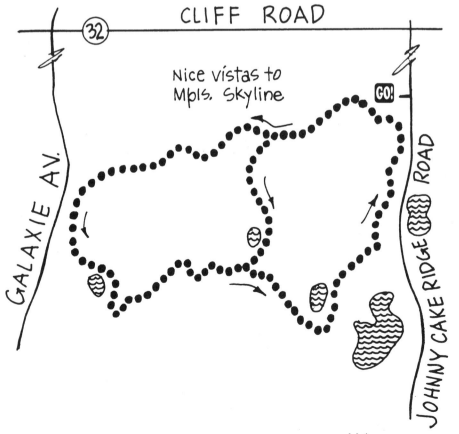

CLIFF ROAD

(32)

Nice vistas to Mpls. Skyline

GO!

GALAXIE AV.

JOHNNY CAKE RIDGE ROAD

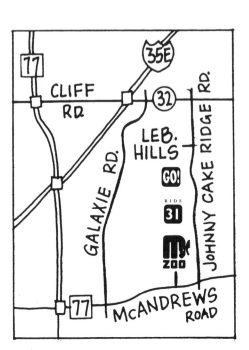

WELCH VILLAGE SKI AREA

Goodhue County. Connects with RIDE 38.

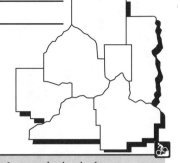

OWNER	Welch Village Ski Area 222-7079			
OPEN	Weekends, 10 a.m. to 4 p.m., Memorial Day through October			
LENGTH	~ – ⬧ 4 miles	**RATING**	Intermediate to expert	
FEE	$5, helmet required	**CAUTION**	Hidden ruts on downhills	

W elch Village is the prettiest local ski area that currently offers mountain biking. It may also be the least organized. Call before heading down to see what's up.

Nestled in the beautiful Cannon Valley, Welch Village has the potential to be a great mountain biking area. There is a 300-foot vertical drop — greatest of any local mountain bike trail — and picturesque surroundings of hardwood forest, exposed limestone cliffs and the Cannon River.

I visited in mid-October of 1994. The season was coming to a close and a race had been held the previous weekend. Though I had called just a couple days earlier, there was no one collecting money, no maps of the trail, and just random directional signs from the recent race.

Undaunted, I still had a fine afternoon of bicycling amidst the beautiful fall colors. This is a tough area for biking and novices need not apply. Head up the relatively gentle slopes on the eastern edge of the ski area and spend some time exploring the trails on top. Be very careful descending. There are some mean-looking ruts that are not easily seen, especially at 20 to 30 miles per hour.

N

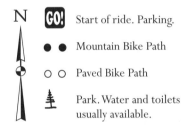

GO! Start of ride. Parking.

● ● Mountain Bike Path

○ ○ Paved Bike Path

🌲 Park. Water and toilets usually available.

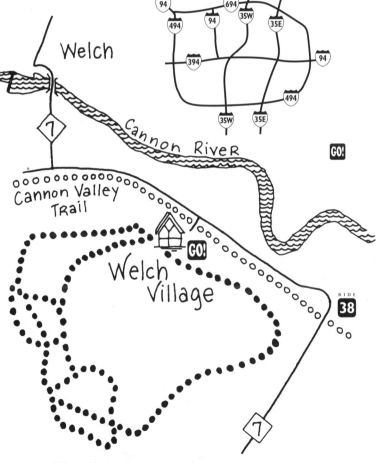

Trail layout varies — Stay on marked Routes

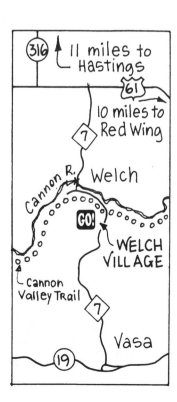

Bicyclists take over Godfrey Parkway at the start of the 1993 Minneapolis Aquatennial Bike Festival. See July events.

ANNUAL BIKE EVENTS

While nobody was looking, the Twin Cities has become a place where people can — and do — ride their bikes twelve months a year. This 'can bike' attitude, and the widespread use of mountain bikes, ensure that there are bicycle trips, tours and races throughout the year.

The following list highlights major annual Twin Cities bicycle events. Hundreds more take place each year so contact your favorite local club (see BICYCLE ORGANIZATIONS chapter) for current activities.

Silent Sports magazine (715-258-5546) is a great place to find out about bike events taking place throughout the Upper Midwest. The **Chequamegon Fat Tire Festival** (715-798-3811) in Hayward, Wisconsin, is one of the most popular. It runs the third weekend of September but fills up early in July.

The **Twin Cities Bicycle Club** (TCBC Hotline is 924-2443) schedules over 400 recreational rides throughout the year. Bicycle races are coordinated through the **Minnesota Cycling Federation** (MCF Hotline is 729-0702) and bicycle advocacy activities are led by the **Minnesota Coalition of Bicyclists** (MCB Hotline is 452-9736).

Most of the larger tours require preregistration and payment. Many fill up early, while others are open until the leader takes off. Confirm early registration discounts, fees, routes, dates, and helmet requirements before going.

January

POLAR BEAR RIDE
New Years Day

Start your bicycling year off right. Begun in 1983, this ride attracts 40 to 50 well-dressed cyclists for a 12-mile round trip ride down Summit Avenue in St. Paul. Starts at high noon in the SW corner of Sears at I-94 and Marion. Phone TCBC at 924-2443. Perennial leader is Bob Hoffman, 430-2676.

BIKE ON ICE RACE SERIES
Saturdays in January

The first annual event in 1995 was sponsored by Erik's Bike and Fitness, 891-6411. This received national press and the shop plans to expand this event for 1996. The first year's race took place on Crystal Lake in Burnsville. There are race categories for all levels of cyclists, men and women.

HUMAN POWERED ICE RACES
Weekend before Super Bowl

The Minnesota Human Powered Vehicle Association (929-2978) sponsors this annual event that began in 1992 on White Bear Lake. Contestants from throughout the Midwest use studded tires, outriggers and the wildest array of "bicycles" you are likely to see to compete in time trials, lap and drag races.

February

TCBC BIKE RIDES
Weekends and Weekdays

Check the TCBC hotline at 924-2443 to find out the schedule. In 1995, February offered *Thursday Thermals* (Edina), a *Soup's on Series* (Bloomington) and a *Vibrant Valentine's Venture*. Slippery road conditions may preclude safe bicycling, but February is a great time to tune up your bike and register for the Minnesota Ironman.

March

MINNESOTA STATE BICYCLE CONFERENCE
Two days mid-March

Sponsored by the Minnesota Department of Transportation and the State Bicycle Advisory Board (296-5269), this annual two-day conference provides an excellent opportunity to learn about the latest developments in bicycle transportation planning, trail funding, traffic calming and bike safety.

April

EARTH DAY
April 22

On April 22, 1970, observers of the first Earth Day rode bicycles through downtown Minneapolis to protest America's addiction to the automobile. Show your gratitude to Mother Earth and leave that polluting beast in the garage for the day.

MINNESOTA IRONMAN
Last Sunday in April

The biggest bike ride in Minnesota is sponsored by the Minnesota Council American Youth Hostels (MN AYH), 924-2443. This Ironman began in 1967, years before the Hawaii triathlon that uses the same name. Minnesota's version is not a race, but a century ride with participation capped at 5,000 riders. You can bike 100 miles or 100 kilometers (62 miles) through the scenic countryside of Wright County. In 1995 a 40-mile route was added. Register early, as the ride is usually filled by mid-March and registration closes by April 1.

COTTAGE GROVE ROAD RACE
Last Sunday in April

While hordes of bike tourers are doing the Minnesota Ironman, the local bike racers are kicking off their season down in Cottage Grove (south Washington County). This annual road race features five laps around a 14-mile circuit. Speeds average over 24 miles per hour. Phone the MCF at 729-0702.

May

BIKE, BUS OR CARPOOL (B-BOP!) DAY
Weekday, later in May

B-BOP Day is held each year during National Transportation Week. The idea is to leave your car at home and use an alternative — like biking — to work. Phone the B-BOP Hotline at 349-RIDE to find out the date and how you can get your company involved. See chapter on BICYCLE COMMUTING.

CLEAN AIR BIKE FESTIVAL
Third Saturday in May

Sponsored by the American Lung Association of Minnesota (871-7332), the Clean Air Bike Festival features country bike tours of 12 to 55 miles in length, a mountain bike race and Health Fair. There is a registration fee for all bike rides but fundraising is only required if you want to win prizes.

ANTIQUE BIKE RIDE
Memorial Day afternoon

This annual event goes back only to 1993, but some of the bicycles that take part go back another century to the 1890s — the first heyday of bicycling. But you don't need a vintage high-wheeler to join the fun. Dig out that old Sting Ray with the banana seat and sissy bars, put on some bellbottoms and head over to Long Lake Regional Park. This short ride is more of a parade than a tour. It is a TCBC ride, organized by Dona and Tom Devine (633-2588).

June

MINNESOTA MS 150 BIKE TOUR
Weekend, early June

A scenic 150-mile fundraising ride from Duluth to the Twin Cities. This ride began in 1980 and its success launched fundraising bike tours around the country. The Minnesota MS 150 has raised over $6.4 million to help fight Multiple Sclerosis. Phone the Minnesota MS Society at 870-1500 to register. They also run an MS 75 in August.

GREAT RIVER RIDE
Three day weekend, late June (and September)

Here is a great trip — and it is a fundraiser as well. Start with a riverboat cruise down the Mississippi to Hastings. Then it's a leisurely 25-mile ride to Red Wing. The next two days you bike either 40 or 70 miles and wind up in Winona. Finish with dinner and take the Amtrak train back home. Phone the American Lung Association at 871-7332.

ORIGINAL SUMMER SOLSTICE METRIC CENTURY
June 21 or 22

The summer solstice marks the longest day of the year and the sun does not set until after 9 p.m. Therefore, you can take off after work (say, 4:45 p.m. from White Bear Beach), bike over to Osceola, Wisconsin, and back — a mere 62 miles — and still make it home for the evening news. A TCBC event.

PAUL BUNYAN DOUBLE CENTURY
Longest Saturday of the year

This is the ride you have been waiting, and hopefully training for. A one-day, 202-mile jaunt from Anoka Senior High School (4:30 a.m.!), around Lake Mille Lacs, and (ideally) back again. This ride began in 1967 and some of those original riders still haven't made it back. Brought to you by those fun-loving folks at TCBC. Make a day of it.

MANITOU DAYS CRITERIUM BIKE RACE
Last Sunday in June

White Bear Lake hosts this annual high-speed bike race on city streets each year as part of their summer celebration. Criterium races are exciting for both spectators and participants as the race is on a short, closed course with numerous turns. Phone the White Bear Lake Area Chamber of Commerce at 429-8593 if you want to watch.

July

WATERMELON BIKE RIDE
July 4th

This is billed as Minnesota's premier family ride and has drawn over 600 riders. Celebrate Independence Day with a relaxed 25-mile ride followed by a picnic lunch. If you get tired of spitting seeds you can do another 25-mile loop. The ride stars in Arden Hills (just north of I-694 on Lexington). Call TCBC at 924-2443.

MIDNIGHT-TO-DAWN METRO BIKE TOUR
Saturday night, mid-July

Now here is a Midsummer Night's Dream of a ride. Participants can choose a 42 or 32-mile route that includes numerous restaurant stops (rider's expense) and a hot breakfast while watching the sun rise over Lake Harriet (included). This is one of the wackier bike tours around and also one of the most popular. It is a fundraiser (but cheap) for the Southwest Community School in Minneapolis. Phone 627-2463 well in advance for a registration form.

AQUATENNIAL BIKE FESTIVAL
Later Sunday in July

This 25-mile family ride enjoys one of the best routes in the Twin Cities as it cruises along the Mississippi, through downtown Minneapolis on Nicollet Mall, around the Lakes and back to Minnehaha Falls along the Parkway. It is popular and relatively inexpensive, with kids under 12 given a price break. Phone the Aquatennial Association at 331-8371 or the Connection at 922-9000 for details.

THE RIDE ACROSS MINNESOTA (TRAM)
Sunday to Friday, end of July

This is a fundraiser for Multiple Sclerosis that attracts over 2,000 participants. It is a well-orchestrated event that gives riders a sense of accomplishment as they span the state for a good cause. The small towns along the way do their best to make this a rolling parade celebrating all that is good about country living. Phone the MS Society at 870-1500 for details.

THE NORWEST CUP
Last Sunday in July

This Minneapolis road race is the hottest bike race in the Upper Midwest. Over 50,000 people come to watch the top riders in the country compete for $75,000 in prize money. The race course loops from the Mississippi River to Loring Park with the race totalling 110 miles. For a small fee families can do a lap on the race course prior to the event as part of the **Norwest Cup Family Fun Ride.** The contract for this race ends in 1995 but promoters promise it will continue. Phone the Minnesota Cycling Federation at 729-0702 for more information on the race. Family Fun Ride participants should call the Minnesota Head Injury Association at 644-1121 for details.

August

WEEKEND ON WHEELS (WOW)
Early weekend in August

WOW is a fully supported, no-pledge ride designed by avid cyclists to let you enjoy a carefree weekend of cycling. The tour was first run in 1981 and currently overnights in River Falls, Wisconsin. Participants can choose daily routes of 30 to 80 miles in length. Cost is moderate. Phone TCBC at 924-2443 for early registration information.

MINNESOTA BORDER TO BORDER TRIATHLON
Four weekdays in August

North America's longest triathlon traverses the state from the small southwestern town of Luverne to Crane Lake on the edge of the Boundary Waters Canoe Area. Begun in 1981, two-person relay teams bike a total of 415 miles the first two days, run 50 miles on day three and then hop into a canoe for a 50-mile paddle down the Vermillion River on the final day. This demanding event requires a support van and is limited to 60 teams. Phone 448-3115 or the MCF (729-0702) for details.

TOUR DE BUMP
August weekend

Hosted by Buck Hill, this is the Twin Cities' premier mountain bike race. The first event in 1989 launched Gene Oberpriller's career. He recalls sailing across the finish line 8 feet in the air going 42 miles per hour and decided at that precise moment to make mountain biking a career. There are several classes of races, and kids and first-timers are encouraged to enter. Phone 435-7174 for registration information.

September

LABOR DAY CENTURY
Labor Day

Jim Weber has been running this annual event since 1988. About 60 to 70 riders show up to bike 100 miles or 100 kilometers (a non-bikers idea of hard labor). The ride takes off at 8 a.m. from the Minnetonka Civic Center and follows a scenic countryside route out to Waconia. The longer route returns via Belle Plaine. Phone the TCBC Hotline for details.

DEFEAT OF JESSE JAMES DAYS
Saturday closest to September 7

On September 7, 1876, the notorious James-Younger gang rode into Northfield and started shooting. Joseph Lee Heywood was killed for refusing to open the bank's safe. Two other employees were wounded, one fatally, and the desperados left two more dead as they were driven out of town. Stop on down to watch the raid be reenacted and take your pick of scenic bike tours that range from 10 to 100 miles. Phone (507) 645-5604.

SAINT PAUL CLASSIC BIKE TOUR
First Sunday after Labor Day

The first annual Saint Paul Classic Bike Tour takes place on September 10, 1995. Warner and Shepard Road are closed to traffic for miles of hassle-free bicycling along the Mississippi River. Two historic routes are featured — a 27-mile Grand Round of the city (see RIDE 27) and a 14-mile family ride that includes the Mississippi and Summit Avenue. Phone 290-0309.

October

CANNON FALLS COLOR CLOVERLEAF
First Saturday in October

Enjoy a fall color excursion in one of the prettier regions of Minnesota. Tours ranging in length from 25 to 100 miles follow the Cannon Valley Trail and continue on country roads. Phone (507) 263-2665.

HALLOWEEN RIDE
Saturday closest to October 31

Boo! This is a house-to-house gobblin' (food) tour with up to 100 riders. Some folks dress up in more eye-catching fare than even the usual neon lycra. This is the last large organized bike ride of the year. Boo hoo. Phone TCBC at 924-2443.

November

FRIGID MADNESS CYCLOCROSS
Sunday in November

The Grand Performance Bike Shop (699-2640) sponsored this event for the first time on Sunday, November 20, 1994, at the Battle Creek (RIDE I) mountain bike area. Cyclocross is a wild sport where it is mandatory to run 10 percent of the course.

December

TCBC BIKE RIDES
Weekdays and weekends

By December, normal folks, during normal times are out hitting the ski trails or propped up in their favorite easy chair. Not that hard-charging TCBC crowd (924-2443). They had ten bike rides scheduled in December, 1994, and most of them went. You could choose from the *Thursday Thermals* (Edina), *John's Generic* (15-25 miles starting at Minnehaha Park with several Mississippi River crossings), a Pasta Ride (Lakewood), and my favorite — *Biking's Better Than The Vikings*. Amen.

The world-class Velodrome in Blaine (785-5600) is popular with many local racing clubs and features the only wood racing track in the country. Dueling tandems are caught here at full tilt during the 1992 Olympic Trials. Left to right are Marty Northstein, Erin Hartwell, Bart Bell (right front) and Tom Brinker.

BICYCLE ORGANIZATIONS

"Never doubt that a small group of thoughtful, committed citizens can change the world — indeed, it is the only thing that ever has."

Margaret Mead

One of the great aspects of bicycling is that you can do it yourself. And you can do it right out the back door. There is no need to drive to a ski area, find a canoe partner or set up a belay. Just you, your bike and some pavement is all that's required. Heck, you could even skip the pavement.

On the other hand, there are times when it is nice to ride with a friend. If your friend can't always keep up, you can join a racing club and meet your match. There can be safety in numbers and less experienced riders will find comfort riding with a local bike riding club. Finally, making communities more bicycle-friendly requires everyone's attention. The streets and trails you ride are almost entirely owned and operated by governments. These are <u>your</u> officials making decisions that affect you.

GET INVOLVED! Here is a list of groups and organizations that can meet your every bicycling need. These are friendly, active folks who are helping to make a difference. Find the group (or two) you feel comfortable with. Stop by a meet-ing, call to get a sample newsletter or try out a ride with a friend. Then become a member. As the Twin City Tandems say — "you can double your bicycling pleasure."

Everyone who is interested in making their streets and cities more bicycle-friendly must take an active role. Lexington Parkway in St. Paul would have a bikeway on it today if more citizens had spoken up. Neighborhood and city council meetings are where decisions on street maintenance, trail construction, signing and striping of bicycle lanes are made. There are always people who will stand up against bicycling. You need to be there as well.

National organizations are helpful in providing ideas on how other communities solve bike issues. Federal funding through the Intermodal Surface Transportation Efficiency Act (ISTEA or "ice tea") has provided millions of dollars in support for bike projects throughout the Twin Cities metro area.

Statewide Advocacy Groups

Minnesota Coalition of Bicyclists
Dorian Grilley, President
P.O. Box 75452
St. Paul, MN 55175
Hotline: 452-9736

A statewide organization that has been working for over ten years to improve bicycling safety, education and access. Their quarterly newsletter, Bicycle Minnesota, *and legislative presence deserve your support. Monthly meetings (7 p.m., 2nd Tuesday) in St. Paul.*

Minnesota Department of Transportation
Jim Dustrude, State Coordinator
395 John Ireland Boulevard, MS 440
St. Paul, MN 55155
Phone: 297-1838   Fax: 296-3311
MNDOT Bikeway Map Sales 296-2216
State Bicycle Program staff coordinate the annual bike conference in late winter and the **State Bicycle Advisory Board** *(297-1838) is helpful on technical issues.*

Minnesota Office of Tourism   296-5029
Call for a copy of Explore Minnesota Bikeways, *maps and more.*

Minnesota Rideshare   349-RIDE
Call to get on the Chain Gang *mailing list.*

MN Community Bicycle Safety Project
Cynthia McArthur, Bike Safety Coordinator
Minnesota Extension Service, 4H
340 Coffee Hall, University of MN
St. Paul, MN 55108
Phone: 625-9719   Fax: 625-1731
Cynthia is a tireless promoter of bike safety and helps run bike rodeos for youth throughout Minnesota. Call her for bike safety materials, programs or speaking engagements.

Legislative Representative
League of American Bicyclists
Representative Phyllis Kahn
100 Constitution Avenue
St. Paul, MN 55155
Phone: 296-4257
The strongest advocate of bicycling at the state legislature for 20 years, Phyllis Kahn is also founder of the Hot Flashes Bicycle Club.

North Central Mountain Bike Group
Gary Sjoquist, chief, cook and editor
1119 Kirkwood Drive
Eagan, MN 55123
Phone: 452-0907   Fax: 454-7906
Gary is a perpetual motion machine and mountain biking's strongest activist. His Off-Road Rider *newspaper promotes responsible mountain biking.*

Women's Public Policy Bicycling Society

Senator Sandy Pappas
Minnesota State Capitol-G27
St. Paul, MN 55155
Phone: 296-1802

Also known as the Hot Flashes Bicycle Club, this loose-knit group of women legislators gets together for Friday morning bike rides, baked goods and female bonding.

Midwest Pedestrian-Bicycle Council

Roger Peterson
P.O. Box 8214
St. Paul, MN 55108
Phone: 379-4970

A new organization that sponsors occasional conferences on "light traffic," the European concept of integrating walking and bicycling as part of the overall transportation plan.

Local Advocacy Groups

Hennepin County Bicycle Advisory Committee

Milt Schoen, Chair
Hennepin County Government Center
Mail Code 013
300 South 6th Street
Minneapolis, MN 55487
Phone: 348-3300
Fax: 348-3932

Current projects include developing a Bicycle Transportation Plan and working with the Light Rail Transit staff on sharing facilities. Citizens welcome. Committee generally meets the second Monday of the month.

Minneapolis Bicycle Advisory Board

Tom Becker, Chair
Room 233 City Hall
350 S. Fifth Street
Minneapolis, MN 55415
Phone: 673-2411
Fax: 673-2149

The most successful bike advocacy group in the state. I came back from Europe in the fall of 1994 and found that Minneapolis was on track to become the Amsterdam of Minnesota. Citizens are welcome at meetings held the first Wednesday of each month.

St. Paul Bicycle Advisory Board

Richard Arey, Chair
534 Laurel Avenue, #6
St. Paul, MN 55102
Phone: 290-0309

Striping bike lanes, working on Bike, Bus Or carPool (B-BOP!) Day, and hosting an annual event — the Saint Paul Classic Bike Tour (first Sunday after Labor Day) — are among the ongoing efforts. We welcome your attendance at our meetings on the first Tuesday of each month.

National Advocacy Groups

Bicycle Federation of America

1506 21st Street NW, Suite 200
Washington, D.C. 20036
Phone: (202) 463-6622

Prime movers in getting federal ISTEA legislation moved through Congress, the Bike Federation contracts with public agencies and advocacy groups in providing training, technical assistance and program support. They have several excellent publications for sale and the Pro Bike News is available by subscription.

League of American Bicyclists

190 W. Ostend Street, Suite 120
Baltimore, MD 21230-3755
Phone: (410) 539-3399
Fax: (410) 539-3496

Founded in 1880 as the League of American Wheelmen, the LAB is a nationwide advocacy group that sponsors bicycle rallies and Pedal for Power charity rides. Members receive the monthly magazine Bicycle USA and the annual Almanac. The local representative is John Jefferson (929-4431).

Rails-to-Trails Conservancy

1400 Sixteenth Street, NW
Washington, D.C. 20036
Phone: (202) 797-5400

The national advocacy group for recreational off-road paths on abandoned railroad corridors. There are several of these in Minnesota. The RTC has been instrumental in saving trails across the country by purchasing corridors that would otherwise be purchased privately and lost forever.

Fred cruises on a recumbent bicycle at a Minnesota Human Powered Vehicle Association meeting. Note the location of the handlebars.

Jerry Hass, 1994

Bicycle Riding Clubs

Groucho's advice notwithstanding, there are plenty of good clubs to join in the Twin Cities. The **Twin Cities Bicycling Club** is the largest, with rides every week of the year. There are specialty clubs like the **Twin Cities Tandem Club** and the **Mississippi Valley Women's Cycling Association**. If you are interested in the old high-wheelers, get in touch with the **Minnesota Wheelmen**. And if you want to ride an equally eye-catching 21st century bicycle, the **Minnesota Human Powered Vehicle Association** is your club.

There are bicycle clubs at several of the larger work places in town, including **3M** and **Ramsey County**. Or, you can go slumming on bike trips sponsored by the **North Star Ski Touring Club** during their off-season.

Club rides are usually open to nonmembers (for a couple dollars or so) and generally require helmets.

Hennepin Parks
12615 County Road 9
Plymouth, MN 55441
Phone: 559-9000
Trail Hotline: 559-6778
Hennepin Parks sponsors a dozen or so bike rides each year. Pre-registration is required and rides cost $3 to $5 per person.

Mississippi Valley Women's Cycling Association
621 East 61st Street
Minneapolis, MN 55417
Kathy at 435-5734
This all-women's group has leisurely Wednesday night rides throughout the summer. Longer rides take place one Saturday each month. Members range from 30 to 55 years in age and receive a ride schedule and list of activities.

Minnesota Human Powered Vehicle Association
Dave Kraft
4139 Brookside Avenue S.
St. Louis Park, MN 55416
Phone: 929-2978
Now for something completely different — try riding a "recumbent" bicycle some time. These bikes are low slung and easy on the back as you ride low to the ground in a sitting position. The MnHPVA is home to techies, dreamers and builders. Biannual rides allow newcomers to sample these exotic, but efficient vehicles. Members receive a newsletter and meet the second Wednesday of each month.

Minnesota Wheelmen
Jon Sharratt
2322 Johnson Street N.E.
Minneapolis, MN 55418
Phone: 781-9954

These guys are the really big wheels of bicycling. They ride the high-wheelers and safety bikes that fueled the first bike craze in the late 1800s. Jim Ogland is the area's chief proponent and led the opening day parade across the 1883 James J. Hill Bridge in his 1888 Columbia 55" Light Roadster.

North Star Ski Touring Club
P.O. Box 4275
St. Paul, MN 55104
Hotline: 643-4453
Here is a big amiable group that enjoys outdoor recreation throughout the year. Rafting the Grand Canyon, trail clearing on the North Shore and, yes, bicycling in the Twin Cities. One friend who's a member confesses she has never been on a ski trip. Become a member and receive the excellent Loype *newsletter.*

Sitzmark Ski and Social Club
Mike Helland
14625 Idylwood Road
Minnetonka, MN 55345
Hotline: 545-1151
Sitzmark has trips and parties throughout the year. With over 600 members, the emphasis is on the social life, but a little exercise never hurt anyone.

Trail Blazer's Bike Club
Suite 122-101, Parkdale Plaza Bldg.
1660 South Highway 100
Minneapolis, MN 55416
Phone: 541-0412 or 545-1188
A well-run group, the Trail Blazers sponsor about 70 rides each summer. Club founder Mike Kiefer welcomes all levels of bicyclists and says, "the only competing we do is to see who enjoys themselves the most." There is no membership fee, but riders make a $2 donation for daytime rides and around $15 for weekend camping rides (sag wagons support as necessary). Call to get on their mailing list.

Twin Cities Bicycling Club
P.O. Box 131086
Roseville, MN 55113
Hotline: 924-2443
Formed under the auspices of Hosteling International-Minnesota AYH (378-3773), the TCBC is one of the premier bike riding organizations in the state, with over 1,000 members and 467 scheduled trips in 1994. Don't worry, they don't all show up for each ride. Rides are rated for all ability levels and each has a trained leader. Members receive the Activity News *newsletter.*

Twin Cities' Tandem Club
Doug and Sara Laird
5445 Maple Ridge Court
Minnetonka, MN 55343-9488
Phone: 935-9337
Double your pleasure, double your fun. This is a large active club. The Twin Cities have a unique community of tandem riders and bike builders. I love riding tandems. Nothing beats going full tilt down a big hill with your eyes closed. Tandems are more efficient and make it a lot easier to converse with your buddy. Members receive a monthly newsletter.

Bicycle Racing Clubs

> *"It is a great environment here. I really believe moving here helped everything."*
> Greg LeMond of Wayzata
> *after winning his third Tour de France*
>
> *"Every car has a lot of speed in it. The trick is getting the speed out of it."*
> A. J. Foyt, *race car driver*

There is nothing quite like the feeling of riding at high speeds in a pack of bicyclists, trading off leads and riding at a pace you could never maintain yourself. Speed, fun, and camaraderie can all be found by joining a racing club. You will also find hard work and the training necessary to compete at your highest level.

The Twin Cities support a fine array of cycling clubs for those who wish to compete and for those who simply want to ride with others at a faster clip than recreational clubs can handle.

The **Minnesota Cycling Federation** (Hotline is 729-0702) oversees, along with the USCF, local club and racing activities. Club sponsors and contacts change frequently and the MCF will send you a complete updated list at no cost. Competition for Juniors begins at ages 10 to 12, seniors compete within the 19- to 34-year old range and the Masters level begins at the ripe old age of 35.

Most clubs are open to newcomers (women and youngsters are especially encouraged to join), membership dues are reasonable and sponsoring bicycle shops offer substantial discounts on bike equipment to members. The top local riders get $3,000-plus racing bikes supplied for their use. Road racing, track racing, mountain biking, cyclocross racing (you actually carry your bike for short stretches), and triathlons are now part of the mix at many clubs.

Spectators especially enjoy criterium races held on city streets, like the **Norwest Cup,** which takes place the last Sunday each July in downtown Minneapolis. Criterium races are also held during **Manitou Days** in White Bear Lake and at the **Crystal Minnesota Frolix.** See the ANNUAL BIKE EVENTS chapter.

There are two approaches when looking for a club to join. People who have some race experience should call to ask for the location of a club's training rides. Many rides start at the sponsor's stores, but **Gopher Wheelmen** have rides starting in the four corners of the metro world, and **Loon State Cyclists** have a north ride and a south ride. Those just starting out should call to determine if a club has beginner's rides — about half of the clubs do. Switching clubs is quite common if the first one does not work out.

The Twin Cities have a world-class bike racing facility in the **National Sports Center Velodrome** in Blaine (785-5600). Located at 1700-105th Avenue NE, this all-wood racing track has hosted Olympic-caliber bike races and is open to the public for club and individual use.

Bennett's Cycle Race Team
John Senum
3540 Dakota Avenue S.
St. Louis Park, MN 55416
Sponsor: Bennett's Cycle
Phone: 922-0311
This 50-member club focuses on mountain biking. They pride themselves on taking beginners through the ranks but field upper echelon racers as well. This year they will have full van support with refreshments at all major races. Members range from 15 to 50.

Black Banana Bicycle Club
Jerry Hiniker
10495 University Avenue NE
Blaine, MN 55434
Phone: 757-8679
Sponsor: Blaine Velo Sports
Jerry Hiniker helped get the Velodrome built in Minnesota. Black Banana is also based in Blaine, so it should come as no surprise that one of the club's focuses is track riding. With this Olympic-caliber facility in their backyard, they have generated some of the area's better track riders.

City of Lakes Cyclists
7144 Chicago Avenue S.
Richfield, MN 55423
Phone: 861-3011
Sponsor: Erik's Bike and Fitness
Erik's Bike and Fitness sponsored a three-day Bike on Ice Race Series, which made the national Velo News. The January, 1995 race on Lake Crystal was won by Andy Dahl, who survived a "critical mid-race flat and numerous crashes." These folks also enjoy mountain bike and road racing in summer.

Como Wheelers
Pete Fleishhacker
779 W. Wheelock Parkway
St. Paul, MN 55117
Phone: 488-9078
Sponsor: Como Bike Shop
Pete was a charter member of the St. Paul Bicycle Advisory Board and has been involved in local bike racing for years. The Como Wheelers hold weekly rides and last year sported a pro racer.

Flat City Cycling Club
Frank Williams
2123 W. 21st Street
Minneapolis, MN 55405
Phone: 927-7039
Sponsor: Kenwood Cyclery
Races are won and lost on blown tires, so Flat City may seem an unusual moniker for a bike club, but never fear. The club has about 60 members, including a half dozen women. The focus has been on road racing, but they are hoping to expand into mountain biking.

Gopher Wheelmen Bicycle Racing Club
Scott Sandberg
1380 North Arm Drive
Orono, MN 55364
Phone: 471-8662
Sponsor: County Cycles in Roseville
Founded in 1934, this is the oldest bicycle club in Minnesota. In fact, a founding member who participated in the old Six Day Bike Races of the 1930s — Kenny Woods — is still a member and still biking as of the publication of this book. This is a solid club for all levels of racing for men and women.

Habanero Bike Club

Mike Pederson
4517 – 47th Avenue S.
Minneapolis, MN 55406
Phone: 729-8898
Sponsor: Hoigaards
Habanero is Latin for cowboy. The club sponsors mountain bike and cyclocross races, which fit the name. Even more rugged than mountain biking, cyclocross races include barriers and hills (even in Minnesota) too steep to ride up. Participants hop off their bikes, throw them on their shoulders and run. Yeee-ha!

L'Etoile du Nord

Doug Regester
5440 Colfax Avenue S.
Minneapolis, MN 55409
Phone: 824-1966
As all Minnesotans know, L'Etoile du Nord is part of our state seal and translates to "Stars of the North" as one member kiddingly put it. But even though they claim to have the "coolest team jerseys in the world," they work on bike advocacy as well as attitude. Members have gotten involved with trail maintenance and an effort to put an indoor track in the Minneapolis Armory. They have an emphasis on track, cyclocross and road racing.

Loon State Cyclists

Daryl Doering
12680 - 138th Avenue N.
Dayton, MN 55327
Phone: 323-1291
Sponsors: XLR8, Wheel Sports of Anoka, Saturn
Loon State Cyclists were voted the United States Cycling Federation's Regional Club of the Year in 1994. This is Minnesota's largest club with 130 members competing at all levels and in all types of races from criteriums to road races. They are making a special effort to recruit junior level and women racers.

Maximum Velocity

Dave Pike
2408 Hennepin Avenue S.
Minneapolis, MN 55405
Phone: 374-3635
Sponsor: The Alternative Bike and Board
A small, but potent off-road racing club founded by national mountain bike champion, Gene Oberpriller. They take their racing, and their fun times, seriously. Sponsored by those radical folks at Alternative Bike.

Minneapolis Bicycle Racing Cub

Scott Flanders
2707 Lyndale Avenue S.
Minneapolis, MN 55408
Phone: 872-6994
Sponsors: Flanders Brothers Bike Shop
If you want a team with attitude, then these are your guys. Most clubs schedule training rides. The Minneapolis Racing Club says, "We'll be out there, catch us if you can." Scott Flanders is a perennial winner in road races and criterium races. Judy Christenson has dominated women's cycling in the Twin Cities and won a national title in time trial events. Scott and Jim Flanders are the only local cyclists ever invited to join the USCF national racing team.

Park Tool Racing Team

Kevin Lennon
25 Union Terrace
Minneapolis, MN 55441
Phone: 544-3321
Sponsors: Park Tool, Trek, and Mendota Cycling and Fitness
St. Paul-based Park Tool is the largest bike tool manufacturer in the world and sponsors this high octane crew. The team embraces a wide range of interests — from mountain biking to road racing — and age groups — from 17 to 50 year-olds with several women riders. They strive for a team effort and assign experienced racers to mentor newcomers.

South Cedar Avenue Bicycling Society

Ken Ring
3316 Sixteenth Avenue S.
Minneapolis, MN 55407
Phone: 729-4596
Sponsor: Phantom Bike Shop
The Phantoms consist primarily of race officials, and the real story here is the Phantom Bike Shop (872-8176). This shoestring operation teaches disadvantaged kids about the business of fixing bicycles — a life skill they can take with them. They rebuild bicycles and sell them inexpensively. Buy their bikes and support this operation.

Squadra Pista

Tom Lee
2051 151st Avenue NE
Ham Lake, MN 55303
Phone: 434-4339
Sponsor: Freewheel and Compu Staff
This is the National Sports Center based racing team. They sponsor an annual track race here and have about 30 members.

St. Paul Bicycle Racing Club

Dan Casebeer
1938 Grand Avenue
St. Paul, MN 55105
Phone: 699-2640
Sponsor: Grand Performance
This club is a reflection of its chief, Dan Casebeer, who not only enjoys a good time, but is also the perennial state time trial champion. Excellent programs in all racing modes are in place for juniors, seniors and women. The club sponsored St. Paul's first cyclocross race at the recently opened Battle Creek Park mountain bike area.

Twin Cities Cycling Club

Dave Hogan (729-0810)
2216 E. 34th Street
Minneapolis, MN 55407
Phone: 888-1427
Sponsor: Penn Cycle
Organized in 1974, this is one of the oldest clubs in the metro area. They have fielded national road racing medal winners in the past, but are now putting the emphasis on their mountain bike race team. Club members are active in keeping local mountain bike trails open and doing trail maintenance.

Bicycle Touring Organizations

> *"In a car you're always in a compartment, and because you're used to it, you don't realize that through the car window everything you see is just more TV.*
>
> *On a cycle the frame is gone. You're completely in contact with it all. You're in the scene, not just watching it anymore, and the sense of presence is overwhelming."*
>
> Robert M. Pirsig
> *Zen and the Art of Motorcycle Maintenance*

The following outfits offer a nice sampling of bike tours here and abroad. For the most complete listing of bike tours in the Midwest, check the back pages of *Silent Sports* magazine in the May to July issues.

Outside, Bicycling, and *Bicycle USA* (membership magazine for the League of American Bicyclists) are all good places to look for national and international bike tours. Some of the local bike clubs (listed earlier) offer special bike tours. Also check the ANNUAL BIKE EVENTS chapter for additional tours.

Action Voyage, Inc.
P.O. Box 131765
St. Paul, MN 55113
Phone: 776-0504
Fax: 776-4782
In just their third season, Valérie (from Normandy, France) and Paul (a native Minnesotan) already have repeat customers. They offer a high quality tour with van support, gourmet meals, and nights spent in chateaus and beautiful inns. They only run a couple of one-week trips in summer and limit each one to 12 adults. More expensive.

American Lung Association of Hennepin County
1829 Portland Avenue
Minneapolis, MN 55404
Phone: 871-7332
Here is a way to take a bike tour, visit some wonderful places, and benefit a good cause. American Lung contracts with bike tour companies to offer these pledge (or pay) rides throughout the world. They also sponsor a Great River Ride from Hastings to Winona each year. Moderate to expensive.

Cycle America
P.O. Box 485
Cannon Falls, MN 55009
Phone: (800) 245-3263
If you have ever wanted to ride from sea to shining sea across these United States then this is the outfit for you. Don Haugo has been running Cycle America since 1988. These are van supported, camping tours (hotel optional) that can be done in week-long, state-wide sections. They also offer bike tours through the western national parks and local Cloverleaf tours of the Twin Cities metro area. Moderate to expensive.

Journeys Inward
Phone: 870-7331
Marilyn Mason runs special, small group tours once or twice a year around the planet. She employs a local expert, like a Masai chief in Africa, to co-lead these trips. Hiking and biking tours are offered. More expensive.

Woodswomen
25 W. Diamond Lake Road
Minneapolis, MN 55419
Phone: 822-3809
Fax: 822-3814
Woodswomen is locally owned, with almost 20 years experience in leading adventure-travel trips for women throughout the world. They have Learn to Bicycle Tour trips in Wisconsin and once you get the bug you will surely want to join them in touring Hawaii, New Zealand or Ireland. I love their motto, "Adventure is the best souvenir." Moderate to expensive.

Bicycle touring is a great way to experience different lands and peoples. Everybody in the Netherlands bicycles and this couple at the Kinderdijk display the more relaxed European approach to bike attire and safety.

Fred's Photos, 1994

Bicycle Trail Associations

The Luce Line State Trail was created as a direct result of citizens forming an association and gathering the political support necessary to fund and build a trail. The Gateway Trail, Cannon Valley Trail and Cedar Lake Park have all followed this lead. The **Minnesota Parks and Trails Council** provides support for these types of groups at the state level, while the **Rails-to-Trails Conservancy** is active nationally. There are active "Friends of Parks and Trails" groups in many local communities.

All of these groups are membership based with revenue going to support trail advocacy, construction and maintenance. In a time of dwindling government support, it is likely that more of these associations will be forming. Membership includes newsletters and invitations to special events.

Cedar Lake Park Association

Laurie Lundy, Project Coordinator
1101 Cedar View Drive
Minneapolis, MN 55405
Phone: 377-9522

There is no better example of a successful trail association than the Cedar Lake Park Association. This small grassroots effort in Minneapolis organized in 1989 to protect some land from developers. Six years, 3,000 members and several million dollars in private, public and foundation money later, a series of trails are being constructed that connect the Minneapolis Lake District with downtown and eventually the Mississippi River. (See RIDE 6.)

Friends of the Cannon Valley Trail

Bruce Blair, Trail Manager
City Hall
Cannon Falls, MN 55009
Phone: (507) 263-3954

The Cannon Valley Trail is not only one of the most scenic in the Midwest, it is also one of the few that is not owned and operated by a state or county agency. The Friends are one of the many ways (including trail user fees) of generating financial and volunteer support for the trail. (see RIDE 30.)

Friends of the Parks and Trails of St. Paul and Ramsey County

1621 Beechwood Avenue
St. Paul, MN 55116
Peggy Lynch, Executive Director
Phone: 698-4543

An active, influential board helps power this citizen advocacy group. Lead by the omnipresent Peggy Lynch, they have pushed for striping bike lanes on Summit Avenue, argued against narrow combined paths on Mississippi River Boulevard and initiated the Midwest's first Yellow Bike Coalition which placed free bikes on the streets of St. Paul beginning September 1, 1995.

Gateway Trail Association

Peter Seed, Organizer
7923 Jamaica Avenue North
Stillwater, MN 55082
Phone: 426-2668

While the Gateway Trail (see RIDES 22 and 23) is one of the newest and most popular local trails, it took several years of work by a group of interested citizens (formerly the Soo Line Trail Association) to get to this point. The Minnesota Parks and Trails Association is the fiscal agent for the Gateway Trail Association.

Luce Line Trail Association

Vern Hahn, President
P.O. Box 102
Watertown, MN 55388
Phone: 1-612-587-3368

A new group that has organized to help develop the west end of the Luce Line State Trail (see RIDE 10) from Winsted to Cosmos. There are 200 members currently rewriting the management plan and looking to represent the interests of all users.

Minnesota Parks and Trails Council

P.O. Box 26243
St. Paul, MN 55126-0243

A volunteer citizens group for over 35 years with a revolving fund of one million dollars, the MPTC is a positive force in establishing and developing parks and trails statewide. They embrace all trail users from bicyclists to snowmobilers and have actively assisted trail association developments.

Rails-to-Trails Conservancy

1400 Sixteenth Street, NW
Washington, DC 20036
Phone: (202)797-5400

National advocates for converting abandoned rail corridors into biking and walking paths. Local rail trails include the Luce Line (RIDE 10), LRT North and South (RIDES 13 and 14), the Minnesota Valley Trail (RIDE 16), Gateway Trail (RIDES 22 and 23) and Cannon Valley Trail (RIDE 38).

EAST METRO BIKE ROUTES

See inside front cover for WEST METRO BIKE ROUTES

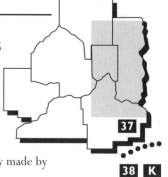

R I D E S

21-40 BIKE TOURS
See pages 64 to 101

R I D E S

H-K  MOUNTAIN BIKE RIDES
See pages 94, and 112 to 115

RATINGS FOR BIKE TOURS

🌀 Easier – Mostly paved, off-road trails

〰 Moderate – Mostly on bike-friendly streets

〰 Experienced – On roads, longer, less protected

LENGTH

Mileage listed below is for a full tour, loop or distinct area. OW (one way) and RT (round trip) mileage is given for linear trails. Note: Longer rides are easily made by connecting two or more routes.

Sample Description (tour user guide pages 26 & 27)

O	BIKE TOUR with RATING and LENGTH
	Oa. Regional Park/Trail or shorter loop described and mapped within tour.

21 SCANDIA SOJOURN	◆ 28.8 MILES
〰 21a. Ostrum Trail Loop	19.1 miles
🌀 21b. William O'Brien to Marine	8.0 miles RT

22 GATEWAY STATE TRAIL	🌀 33.8 MILES RT
〰 22a. Cathedral to I-694	21.8 miles RT
🌀 22b. Arlington Trailhead	14.4 miles RT

23 GATEWAY TRAIL TO STILLWATER	🌀 19.5 MILES
🌀 23a. Round trip to Pine Point	15.0 miles RT

24 JERRY'S RIDE	〰 27.0 MILES
〰 24a. Bald Eagle Lake Loop	15.6 miles

25 FORBIDDEN CITY CIRCLE	〰 24.1 MILES

26 LAND OF LAKES	〰 22.0 MILES
🌀 26a. Lake Phalen Regional Park	4.7 miles
🌀 26b. Short Loop Around Two Lakes	10.0 miles
〰 26c. Medium Loop to Lake Owasso	17.0 miles

27 SAINT PAUL GRAND ROUND	〰 28.2 MILES
🌀 27a. Mississippi River Boulevard	10.8 miles RT
🌀 27b. Como Regional Park	4.1 miles

28 SAINT PAUL SAMPLERS	〰 32.5 MILES
🌀 28a. Summit Avenue to Cathedral	9.0 miles RT
〰 28b. Summit to Lake Phalen Loop	21.9 miles
〰 28c. Mississippi River to Summit Loop	14.6 miles
🌀 28d. Hidden Falls-Crosby Farm Regional Park	8.0 miles

29 WEST SIDE WINDER	〰 10.8 MILES
🌀 29a. Harriet Island-Lilydale Regional Park	6.0 miles RT

30 THREE BRIDGES BIKEWAY	〰 29.3 MILES
🌀 30a. Minnehaha Falls through Fort Snelling Park	9.6 miles

31 BIKE TO THE ZOO	🌀 56.6 MILES OW
🌀 31a. From Fort Snelling	24.0 miles RT
🌀 31b. From Marie Avenue	25.0 miles RT
🌀 31c. From Minnesota Valley Refuge Visitor Center	22.2 miles RT
🌀 31d. From Old Shakopee Road	17.0 miles RT
🌀 31e. From Dairy Queen on Highway 13	12.8 miles RT
🌀 31f. From Patrick Eagan Park	12.2 miles RT

32 PATTI ROCKS THE RIVER	◆ 25.5 MILES
🌀 32a. Indian Mounds to Battle Creek	5.0 miles RT

33 DAKOTA TRAILS	◆ 39.4 MILES
〰 33a. Red Rock and Return	21.2 miles
🌀 33b. Battle Creek Regional Park	4 miles

34 WONDERFUL WOODBURY	🌀 14.2 MILES
🌀 34a. Half Wonderful Loop	10.0 miles

35 STAGECOACH TO STILLWATER	◆ 43.9 MILES
〰 35a. Short Loop to Stillwater	25.4 miles
〰 35b. Afton and Hudson and back	30.4 miles
🌀 35c. Lake Elmo Park Reserve	5.5 miles

36 LOST VALLEY TOUR	◆ 41.1 MILES
◆ 36a. Valley Creek Cutoff	32.7 miles
〰 36b. Half Lost Loop	19.6 miles

37 CHIMNEY ROCK RAMBLE	〰 24.0 MILES

38 CANNON VALLEY TRAIL	🌀 40.0 MILES RT
🌀 38a. Welch to Cannon Falls	20.0 miles RT
🌀 38b. Welch to Red Wing	20.0 miles RT

39 MISSISSIPPI RIVER GORGE RIDE	〰 19.4 MILES
🌀 39a. Ford Parkway Short Loop	8.5 miles

40 RAGS TO RICHES RIDE	〰 22.8 MILES
🌀 40a. Short Loop around Silver Lake	14.4 miles

MOUNTAIN BIKE RIDES Rating for terrain/distance

37 CHIMNEY ROCK RAMBLE	〰 24.0 MILES
H LAKE ELMO PARK RESERVE	🌀 - 〰 12.0 MILES
I BATTLE CREEK REGIONAL PARK	〰 2.5 MILES
J LEBANON HILLS REGIONAL PARK	〰 - ◆ 2.1 MILES
K WELCH VILLAGE SKI AREA	〰 - ◆ 4.0 MILES
AFTON ALPS SKI AREA	◆ 7.0 MILES

Great new area! See RIDE 36, page 94.